Cognitive Behavioural Therapy for Mental Health Workers

Cognitive behavioural therapy is an effective and frequently used psychological treatment. *Cognitive Behavioural Therapy for Mental Health Workers* offers the reader a good overview of CBT, allowing them to develop an understanding of the patient's problems, utilize the approach effectively, prepare for supervision and integrate CBT skills into everyday practice.

This clear, comprehensive introduction written by experienced clinicians, describes how to use CBT within the busy clinical environment. Subjects covered include:

- the therapeutic relationship in CBT
- treating anxiety disorders and depression
- developing further CBT skills
- utilizing CBT in different mental health settings
- recent developments in practice.

This straightforward guide will be essential for all mental health workers who are new to CBT, including nurses, occupational therapists and counsellors as well as anyone training in mental health professions.

Philip Kinsella is a principal cognitive behavioural therapist specializing in adult mental health and general hospital liaison work. He has extensive experience in supervising and training mental health workers who are beginning to learn CBT. He is the author of *Cognitive Behavioural Therapy for Chronic Fatigue Syndrome* (Routledge, 2007).

Anne Garland is a nurse consultant in psychological therapies in Nottingham. She is recognized nationally for her expertise in the training and delivery of cognitive therapy in primary care, community teams, inpatient units and specialist psychotherapy services. She has published widely in the CBT field.

Cognitive Behavioural Therapy for Mental Health Workers

A BEGINNER'S GUIDE

Philip Kinsella and Anne Garland

Routledge
Taylor & Francis Group

LONDON AND NEW YORK

First published 2008 by Routledge
27 Church Road, Hove, East Sussex BN3 2FA

Simultaneously published in the USA and Canada
by Routledge
270 Madison Avenue, New York NY 10016

Reprinted 2009

Routledge is an imprint of the Taylor & Francis Group, an Informa business

Copyright © 2008 Philip Kinsella and Anne Garland

Typeset in Goudy by RefineCatch Limited, Bungay, Suffolk
Printed and bound in Great Britain by TJ International Ltd, Padstow, Cornwall
Paperback cover design Sandra Heath

This publication has been produced with paper manufactured to strict
environmental standards and with pulp derived from sustainable forests.

British Library Cataloguing in Publication Data
A catalogue record for this book is available from the British Library

Library of Congress Cataloging in Publication Data
Kinsella, Philip, 1957–
   Cognitive behavioural therapy for mental health workers: a beginner's guide /
Philip Kinsella and Anne Garland.
      p. cm.
   Includes bibliographical references and index.
   ISBN 978-1-58391-869-2 (hardback) – 978-1-58391-870-8 (paperback)
1. Cognitive therapy.   I. Garland, Anne.   II. Title.
   [DNLM: 1. Cognitive Therapy – methods.   2. Mental Disorders – therapy.
3. Psychotherapy, Brief.   WM 425.5.C6 K56c 2008]
   RC489.C63K46 2008
   616.89′14 – dc22   2007036604

ISBN: 978-1-58391-869-2 (hbk)
ISBN: 978-1-58391-870-8 (pbk)

Dedication

To my mother, Mrs Anne Kinsella. Also to Hazel, Fiona and Duncan with thanks for their support (PK)

Contents

Figures

Tables

Worksheets

Introduction

With the increasing interest in cognitive behavioural interventions, the authors have written this book to help mental health clinicians use these methods in their day-to-day practice. We have tried to write it in an accessible and practical style, describing specific methods for implementing cognitive behavioural interventions, discussing potential difficulties in using these methods and suggesting possible solutions to these difficulties.

Cognitive behavioural therapy (CBT) is a structured time-limited (average 6–18 sessions), evidence-based psychological intervention that aims to address patients' current problems. The therapy is problem focused and goal oriented, in that problems are explicitly identified and specific goals are agreed in order to tackle the problems identified. Problems and goals are usually described in terms of the patient's thought patterns, emotions, behaviour and in terms of day-to-day functioning. All aspects of treatment are clearly explained and the therapist and patient work together using various strategies within an agreed timeframe.

According to Blackburn and Twaddle (1996), the key elements of CBT are a shared psychological understanding of the patient's current problems (this is referred to in the CBT literature as a CBT *formulation*, e.g. Butler, 1998; Persons, 1989); active collaboration between patient and clinician with a full sharing of information; a questioning style that aids patient understanding (this is referred to as Socratic questioning in the CBT literature, e.g. Padesky, 1993); and gaining knowledge from experience particularly that which occurs outside the session.

As with all psychological interventions there is some healthy debate within the field of CBT as to where the emphasis in treatment should lie. Some of the issues that are debated in day-to-day practice are: the importance of cognitive versus behavioural interventions, the importance of the therapeutic relationship, and the 'suitability' of the patient's presentation for cognitive behavioural interventions. To some extent the way clinicians address these issues of emphasis is a reflection of the CBT training they have undertaken, and the CBT clinicians, trainers and supervisors whose theoretical perspective and clinical skills have influenced their practice.

These differences in emphasis are reflected in the CBT literature, with distinctions being made between behavioural and cognitive interventions. To take the example of panic disorder and agoraphobia, the original model targeted avoidant behaviour and was underpinned by conditioning theory (Marks, 1987) and the treatment rationale was based on the principle of graded exposure to the stimulus leading to habituation. The model developed by Clark (1986), targets cognition and emphasizes behavioural experiments to test out whether the patient's panic-related cognitions regarding panic symptoms are accurate. Meanwhile, Barlow (1993) would advocate a combination of these two interventions but would emphasize a more behavioural theoretical position. There is strong evidence for the effectiveness of both models in clinical trials (Simos, 2002), so it can be difficult to decide which model to use. In planning treatment clinicians often follow the methods they have been originally trained in.

However, for both novice and experienced CBT practioners these issues can give rise to tensions and dilemmas, which, from a pragmatic perspective, need to be resolved by each individual clinician herself. This resolution requires knowledge and practical experience of using CBT and we would encourage the reader to discuss the issues with colleagues, CBT trainers and CBT clinical supervisors as a first step in trying to consider your own personal perspective in relation to these issues. What the authors would encourage you to do in this quest is to remain true to the spirit of the scientist–practioner model (Barlow et al., 1984; Salkovskis, 2002) that lies at the heart of CBT. This model is founded on the principle of the individual practioner questioning, investigating and evaluating their own practice on a daily basis in order to develop effective and efficient treatment interventions.

In an attempt to at least acknowledge these differences and to try and reconcile the dilemma, there has been an attempt in this book to set certain core CBT principles as its foundation. Thus, there is a strong emphasis on developing CBT assessment skills and the basic principles of making psychological sense of patients' problems within a CBT framework. The authors would also spend time helping the patient define their current problems in concrete terms and defining goals in relation to these problems. They would put emphasis on the importance of the therapeutic relationship within the theoretical framework of CBT. The reader is encouraged to develop a good sense of the evidence base that supports CBT interventions and to use this as a basis for their own decision making regarding what CBT interventions to use with individual patients. However, the reader is also encouraged to approach the evidence base with a critical eye and to accept that some of the evidence is inconclusive. With ongoing research into the effectiveness of CBT, new treatment interventions emerge and clinicians need to update their theoretical knowledge and practical skills accordingly. It is also important to note that CBT is *not appropriate* for all problems and all patients.

At a pragmatic level the authors would agree, following Padesky and Greenberger (1995), that intervention can occur in any one of five areas namely environment, thoughts, feelings, physical sensations and behaviour. Padesky's work is based on the Beckian model of CBT (Beck, 1976; Beck et al., 1985) and it is this theoretical perspective that underpins this book.

Where to intervene in the five areas is a *clinical judgement* based on the assessment, formulation, goals and evidence-based practice. An 'ideal' CBT intervention would lead to fundamental and permanent changes in the patient's thoughts and beliefs in association with long-term changes in behaviours, emotions, physical sensations and environment. This is, of course, not always the case for every patient for various reasons. These reasons may include pragmatic ones like the wishes of the patient, the resource available to treat him and the level of training of the clinician. In addition, it is important to consider the current limitations of CBT theory and interventions to address mental health problems.

There is strong evidence of the effectiveness of CBT interventions with a wide range of disorders. For example, there is now evidence for varying degrees of effectiveness in panic disorder with and without agoraphobia, obsessive compulsive disorder, generalized anxiety disorder, social phobia, specific phobias, acute and chronic depression, posttraumatic stress disorder, eating disorders, bulimia nervosa, sexual dysfunction, alcohol and drug dependence and other conditions. (See Roth and Fonagy, 1996 for a review.)

There is variability in the strength of evidence in these disorders and the degree of recovery that can be expected with each disorder. These issues are very relevant in making decisions to use CBT interventions and need to be considered before embarking on their use. It is also useful to make a distinction between using CBT interventions to *treat* a particular problem versus using the interventions to more effectively *manage* a chronic problem.

In terms of content, the book will present a straightforward description of CBT approaches and procedures that should be readily understandable to mental health clinicians who are interested in developing skills in CBT assessment and clinical interventions. The text will aim to be practical and solution focused. The authors' clinical knowledge and expertise will be fed into the text and will be identified as such; the authors hope to describe what we refer to as *clinical wisdom*, that is, the knowledge and skills qualified CBT practioners routinely draw on when using CBT interventions that are not routinely described in CBT books. Best clinical and evidence-based practice will, however, be followed. Detailed discussion of research and theoretical issues is beyond the scope of this text. The interested reader can access such information from the literature cited in the comprehensive reference list at the back of the book.

We first describe what CBT is, emphasizing, the importance of structure in the CBT process and look at how to carry out a detailed CBT, assessment, factors to consider in terms of the suitability of a particular problem for CBT, and how to engage the patient in using CBT interventions. Later we describe how to develop a CBT case formulation as a means of making psychological sense of the patient's current problems. The task of agreeing clear treatment goals will be described. The concept of the therapeutic relationship from a CBT perspective will be explored and we go on to describe how to identify and work with negative thoughts and beliefs, and the variety of behavioural, disputational, imaginal and emotional techniques that can be used, and the typical problems that arise. We also examine treatment of anxiety and depression and the reader will be helped to overcome common pitfalls that occur when using CBT interventions to tackle these problems. The book will then describe other commonly used CBT methods drawn from the broader schools of CBT, for example problem solving and assertiveness.

We explore how CBT principles and practices can be integrated into routine mental healthcare. The issue of managing patients whose problems are not readily tackled using CBT interventions, but for whom a CBT formulation may be helpful, is addressed. Chapter 11 recommends how the CBT approach can be integrated into generic mental health roles, and methods for fostering a CBT culture in mental health teams and inpatient units will be discussed. The final chapter is designed to help the reader find ways to access and use CBT clinical supervision and training optimally. Case descriptions, patient and clinician dialogues and problem-solving exercises will be used to aid readers' understanding.

As with books the authors read themselves, we would hope that this book will be interesting and useful. Following the therapeutic style of CBT, it is requested that you spend a little time reflecting on the contents of each chapter when you have finished reading it and, more particularly, that you complete the practical exercises that we have included. It is tempting to bypass these exercises in a book, but if you spend a little time doing them, they will enhance your learning and help you relate the text to your own practice.

We hope you enjoy the book.

Philip Kinsella
Anne Garland

What is cognitive behavioural therapy?

There is nothing either good or bad but thinking makes it so.

Shakespeare, *Hamlet, Act II, Scene 2*

The description is not the described.

Krishnamurti (1996)

Chapter contents

- CBT is a structured, evidence-based treatment
- There are various schools of CBT but the treatment arising from Beck's work is focused on here
- CBT understands problems by considering the interaction between environment, thoughts, feelings, physical sensations and behaviours
- There are three levels of thinking; negative automatic thoughts, rules for living and core beliefs. Treatment is focused on modifying these three levels of thinking and associated unhelpful behaviours with the aim of alleviating negative feelings and physical reactions associated with anxiety and depression
- The key elements of CBT include a collaborative understanding of how current problems are being maintained and the use of specific interventions both in and out of treatment sessions in order to tackle such problems

INTRODUCTION

Cognitive behavioural therapy (CBT) is a highly structured, evidence-based treatment that aims to address patients' current problems. The treatment is goal oriented, in that goals are agreed between the patient and clinician usually in terms of improving the patient's distressing emotional states and unhelpful patterns of thinking and behaviour. All of these may interfere with the patient's day-to-day functioning. Each aspect of treatment is explicitly discussed and the patient and clinician work together to solve the patient's problems using a range of interventions informed by a coherent cognitive behavioural treatment rationale and working within an agreed, short-term (average 12–18 sessions) timeframe. Central to the cognitive behavioural model is the idea of a normalizing treatment rationale. Thus, the emotional responses that characterize anxious and depressive states are seen to exist on a continuum with normal emotional reactions that we experience every day. Thus, when looking at the evidence base for CBT treatments there is a wealth of research data that demonstrate many of the cognitive and behavioural features of common mental health problems are also present in individuals who do not meet the diagnostic criteria for such problems. Examples include the frequency of reported intrusions (a feature of obsessive compulsive disorder and generalized anxiety disorder) in the general population; experiments in mood induction demonstrating a link between low mood and negative thoughts in both depressed and non-depressed subjects; the tendency for all humans when anxious to pay more attention to the object or event that is the focus of our fear, as demonstrated in threat cue detection experiments. For a comprehensive review of this literature the interested reader is directed to Williams et al. (1997). So what is the difference between a normal human response to distress and the nature of the response that is seen in mental health problems? The difference is that in mental health problems these emotional responses are seen as more intense, persistent and out of proportion with our usual responses.

It needs to be acknowledged that there are many different 'schools' of cognitive behavioural therapy. Gilbert (1996) identified at least 16 schools of CBT, each of which places different emphases on behavioural and/or cognitive elements and/or interpersonal factors within CBT theory and practice. For example, if the reader compares the work of Marks (Marks et al., 1983) with that of Barlow (Barlow et al., 1989) and Clark (Clark et al., 1999) in the treatment of panic and agoraphobia as an example, the treatment methods, while sharing some commonalities, also contain some divergent theoretical principles and interventions. In addition, some CBT models are more evidence based than others and it is a mistake to assume that the acronym CBT is synonymous with the idea of its treatments being evidence based. For example, a series of randomized controlled trials in the area of depression validated the original work of Beck and colleagues (Beck, 1976; Beck et al., 1979) but there is some debate over the conclusions drawn regarding the efficacy of the original CBT for depression studies (see Williams, 1997, for a meaningful discussion of these issues). Meanwhile, Young's schema-focused cognitive therapy (Young, 1994), while drawing on some of Beck's original theory and treatment methods has also introduced new interventions and has yet to be empirically validated. Similarly, the rational emotive behaviour therapy invented by Ellis (1962) and developed by Dryden and associates in the UK (Dryden 1995) has less supporting evidence.

This book aims to describe the basic principles of CBT theory and its related treatment methods. Most emphasis is placed on the cognitive therapy of Beck and colleagues (1976, 1979) and the British scientist–practitioners who have over the last 20 years significantly advanced the evidence base of CBT treatments for common mental health problems. A small sample of this vast literature, relevant to the disorders discussed in this book is as follows: in the field of anxiety disorders, Clark (1986), Freeston et al. (1996), Salkovskis (1989), Wells and Clark (1997). In depression, Fennell (1997), Gilbert (1992), Scott (1992), Teasdale (1993), Williams (1997). It is the work of these, mainly British, scientist–practitioners that has so greatly influenced the authors' clinical work and thus forms the basis of the theory and practice described in this book. However, it is also important to acknowledge the significant contribution the behavioural psychotherapy tradition has made to the interventions described. Behaviour therapy would undoubtedly have been a central aspect of the clinical training of the scientist–practitioners named previously and was the initial psychotherapy training undertaken by the authors. This field includes the work of an earlier generation of researchers such as Gelder and Marks (1968), Marks (1987), Rachman (1980); and, in more recent times, Davey (1992) and Ost (1989). The book is written to encourage the reader to engage with CBT in the spirit of the scientist–practioner (Barlow et al., 1984; Salkovskis, 2002). This model encourages the clinician to approach their work with an enquiring mind and not only to use interventions that have been empirically established as valid using the scientific method, but to generate further research data by investigating the efficacy of their own clinical practice using the scientific method.

THE GENERIC COGNITIVE BEHAVIOURAL MODEL

The starting point for making sense of CBT is to consider its generic principles. Thus, at a very basic level CBT looks at the inter-relationship between five elements: environment, thoughts, feelings, physical sensations and behaviour. This is usually described as a *vicious circle* and it is this metaphor that is used as a basic treatment rationale when first introducing patients to CBT as a model. In CBT, all disorder-specific models such as panic disorder (see Chapter 8), are presented as a vicious circle with these elements represented. The scientist–practitioner model would encourage the clinician, wherever possible, to use a disorder-specific model to introduce the patient to the CBT treatment rationale. This will be discussed later in the book.

However, in order to understand the fundamental principles of CBT it is useful to think about first principles. Thus, in its most generic form the CBT model can be represented, as it is by Greenberger and Padesky (1995), as a vicious circle connecting events in the environment with our thoughts, feelings, physical sensations and behaviour. This is illustrated in Figure 1.1.

THE THREE LEVELS OF THINKING (COGNITION) IN CBT

Within the CBT model there are three levels of thinking (in CBT textbooks this is referred to as *cognition*), which over the last 30 years have been defined, described and elaborated in a variety of ways. Key texts for the interested reader are by Beck and colleagues (1976, 1979) and Beck (1995) and Padesky and Greenberger (1995). The language used to describe these levels of thinking can seem complex and confusing to both clinician and patient. Therefore, here there has been an attempt to simplify the language and the following terms have been used to label the three levels of thinking:

- negative automatic thoughts (NATs)
- rules for living
- core beliefs.

From a theoretical perspective these three levels are connected and this is best explained

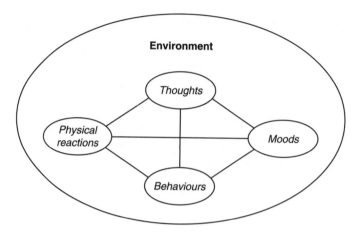

Figure 1.1   Five aspects of your life experiences (© 1986 Center for Cognitive Therapy, Newport Beach, CA)

using a metaphor. If we were to consider the three levels in terms of a fountain then the core beliefs would represent the powerful bore that forces the water out of the ground. The rules for living would represent the founts of water that directly emerge from the bore and give the fountain its form and shape. Finally, the negative automatic thoughts (NATs) would represent the hundreds of droplets of water that are thrown off as each fount, driven by the power of the bore, reaches its full height. Expressed in psychological terms the core beliefs represent our fundamental sense of self and are key to how we see ourselves, others and the world and are associated with high levels of emotion. The rules for living act as principles that guide an individual's behaviour and govern how we act and interact in the world in a way that builds and further develops our sense of self, i.e. who we are. The NATs are the direct product of both our core beliefs and rules for living and represent how we make sense of our experiences in everyday situations. We will now consider each of these levels in more detail.

First level: negative automatic thoughts (NATs)

The first level is usually referred to as *negative automatic thoughts (NATs)*. At this level cognitive theory identifies two aspects to thinking:

- thought *content*, that is, *what* we think
- thought *processes*, that is, *how* we think.

These will now be considered in turn.

What we think: thought content

In Beck and colleagues' model (1976, 1979) NATs are defined as an individual's appraisal of a specific situation or event. As such this level of cognition represents what is going through an individual's mind in a particular situation and may be associated with pleasant, unpleasant or neutral feeling states. Within the CBT model the NATs that the clinician is most interested in are those that are most closely associated with high levels of negative feelings such as anxiety, low mood, guilt, shame and anger and the like. Hence the use of the label NATs. NATs can occur in two forms:

- as *words*
- as *images or pictures in the mind's eye.*

Each disorder-specific CBT model identifies different themes in terms of the content of NATs (and rules for living). Thus, for example, in panic disorder (Clark, 1986) the content theme in NATs is *a catastrophic misinterpretation of bodily sensations where danger is imminent* and typical NATs are:

- *verbal or words*, e.g. 'I'm going to faint', 'I'm having a heart attack'
- *an image or picture in the mind's eye*, e.g. image of self collapsing in the supermarket and people standing over you staring at you and not helping. Imagery is a key cognitive component of anxiety disorders.

How we think: information processing biases

In Beck's original model (Beck, 1976; Beck et al., 1979; Beck et al., 1985b) these information processing biases are referred to as 'thinking errors' or 'cognitive distortions'. Within Beck's clinical model, the content of each NAT is said to contain information processing biases and particular types of information processing bias can be identified in relation to depression and anxiety. The most important ones are as follows.

When mood is depressed:

- thought processes are more *negative* and often *focuses on past events*: 'I've never been good at my job'
- thought processes are *more black and white*: 'if there's any mistakes in that essay it's not worth finishing'
- we have difficulty thinking in *specific* terms and tend to make *overgeneralizations*, using one specific incidence to jump to a general usually negative conclusion about ourselves, other people or events in our lives: 'my boss didn't like that work; he probably won't like anything I do'
- we more easily *recall negative memories* from the past and it is harder to recall positive memories
- our thinking about *past* events can become *ruminative*, that is we turn the same thing over and over again in our minds repeatedly
- we are *more much sensitive to criticism* and see this where perhaps it is not intended, tending to *take things personally* whether they are meant this way or not.

When mood is anxious our thought processes are:

- more *negative* and often *focuses on future events*: 'if I go for this interview I'll make a fool of myself'

- automatically looking for what is potentially *threatening or dangerous* to us
- *only focusing on the threat* at hand with a *narrow perspective* and not taking in other information
- *overestimating the risk* in a situation
- *underestimating the likelihood of our dealing* with the situation
- focusing on the *worst possible outcome* often stretching weeks, months or years into the future
- dominated by *worry* about *future events* and we turn the same thing over and over again in our minds.

Generally, nowadays, these are referred to as *information processing biases* and this is the term the authors will use in this book. The categories defined by Beck in his original work are derived from clinical observation. Over the last 30 years ongoing research in the field of cognitive science has developed evidence to support Beck's clinical observations and further elaborate how information processing biases maintain mental health problems. Examples of this research evidence exist (see Williams et al., 1997 for a comprehensive review) to support the idea that in anxiety and depression, *how* information is processed is biased in a way that means only certain types of information are taken on board or are given more attention and weight. These processing biases are viewed as central to the maintenance of emotional disorders by keeping the focus of attention on negative or threat-related information and not attending to or discounting contrary information. For an excellent text on the clinical application of this aspect of cognition, see Harvey et al., 2004. For example, staying with the cognitive model of panic disorder (Clark, 1986), there is research evidence (for an interesting discussion, see Barlow, 2004) to show that patients with panic disorder more readily detect and pay attention to changes in bodily sensations than non-anxious controls. Thus, if the panic prone individual experiences a sensation of light-headedness, they not only detect this more quickly than non-panic-prone individuals, but they are more likely to appraise this as dangerous and threatening and they will conclude 'I'm going to faint'. They are more likely to do this than ignoring the sensation or ascribing a more benign explanation to the sensation, such as 'it's just a feeling, it will pass'. In the literature this is referred to as threat cue detection (Barlow, 2004; Williams et al., 1997) Similarly in depression, research evidence shows that not only is the content of thought negative but also a key processing bias that is central to the maintenance of depression is black and white thinking (see Williams et al., 1997).

Anxiety and depression are discussed separately here, however, in the reality of clinical practice where patients frequently present with comorbid anxiety and or depression then patients may experience a combination of these symptoms. This area represents the cutting edge of current CBT research. As the literature in the field of information processing biases and their role in the maintenance of mental health problems expands, some researchers are calling for the development of what is termed transdiagnostic models that take into account the clinical observation that these information processing biases are common across a range of anxiety disorders or in comorbid presentations of anxiety and depression. These information processing biases are discussed further in Chapters 8 and 9.

Patient example

Julie, who has a diagnosis of panic disorder, experiences panic attacks on a daily basis. When a panic attack happens Julie experiences a range of physical sensations including palpitations, breathlessness and dizziness. She perceives these symptoms as being dangerous and reports the following NATs that within the cognitive model of panic disorder (Clark, 1986) would be described as *a catastrophic misinterpretations of the bodily sensations*. Examples of these bodily sensations and the related NAT are as follows:

- palpitations – 'I'm having a heart attack'
- breathlessness – 'I'm going to die'
- dizziness – 'I'm going to faint'.

Julie also described an image of herself alone at home, writhing in excruciating agony and trying to crawl to the telephone to summon help.

Patient example

John has a diagnosis of acute depression characterised by low mood, lack of enjoyment, poor concentration and memory, tiredness and lethargy, loss of libido and irritability. John has withdrawn from most of his social activities and spends most of his time in bed. With much effort John arranges one day to meet a friend, Bert, to go out for the day. At the last minute his friend telephones and informed him he will have to postpone their trip, as he has been called away on urgent business. John feels very low in mood. His NATs are:

- 'This always happens to me'
- 'There is no point in trying to do anything; it always ends up a mess'
- 'I bet Bert isn't really going to work, I bet he got a better offer'
- 'He is probably sick of me'
- 'I'm such awful company'
- 'I'm so useless'
- 'I might as well give up; nothing is ever going to change'
- 'My life is pointless.'

John's thoughts are negative in content across three domains, namely a negative view of self, world and future (Beck et al., 1979), and the way in which information is processed is black and white and personalized.

Second level: rules for living

In Beckian theory this second level of thinking is referred to variously as dysfunctional assumptions (Beck, 1995; Beck et al., 1979) or, in more recent years, conditional beliefs (Greenberger and Padesky, 1995). For the purposes of this text the authors have simplified language and termed this level of cognition *rules for living* which are defined as rules that guide behaviour and action. This also represents a more user-friendly language when working with patients.

In CBT there are two types of rule, as follows:

- The first are those phrased as a *conditional statement*: 'if . . . then . . .'. To return to our case example, Julie lived by a rule that guided much of her decision making and avoidance behaviour, as follows: 'If I am not in control at all times something bad will happen.' At this second level of thinking the theme of *control* is key to understanding CBT models for anxiety disorders.
- The second type of rule relates to those phrased as 'demand' statements. John held the rule: 'I should be perfect.' This does not have the conditionality of 'if I do X then Y will follow', but is simply held as a demand the individual expects himself or herself to follow. Rules, which are phrased as demand statements, are often associated with a strong sense of duty and morality and are often harder to tackle in treatment.

These rules for living are directly linked to the behaviours we engage in in order to maintain self-esteem and a sense of safety and security. Thus, provided we can meet the conditions or demand laid out for us by our rules, our self-esteem and sense of safety and security remains intact and we function well. However, if for any reason our ability to keep to the conditions or demand within our rules is compromised then, according to Beckian theory, this makes us vulnerable to anxiety and depression. Also, the childhood circumstances (see following patient example) that lead to the development of these rules can mean that the demands of our rule are ultimately unrealistic and increase our vulnerability further.

There are two important distinctions to be made between NATs and rules for living, as follows:

- While NATs represent our appraisal of a specific situation or event, rules for living *apply across situations*.
- While NATs are biased in terms of content and process, rules for living are *value judgments*, which rather than being inherently right or wrong are to a greater or lesser degree helpful or unhelpful.

In keeping with the normalization model described previously, we all have such rules that guide our behavioural choices. Indeed Beckian theory holds that these rules are directly derived from our upbringing and often reflect culturally shared values from family, school, religion, social class and the like. A defining feature of such rules is that the person holds them rigidly, often with a high degree of conviction and it is this inflexibility that is often problematic rather than the content of the rule itself.

Given that a defining feature of rules for living is that they operate across situations, then they tend to exert an influence over several areas of a person's life. The behaviours an individual does and does not engage in are useful markers for identifying the themes in rules. More in-depth discussion of the themes to the cognitive content of rules for living can be found in Chapter 7.

Third level: core beliefs

In Beckian theory, this third level of cognition is referred to variously as underlying assumptions (Beck et al., 1979) or, in more recent years, unconditional beliefs (Greenberger and Padesky, 1995) and schemas (Young, 1994). In this text, for consistency, they are referred to as core beliefs. These represent the mechanism by which information is processed by the individual that drives the psychological component of emotional disorders, of which the rules for living are a related process and NATs are a product. These core beliefs relate to domains about self ('I am bad', 'I am a failure'); self in relation to others, ('I am inferior'); other people ('people are not to be trusted', 'other people are better than me'); and the world ('the world is competitive', 'the world is not fair'). These are considered to be more global in their sphere of influence and have an absolute quality in that people tend to hold them as unquestionable truths. Thus, the individual finds it hard to distance themselves from the belief, and defines himself, others and the world by the belief.

To return to our case examples: thus, rather like the everyday givens we live by that grass is green or the sky is blue, Julie sees herself as vulnerable, other people as unreliable and the world as dangerous. Meanwhile, John sees himself as a failure, others as superior to him and the world as hostile and cruel.

Beckian theory holds that core beliefs are formed in childhood and adolescence as a result of experiences in our lives. While traumatic events such as abuse or bereavement in childhood can clearly lead to the development of strongly held core beliefs regarding self, others and the world, most people's beliefs at this level are a product of their general environment during childhood, which will be a mixture of beneficial and negative experiences. Young (1994) describes core beliefs as being the product of a general noxious environment rather than the result of any one-off traumatic event. According to Beckian theory (Beck, 1976; Beck et al., 1979; Padesky and Greenberger, 1995), it is our rules for living and core beliefs that represent the individual's psychological vulnerability to depression and anxiety. Thus, these beliefs may lie dormant but are activated by critical events that are related to them.

Patient example

Thus, for Julie, the onset of her panic symptoms coincided with the sudden death of her father from a heart attack (an event that was unexpected and over which she had no control). Since his death she had become anxious and noticed an increase in bodily sensations (a normal aspect of the grief process), in particular, palpitations. Julie perceived these to be abnormal and she became more preoccupied with her own health and that these symptoms may be indicative of imminent catastrophe, expressed in her NATs (see earlier). These events activated her core belief 'I am vulnerable' and activated her rule for living: 'If I'm not in control I'll be overwhelmed.' During her childhood Julie's mother was somewhat overprotective. Whenever Julie showed the slightest sign of ill health she was kept home from school and taken to the doctor. As she got older her mother lectured her on the importance of keeping herself safe, telling her to be careful crossing the road, not to talk to strangers and not to take risks regarding her safety. These lectures would be supported by examples of what could happen to her should she not be careful. Similarly her mother protected her from any situation that made her anxious and encouraged her to avoid activities that raised her anxiety levels, such as reading in school assembly.

Patient example

In John's case, the onset of his depression followed his being made redundant from work, which activated his core belief that he is a failure and that other people who kept their jobs in the company did so because they are superior to him. He perceived that now he was no longer employed he had lost value and purpose and people would no longer want to associate with him. Hence his rule for living: 'If someone alters their plans it's because they got a better offer.' John's family environment was strict and his parents had high expectations of him in terms of his performance and attaining status. He recalled occasions in his childhood when his achievements were downplayed and he was compared to his peers unfavourably in terms of the status they achieved. He remembered one occasion when his father became angry because he had not been chosen for the school first team in rugby, but another boy in his class, who was the son of a work colleague of his father, *had* been chosen and his father told him he was humiliated because his work colleague now had 'one up on him' and therefore wouldn't want to mix with him. Similarly when he obtained eight grade A and one grade B in his GCSE results and came second in the school his parents expressed their disappointment that he had not been first.

In terms of the evidence base there is equivocal empirical data to support Beck's original hypothesis that rules for living and core beliefs represent a trait cognitive vulnerability to depression and anxiety disorder (Beck 1976; Beck et al., 1979; Beck et al., 1985). What data do exist (for a comprehensive review see Williams et al., 1997) support the idea that such constructs are mood-dependent phenomena that disappear once anxiety and depression lifts. However, there is some evidence in the depression literature to support the role of a need for social approval as being relevant in the onset of depression (Hammen et al., 1985; Hammen et al., 1989). There is currently much debate regarding the implications of such data for the practice of CBT. It is the authors' view that working with rules for living in relation to the maintenance of current distress has clinical validity. Thus, if we return to Julie and her rule, 'if I am not in control I will be overwhelmed', this rule informs her action of mentally scanning her body for what she deems to be potentially dangerous bodily sensations (thus influencing how she processes information) and leads her to engage in active strategies (checking her pulse every hour, monitoring her heart rate and lying down if they are 'too fast') in order to try and minimize (control) the likelihood of experiencing any unpleasant bodily sensations and subsequent panic attack.

How is this theory applied in practice?

The overall aim of CBT is to modify each level of thinking. There is an assumption that work always starts at the level of NATs, working with both content (*what* a person thinks) and process (*how* a person thinks). This is based on the idea that these are:

- central to the maintenance of current problems
- the most readily accessible aspect of thinking
- the one that can most readily be tackled, resulting in the most rapid symptom relief.

A further reason for not tackling rules for living and core beliefs in the first instance is that these are more closely associated with our core sense of our selves and self-esteem, and tackling these is likely to give rise to high levels of emotion that may worsen rather than alleviate distress. Thus, the individual needs to be equipped with skills to manage such emotion. These skills are derived from work carried out at the level of NATs. The skills learned at this point in treatment are crucial if patient and clinician take the decision to carry out work on modifying rules for living and core beliefs. Any attempt to work on these will lead to a temporary exacerbation of low mood and anxiety. This is normal and necessary for this work to take place. However, the patient needs to have a good grasp of the CBT skills used to tackle NATs and unhelpful behaviours so these can be used to manage the high levels of emotion that arise when working on rules for living and core beliefs. Importantly, there is an assumption in CBT that all three levels of thinking are interconnected. As such, modifying NATs leads to increased flexibility in the rules for living and in turn direct work on these rules makes the processing mechanisms in core beliefs more flexible and adaptive. Thus, in short-term cognitive therapy (6–18 sessions) there is an assumption that the processing mechanisms in core beliefs are sufficiently adaptive and that no direct work needs to be carried out on this level of thinking. However, as rules for living can play a key role in the maintenance of unhelpful behaviours that also maintain anxiety and depression then work at this level is required in order to reap lasting gains for the individual receiving treatment. It is, in our opinion, a common mistake for people beginning to use CBT to think that CBT is 'about' verbally disputing some of the patient's NATs. Although this is an element of CBT, it is really about identifying, understanding and breaking the vicious circle that is established between events in the individual's environment, the person's cognition (NATs generated by rules for living and core beliefs) feelings, physical sensations and behaviour (Greenberger and Padesky, 1995).

KEY ELEMENTS OF CBT

Blackburn and Twaddle (1996) describe the key elements of CBT as follows:

- The importance of a shared psychological understanding of the patient's problem. In the CBT literature, this is referred to as formulation (Butler, 1998) or conceptualization (Persons, 1989).

- The emphasis on the patient's distinct experience.
- The collaborative nature of the therapeutic relationship (more recently the inter-personal dynamics between clinician and patient has been emphasized, for example Safran and Segal, 1996).
- Active involvement of the patient, particularly in devising homework tasks.
- The use of *Socratic questioning* (Padesky, 1993). This essentially means using a specific questioning style within a specific structure in such a way that a dialogue occurs that promotes problem solving and self-understanding, which is then used as a basis for taking action.
- Explicitness of the clinician – usually most aspects of treatment are explained to and shared with the patient.
- The emphasis on empiricism, which means gaining knowledge from experience, and using this to guide future action.
- The importance placed on what happens outside the session through the use of homework assignments.

WHAT TYPE OF PROBLEMS WILL BEST RESPOND TO CBT INTERVENTIONS?

An important consideration in deciding which patients will benefit most from treatment is the evidence base for CBT. The cognitive behavioural model has a long tradition of evalu-ating its efficacy and there is a robust set of research evidence demonstrating its utility in the treatment of a variety of mental health problems and chronic physical illness. For an overview of this literature, see the Department of Health (DoH) (2001).

Increasingly, cognitive behavioural interventions are being used to manage severe and enduring mental health problems such as bipolar disorder (Scott et al., 2001), schizo-phrenia and psychosis (Chadwick et al., 1996) borderline personality disorder (BPD) (Linehan et al., 1991) and anxiety in dementia (James, 1999). It is vital that cognitive behavioural interventions are not seen as a panacea for tackling all mental health problems and an important consideration is the goal of the intervention to be made. Namely, is the goal to treat the problem the individual is experiencing so that they become largely symp-tom free or is it to help the individual to better manage a chronic and enduring illness? For many patients and clinicians the latter is often a more realistic goal.

The CBT assessment process can be applied to any patient presentation including those who present with bipolar disorder, psychosis, personality disorders and Alzheimer's in its early stages. The same is not necessarily true for CBT interventions. Decisions regarding which patients will benefit from a CBT intervention can be complex and a number of factors play a role. These include: the nature of the presenting problem and its chronicity; the degree to which the patient accepts the cognitive behavioural treatment rationale and can work within its principles; personality factors; and the level of hopelessness and pessimism in the patient's presentation. A pragmatic discussion for the clinical implica-tions of such factors can be found in Safran and Segal (1996). In addition, factors such as the level of clinician's adherence to the CBT model, the quality of CBT training under-taken and the level of skill in delivering the intervention (Burns and Nolen-Hoeskema,

1992; DeRubeis and Feeley, 1991), and the clinician's optimism/pessimism regarding the patient (Williams, 1992) also exert a significant impact on treatment response.

There is much research still to be done in order to increase further the effectiveness of CBT interventions. In the spirit of the scientist–practioner model (Barlow et al., 1984; Salkovskis, 2002) this ongoing commitment to developing the evidence base of interventions and examining our own clinical practice lies at the heart of the CBT model. Equally the dissemination of the existing interventions and skilling the workforce in their implementation is still in its infancy.

Chapter summary

CBT is an evidence-based structured psychological intervention that addresses the patient's current problems. Problems are understood by considering the relationship between environment, thoughts, feelings, physical sensations and behaviour, maintained as a vicious circle (Greenberger and Padesky, 1995). Problems can also be made sense of within the framework for disorder-specific models and this is detailed further in Chapters 8 and 9. There are various schools of CBT, but the approach taken here is based on both the original work of Beck (1976; Beck et al., 1979; Beck et al., 1985) and the work of a number of British scientist–practitioners who have made a significant contribution to the advancement and accessibility of CBT treatments. The model describes three levels of thinking: negative automatic thoughts, rules for living and core beliefs about the self, others and the future. The key elements of CBT are a shared understanding of the patient's problems, a collaborative approach and an emphasis on homework and learning from experience. There is a strong research evidence base for the effectiveness of the approach, particularly with anxiety and depression, but individual patient outcome will be influenced by the skills of the practitioner and the commitment of the patient.

2

CBT style, structure and materials

THERAPEUTIC STYLE OF CBT

In CBT, perhaps more than in any other psychological intervention, there is an emphasis on an active, directive problem-solving style that focuses on here and now problems. The defining features of a CBT intervention are that it is:

- time limited
- active, directive, focused and structured
- coming from a problem-solving stance
- goal directed
- educational
- collaborative
- action oriented.

The aim is to describe problems in terms of the five interconnected domains of the vicious circle (environment, thoughts, feelings, physical sensations and behaviour) and use practical strategies to proactively tackle the problems identified, using specific goals as the measure of change. In this respect, CBT is not just about talking, it is about *taking action*, with a strong emphasis on the patient being the person who instigates change. Thus, there is an intrinsic self-help focus to any CBT intervention. The aim is to teach the patient a set of skills that can be used on a long-term basis to effectively tackle or manage problems.

Taking this into consideration, the clinician using CBT interventions needs to adopt a specific therapeutic stance. Thus, while the therapeutic relationship is important, this is not seen as the vehicle for change in CBT, but rather the skills the patient acquires during treatment and the independent use of these outside the session. Therefore, while it is important for the clinician to demonstrate the non-specific skills necessary to develop a productive therapeutic bond (see Chapter 4), this is insufficient. The clinician also needs to have specific practical skills at their disposal and be able to teach the patient to use these skills outside the treatment setting.

Collaboration

Fundamental to the active, directive, problem-solving style described earlier is the process of collaboration. In this respect, the clinician and patient are seen as equals who both bring important knowledge to the treatment process. The patient brings his understanding of his problems and difficulties, and the clinician brings her knowledge of CBT interventions to share with the patient. Intrinsic to the CBT definition of collaboration is the concept of equal responsibility sharing and this is made explicit at the beginning of treatment, and is exemplified in how each CBT session is structured (see 'agenda setting', later). In this respect, an important skill for the CBT clinician to develop is to effectively manage this sharing of responsibility. Most clinicians are trained to take a benevolent stance toward the patient in which more responsibility for the intervention lies with the clinician. Thus, when the patient fails to attend sessions repeatedly, cancels frequently, is late for appointments or does not complete homework assignments this is not usually addressed and there are no consequences for the patient should they persistently approach healthcare appointments in this way. Within a CBT model, it is made explicit between clinician and patient at assessment what behaviours are expected of both parties in order to maximize the chances of CBT being effective. These are:

- attending sessions as agreed, usually weekly for standard CBT interventions
- attending sessions on time
- completing homework assignments
- planning how to use the session time effectively.

A further consideration in establishing a collaborative style is ensuring that both clinician and patient participate actively in the session. Thus, it is usual in a CBT session that there is a 50:50 split between the clinician and patient in terms of how much each party speaks. Many clinicians define collaboration as always agreeing with the patient and not challenging them in any way, but collaboration is about active participation and negotiation. For many CBT interventions, some aspects of the treatment are non-negotiable, that is there are certain aspects of the intervention that, if they are not carried out as intended, will mean that the intervention will be ineffective. It is usually these aspects of treatment that the patient (due to the nature of his problems) and often the clinician (because it inevitably means engaging the patient with his distress) will want to avoid. In a CBT model, the clinician needs to develop the necessary skills to negotiate and engage with the patient (and herself where necessary) to enable the patient to use the CBT intervention in a meaningful way. Thus, the clinician seeking to utilize CBT skills effectively with mild to moderate mental health problems needs to:

- Understand and accept the treatment rationale for any given CBT intervention.
- Have the necessary skill and knowledge to convey a treatment rationale to the patient which instils confidence and hope.
- Be willing to address her own avoidance regarding any CBT intervention she feels unable to implement.
- Implement CBT interventions as intended within limitations of the complexity of the patient's presentation.

Exercise

Here is a description of a panic provocation exercise, which is part of the CBT treatment protocol for the treatment of panic disorder. Once you have read it, reflect on your thoughts and feelings about using it with a patient:

- What would it be like to use this with a patient?
- What are your thoughts about it as an intervention?
- What are your concerns?
- What action might you need to take to address any difficulty you have with the intervention?

This intervention is used to help the anxious patient who experiences panic attacks and who believes the symptoms of panic are a sign of imminent catastrophe, e.g. 'I'm going to die/faint/have a heart attack'. As a result, the patient uses safety behaviours (for example, sitting down or always carrying water to sip or reciting a mantra such as 'I will be okay') believing the safety behaviour prevents the feared catastrophe from occurring. A clinician using this intervention would deliberately induce a substantial number of panic symptoms (breathlessness, palpitations, dizziness, dry mouth, jelly legs, tingling sensations etc.) in the patient, by, for example, asking him to rapidly over-breathe for 30–60 seconds. The aim is to deliberately induce panic symptoms in such a way that the patient activates his catastrophic panic-related thoughts (e.g. 'I'm going to faint/die/have a heart attack'). For example, during the process of over-breathing the patient reports feeling dizzy with jelly legs and tingling sensations in his head and reports the thought 'I am going to faint'. You then direct the patient while experiencing these sensations to drop his safety behaviours for example sitting down, or sitting down and remaining still (e.g. instruct him to stand on one leg and deliberately sway around) in order to test out the accuracy of his panic related thought: 'I am going to faint'.

Socratic questioning and guided discovery

Wills and Sanders (1997) describe guided discovery as a process, which uses a questioning format (Socratic questioning) that involves the clinician and patient working together to see if there are different ways of viewing things. Socratic questioning is the method of information gathering used in CBT while guided discovery is the process by which problems are identified, examined and solved. In their definition, the authors are considering these two methods only in terms of making an intervention, but their use is fundamental to CBT at assessment, and as part of agenda and homework setting as well as treatment interventions. The purpose of Socratic questioning is to gather information and to invite the patient to devise plans to use the information gathered to generate homework exercises and/or behavioural experiments.

In their early work, Beck and colleagues (Beck et al., 1979) define Socratic questioning as a method for asking questions in a structured way in order to draw general conclusions from specific facts or instances. In traditional CBT language, this is called inductive reasoning with the aim of directing the patient toward a (predetermined by the clinician) view of a problem situation. It is this definition that leads some authors to emphasize the logical and rational aspects of CBT, and some critics to suggest CBT emphasizes an unrealistic shift from negative to positive thinking. However, Padesky (1993) in a celebrated keynote address entitled 'Socratic questioning, changing minds or guided discovery?' took the process back to its origins in the philosopher Socrates' work and significantly advanced the practical application of the method. In her keynote address, Padesky emphasizes the exploratory nature of Socratic questioning in which patient and clinician collaboratively explore a problem examining it from different perspectives in order to construct a range of viewpoints that can then be tested out for their validity in the patient's life.

In this method, Socratic questioning and guided discovery always focus on a specific example of a recent problem situation that is located in time, place and person. Examination of this concrete example is then generalized to other problem situations in order to identify key themes (patterns of thinking or behaviour) so that the patient can apply the new information discovered to evaluate previous conclusions or to construct new ideas to be tested. The clinician uses the method in a way that draws the patient's attention to information relevant to the issue being discussed, but which may be at the time outside the patient's current focus of attention. Thus within Padesky's definition of Socratic questioning and guided discovery, rather than emphasizing one 'right conclusion that fits all circumstances' there is rather an ongoing process of examination of problem situations with new information and ideas being generated, revised and retested in the light of different experiences. A key aspect of this process is teaching the patient the skill of using Socratic questions to question their thoughts and perceptions in a problem situation, rather than, as many people do, operating on an assumption, usually worded as a prediction and on the basis of this assumption engaging in avoidance. Thus, for Padesky, equipping the patient with this skill gives them the opportunity to use it on a long-term basis months and years after CBT treatment has finished.

Exercise

Return to the first practical exercise and identify whether any of your reflections on the intervention contain assumptions. Common examples novices to CBT report are: 'It is potentially dangerous to the patient', 'I will upset the patient and damage our therapeutic relationship', 'I will make a mess of the intervention and do the patient harm'. In a CBT model the aim is to identify such predictions (or assumptions) and test their validity by carrying out a behavioural experiment.

NB Obviously, before you implement any CBT intervention you need to be trained to use it and have access to appropriate clinical supervision. So at this stage we are not suggesting you go out and try panic provocation unless you have specific training and clinical supervision but as you read this book try and identify what assumptions or predictions you make in relation to CBT theory and/or practice. Try to record them and consider the impact they have in terms of how you act as clinicians trying to use a CBT approach.

Padesky (1993) identifies the characteristics of good Socratic questioning as follows. There is an open questioning style with the aim of the majority of questions beginning with the word 'what'. For example consider the following two questions:

- Do you like bananas?
- What is it about bananas you like?

The first question is likely to elicit a yes or no response. The second questions focuses the person being questioned on considering what it actually is about bananas they like, for example, 'they are a tasty, filling and healthy snack'. This reply then enables you to use the information to question further, for example, 'What is it about a snack being healthy that is important for you?' and the person might answer, 'I feel better about myself if I eat healthily; eating chocolate makes me feel guilty'. As you can see this opens an opportunity to explore the feelings of guilt about eating chocolate which may lead to information about particular food rules the person holds. The overall aim in using Socratic questioning and guided discovery is to elicit the idiosyncratic meanings the individual holds and using 'what?' questions as a starting point is the optimal way of achieving this.

With this in mind, within Socratic questioning there is an avoidance of using questions beginning with the word 'why?' The use of the word often leads to vague answers. For example, compare the following two questions:

- Why do you put yourself down?
- What is it about yourself that leads you to put yourself down?

The first is likely to elicit answers such as 'I don't know' or 'it is the way I am'. The second focuses the patient's attention on self and what aspects of self lead them to put themselves down. Thus the reply might be 'I don't like myself'. Once more this naturally opens up an opportunity for further questions, for example, 'When you say you don't like yourself, what aspects of self do you not like?' or 'What experiences have led you to conclude you don't like yourself?' The second method is going to elicit much more, detailed, rich and emotionally relevant information.

Here is an example of the use of Socratic questioning to explore a problem situation with a patient:

P Susie [her 3-year-old daughter] is always misbehaving and I handle it really badly.
C Can you recall a time over the last few days when in your mind she has misbehaved and you have not handled it well?
P Yes, yesterday she threw yoghurt at the cat and then kicked it.
C How did you handle the situation?
P I didn't do anything, just cleaned it up. I find it so hard to tell her off.
C What is it about telling Susie off that you find hard?
P I'm not sure.
C How do you feel at the prospect of telling her off?
P Anxious and guilty.
C Okay, did you have any of those feelings yesterday?
P A bit.
C Let's focus on those feelings. Which feeling is generally the strongest?
P Guilt, definitely.
C Okay. What is it about telling Susie off that makes you feel guilty?
P I must be a really bad mum if I have to tell her off.
C That's an interesting thought, what is it about telling her off that makes you a bad mum?
P Well, a good mum would be able to control their child so she didn't do things that meant I had to tell her off; it's my fault.
C There seem to be some important ideas here, a relationship between the idea that part of being a good mum is never having to tell Susie off and being in control of Susie's behaviour and the fact you don't have control is your fault. Have I understood you correctly?
P Yes, Susie's behaviour is a reflection of me as a mother. Children only misbehave when the parent is not in control, therefore it is my fault, and I'm a bad mother, I have no control.
C So are you saying here 'if my children have to be told off it is my fault because I have no control'? This seems to be directly related to your sense of yourself as a bad mum.
P Yes.
C This sounds like an area we need to focus on and try and find ways of influencing how you deal with Susie misbehaving in terms of how it affects you. What is your view?
P I need to do something – I'm so useless.
C Don't be hard on yourself, at times it's hard work being a parent, let's try and examine the situation in more detail and see if we can find a different way of tackling the problem.

STRUCTURE OF TREATMENT

As you will be beginning to understand, CBT is a highly structured intervention and as such has a number of features:

- a clear and well planned treatment rationale
- a structure that guides the patient in such a way that they learn to tackle their problems themselves
- it teaches the patient to use specific skills to solve problems
- it emphasizes the independent use of these skills outside of the treatment session
- it provides the patient with sufficient structure in the session that they can learn the necessary skill to a level it can be used independently
- it encourages the patient to attribute improvement in their problems to the skills they learn and not the clinician.

This structure is present and can be observed from the beginning of the assessment process, through treatment and into relapse prevention and follow-up as well as in each individual CBT session. In this respect, it is possible to clearly identify different phases in the process and to offer guidance on how much time is usually devoted to each phase. This is now shown:

> assessment of problems (1–3 sessions each of 1-hour duration)
> problem and goal setting (1–2 weekly 1-hour sessions)
> making psychological sense of the problems (ongoing throughout treatment)
> CBT intervention (6–15 weekly 1-hour sessions)
> relapse prevention (2–5 fortnightly 1-hour sessions)
> discharge into follow-up (2–5 sessions 1 month, 3 months, 6 months, 12 months, of 30 to 60 minutes' duration).

Once a decision has been taken to offer CBT to a patient, then an explicit treatment contract will be negotiated. An average treatment contract for problems of moderate severity (e.g. acute depression of up to 6 months' duration) is between 8–15 sessions excluding the assessment and follow-up session, which are additional. However, with problems of mild severity (e.g. panic disorder without agoraphobia with an onset in the previous 3 months) treatment could be as little as 2–3 sessions, while with more complex presentations (e.g. chronic obsessive compulsive disorder with a duration of 4–5 years) treatment could be 25 or more sessions. In some circumstances, a trial of treatment might be offered. Such circumstances include when the clinician is unsure whether the patient has the resources to tackle their problems in the way a CBT intervention would ask (e.g. facing up to high levels of anxiety and being able to tolerate this) or where the clinician has concerns that CBT may exert a detrimental effect on the patient's emotional well-being. A typical trial might be 4–8 sessions. It is important that once the treatment contract is offered then the clinician manages it effectively. This is usually achieved by building in regular review sessions, for example every 3–5 sessions. At these review sessions progress towards treatment goals are measured and discussion takes place regarding changes made and any obstacles to change. Review sessions also provide an opportunity to renegotiate the treatment contract either offering more sessions or fewer depending on how treatment is progressing. This process gives a clear message to the patient that treatment is time limited and that if progress is not being made then this needs to be proactively addressed.

STRUCTURE OF CBT SESSION

If you were to watch a video of a CBT session, you should be able to readily observe the session structure in terms of there being a clear beginning, middle and end to the session. You should also be able to observe the clinician being active and participative in the session in terms of time keeping and maintaining appropriate control over the focus and pacing of the session. The ability to do this effectively requires certain skills, which include an ability to set and stick to an agenda, time-keeping skills and an ability to structure the session in order to use the time effectively. This requires the clinician to have the confidence and skill when necessary to interrupt the patient if they are digressing from the chosen topic of the session or to direct the session if it is descending into a vague and unfocused discussion as opposed to the structured active intervention it is meant to be.

There now follows an outline of the typical structure of a CBT session of 60 minutes' duration. It is presented as a series of steps with guidance on how much time should be spent on each step.

Typical step structure

Step 1: review patient's current mood state

This is a general enquiry of how the patient has been since the previous session which may help to identify items for the session agenda (2–3 minutes).

Step 2: set agenda for session

This is the means by which the session is structured. There are usually standing items such as reflections on previous session, review of homework and main topic for current session (5 minutes).

Step 3: homework review

This is the opportunity to discuss the week's homework in terms of outcome, difficulties and conclusions. Even if homework is not completed, time needs to be spent reviewing the reasons for non-completion and applying appropriate problem solving. This also enables planning for further action on the basis of the outcome of a particular homework assignment or repetition of particular homework activities if they have been especially beneficial. Encouraging the patient to make a written summary of learning from homework to take away is vital (5–20 minutes depending on the stage of treatment).

Step 4: main task of session

This would be chosen in terms of the current problem from the problem list which is being tackled. It may be developing a particular skill (e.g. modifying negative automatic thoughts

(NATs) or carrying out a behavioural experiment (e.g. inducing panic symptoms to test catastrophic panic-related NATs) (20–25 minutes).

Step 5: session feedback and homework

This involves enquiring how the patient is feeling and summarizing learning from the session. This is followed by negotiating the homework for the coming week, which usually arises from the results of the previous week's homework and the work carried out in the session. A written record of the homework needs to be made and if particular skills have been taught then written instructions on how to use these outside the session need to be given (e.g. handout on how to modify NATs and blank diary sheets to fill in). It is then useful to help the patient summarize what has been both helpful and unhelpful about the session and to enquire as to whether there is anything that has occurred in the session that has been especially upsetting to the patient. If anything is identified or if important topics have arisen for which there is insufficient time to address then these should be prioritized on the next session's agenda (10–15 minutes).

You will note in this description of session structure two methods that are seen as central to the maintenance of structure in CBT, these are agenda setting and the use of homework. We will now briefly consider each of these in turn.

Agenda setting

The setting and management of an agenda to guide each CBT session is a key skill that clinicians using CBT interventions need to develop. It is a means by which important aspects of the CBT structure are brought to life in the treatment process, and it fosters collaboration, which is the cornerstone of the therapeutic relationship in CBT. By engaging in the act of setting an agenda at the beginning of each session it sends an explicit message that there is a shared responsibility between patient and clinician for the content of the session. Similarly, sticking to the agenda as the session progresses helps keep the activity of each session consistent with the overall goals of the intervention. The use of agenda setting also allows for the targeting of new problems as they arise in treatment and importantly keeps treatment in line with the overall psychological formulation that guides every CBT intervention.

The act of setting an agenda often feels very unnatural to many clinicians. Its use is not generally part of any core professional training and many clinicians when introduced to the idea struggle to implement it as intended within the CBT therapeutic process. Some clinicians argue it is too business-like and detracts from the establishment of the thera-peutic relationship. Agenda setting is a good example of the stylistic qualities of CBT that necessitate patient and clinician acting as a team, speaking in equal measure and when necessary the clinician taking charge of the session if the content is straying from the agreed agenda. This requires the skill of politely interrupting the patient and, if necessary renegotiating the agenda if the patient feels the new topic that has arisen in the course of the session requires immediate attention, and the agenda set at the beginning of the session is to be put to one side.

Exercise

Take time to reflect on your own thoughts and feelings about interrupting a patient who is straying from an agreed topic for discussion in a session.

What are your predictions about interrupting the patient? Try and write these predictions down.

Can you see any advantages to interrupting a patient who is digressing?

Can you see any disadvantages?

Can you identify any situations where it may be important to interrupt the patient who is digressing?

Can you identify any situations where it might be better to allow the patient to digress?

How to set an agenda

There are five clear steps to agenda setting:

1 Set the agenda at the beginning of each session, spending usually 2–3 minutes and ideally no more than 5 minutes. The agenda should be written down and ideally within view of both patient and clinician throughout the course of the session.

2 Prioritize the agenda items and be realistic about how much can be covered in the time allocated to the session. If the usual length of each session is 60 minutes then usually 1–2 items can be covered. Bearing in mind that within the time allocated the standard agenda items that appear on a session agenda on a weekly basis (see 1) also need to be included.

3 Identify how much time within the session is going to be devoted to each item on the agenda, remembering that the session review and the review and setting of new homework on average takes up 15–20 minutes of the session, and can take up to 30 in the early stages of treatment. How much time is to be devoted to each item on the agenda should be written next to the appropriate item.

4 Adhere to the agenda while maintaining collaborative flexibility as appropriate to the needs of the patient as they change within the session.

5 Review the agenda at the end of the session to identify what has been covered and what needs to be placed on the agenda for the next session.

Here is an example of agenda setting presented as a dialogue between clinician and patient:

C Okay James, from your point of view, what do we need to focus on in today's session?
P I'm not sure.
C Let's see, how did you get on with the diary we agreed you would keep?
P Ah, yes, I didn't do it.
C Okay, it may be helpful to spend some time thinking about what prevented you from doing it. What is your view?

P   I feel awful, I'm sorry I didn't do it.

C   As we have discussed before, helping you to deal with your problems outside of the CBT sessions is an important part of treatment. It would seem important to discuss what was difficult about keeping the diary, I get a sense listening to you that you feel upset you have not done it and you may feel tempted to try and not think about the reasons for not doing it. But I think we really need to look at that if the treatment is going to be helpful.

P   [sighs and nods] Okay.

C   So item one is review of homework and identifying reasons for not doing it. What else do we need to look at today?

P   I had an awful day on Wednesday; my mood was really low and I had an argument with my wife. I've been feeling pretty awful about myself since.

C   Sounds like there are a number of things we could focus on: your mood, the argument and feeling awful about yourself. If I asked you to sum up the main problem, what would that be?

P   I just don't understand how everything gets so out of control, my mood, my thoughts and my temper – it happens too often.

C   So a sense of feeling out of control in terms of your mood, thoughts and temper and using Wednesday as an example, it may be helpful to relate this to the diary you were going to keep for homework which was about trying to record your negative automatic thoughts. How does that seem?

P   Okay.

C   So our two items are reviewing the difficulties you had with keeping the diary and your sense of a lack of control over your mood, thoughts and temper based on trying to understand what happened on Wednesday and perhaps seeing if we can relate that back to the homework exercise. Then we can think about what we could do to build on what we cover in the session today and when we meet next week. How much time do we need to give to each item?

P   I think most time to what happened on Wednesday. I want to do something about it.

C   Okay, how about 10 minutes on the homework review, 35 minutes on the incident on Wednesday and your sense of feeling you have no control over your mood, thoughts or temper? Then we can spend 10 minutes on reviewing what has been learned in today's session and the homework for the next week. How does that seem?

P   Fine.

C   Okay, will you help me keep time? As you know time keeping is not my greatest skill, but with your help, I may improve! [clinician smiling and joking with the patient]

The written agenda would look like this:

1   Review of homework – identifying difficulties in carrying out agreed homework (10 minutes).

2   Incident on Wednesday – sense of no control over mood, thoughts or temper (35 minutes).

3   Review of session and setting of homework for next week (10 minutes).
     (**NB** 5 minutes would have been spent setting the agenda thus the whole session covers 60 minutes).

This is a relatively straightforward example. The patient with minimal encouragement engages in the process and makes a contribution. However, this behaviour usually has to be shaped in the early stages of treatment. This is generally achieved by sharing with the patient a basic rationale for setting an agenda. The following box contains an example of how agenda setting may be introduced to the patient.

> 'As you are aware we have agreed to meet initially on a weekly basis for 12–15 sessions of CBT. Each session lasts for an hour. This may seem like a long time but the time can go very quickly once we start talking about your problems and how to tackle them. In order to use the limited time we have as wisely as possible one of the things we do at the beginning of each session is to set an agenda. Now that might seem a bit daunting but all this means is we are going to decide what are the most important things for us to focus on in each session and write these down as a list. We then use the list to guide the session. One of the things I will ask you at the beginning of each CBT session is how you would like to spend the time we have set aside. This might also seem a bit anxiety provoking but this is really to give you opportunity to take part in the planning of the session so we can ensure the problems that need addressing in the treatment are tackled. I also will suggest items for the agenda based on particular problems we are trying to solve. This way we can be sure we are working together to address your concerns. Most people find this process odd at first but eventually find it helpful in focusing our work together. How does this seem to you as way of deciding how we use our time each week?'

Difficulties in agenda setting

In our current healthcare settings, generally speaking patients attend appointments with the idea that they are passive recipients of treatment and the clinician is going to sort out their problems for them. In this respect, many patients struggle with being asked to participate in treatment and make an active contribution to the intervention. This is often brought into sharp focus by how patients respond to being asked to participate in setting and sticking to an agenda. For patients with low self-esteem it can make them feel highly anxious. They may worry about appearing foolish or making a mistake and therefore respond to the opportunity to participate with statements such as 'I don't know'. Some patients may respond with hostility particularly if they are interpersonally sensitive and perceive others as trying to catch them out or humiliate them. For patients who have spent a lifetime putting others' needs first they may never have been able to develop an internal sense of their own point of view. Thus the patient, when asked to contribute to an agenda, may genuinely not know how to respond as they have no opinion to bring which can result in anxiety and bewilderment.

All these examples illustrate the point that how a patient responds to the invitation to participate in setting an agenda can tell both patient and clinician a great deal about the rules for living and core beliefs that inform the patient's actions and interactions. Therefore whenever setting and sticking to agenda becomes problematic this is an opportunity to begin to make psychological sense of the patient's problems (see Chapter 3 for detailed discussion of this process in CBT) as they manifest themselves in the patient's interactions with the clinician and the CBT methods. Generally speaking, the more complex a patient's presentation, particularly where there is chronicity, high levels of hopelessness and helplessness, avoidant coping strategies or where personality factors need to be considered, then setting an agenda and sticking to it may be more difficult to manage. However, it is especially important that the clinician try to actively address these difficulties when they arise and not abandon the act of agenda setting, which is fundamental to the structure and process of CBT. The key to good agenda setting skills is to be able to remain sufficiently structured that the session is coherent with a clear beginning middle and end and where problems are actively addressed. This needs to be achieved while being faithful to the spirit of collaboration that is enshrined within the CBT model thus ensuring a flexible approach within the session. This said, a skilled clinician should be able to identify when it is essential to abandon an agenda (and not necessarily explicitly address this with the patient until the end of the session) because an important topic has arisen during the course of the intervention. Examples include if the patient discloses thoughts of harm to self or others (e.g. suicidal thoughts or risk of harm to children or vulnerable adults) then this should always be given priority and it would not be wise to interrupt the patient to refocus them on a predetermined agenda. In a similar vein a patient may begin to disclose highly emotional material related to experiences in childhood or adulthood that may be key to understanding their distress. Examples may include childhood sexual abuse, adult sexual assaults, painful memories of childhood losses such as death of a loved one or expressions of acute distress unrelated to items on the agenda. Again, the patient should be enabled through sensitive and empathic collaboration using Socratic questioning and guided discovery to articulate the meaning of their distress and to make use of this material within the CBT formulation of their current problems (see Chapter 3).

HOMEWORK ASSIGNMENTS

Homework assignments are an essential feature of all CBT interventions. The effectiveness of every CBT intervention is determined by the degree to which the patient is able to use the psychological understanding and practical skills that are learned in treatment sessions in problem situations in their everyday lives. As Kazantzis et al. (2005) observe, homework assignments are not just additions at the end of the session but a defining feature of this model of working and should be present in *every* session. It is indeed difficult to conceive of an intervention being labelled as CBT without the use of homework assignments. Kazantzis et al. (2005) continue by identifying a number of benefits to the use of homework assignments, which include:

- promotion of transfer of skills from the CBT session into problem situations the patient is trying to tackle
- enabling the patient to take responsibility and ownership for their improvement in treatment
- allowing for the generalization and maintenance of cognitive and behavioural skills and it is this process that is crucial to the long-term benefits of CBT.

There is a wealth of research data on the role and effectiveness of using homework assignments in psychological therapies (see Chapter 2 in Kazantzis et al., 2005, for a full discussion). While extensive discussion of this is beyond the scope of this text there is evidence to suggest that treatment interventions that include homework assignments as a component are more effective than those which do not use homework assignments. Further, patients receiving CBT interventions who complete homework assignments obtain better treatment outcomes than those who do not complete such assignments (Addis and Jacobson, 2000; Bryant et al., 1999).

Given that homework is such a vital part of every CBT session the burden of responsibility for its inclusion lies with the clinician. A key goal therefore is to establish a routine at the start of each session (as part of the agenda) whereby the previous session's homework is reviewed and learning from this summarized and used in the current session and/or future homework assignments. The patient makes written summaries of learning, ideally, but if the clinician does this written summarizing then this is given to the patient to take away from the session. This usually takes the form of an action plan of how this learning is going to be applied in the patient's everyday life. Clearly, a major challenge in treatment and a key skill the clinician needs to develop is engaging the patient in using and learning from homework assignments. There are several steps the clinician can take to optimize the effectiveness of homework assignments in CBT sessions. These are discussed below and examined in greater detail in Garland and Scott (2005):

- *Giving a rationale for homework that emphasizes the 'no lose' scenario.* This is best achieved by presenting the homework assignment as an experiment not a test. Thus, the rationale includes the idea that if the homework assignment is successfully completed then this is a step toward understanding and solving the problems the patient brings to treatment. However, equal and explicit emphasis is given to the idea that there may be obstacles to completing homework and these also need to be understood. Thus whether or not the homework is completed something can be learned about the patient and their problems.
- *Making homework assignments achievable.* Breaking problems down into manageable tasks is an important part of the problem-solving rationale on which CBT is based. Many of the symptoms of anxiety and depression will impact significantly on the person's ability to engage in homework assignments. It is therefore vital that such assignments are tailored to make an allowance for the impact of symptoms such as poor concentration and memory, as well as practical obstacles such as caring for a young family or working. The emphasis here is not that these obstacles mean that homework assignments are not actively and consistently used, but they are devised in such a way as to maximize the patient's chances of completing them.
- *Making use of the structured approach to treatment.* This is achieved by using other standard elements of CBT structure to guide the use of homework. Thus, agenda setting in which reviewing homework and the setting of further homework is always present. Specifically designed homework summary sheets are used to record learning both in and between sessions. Homework assignments usually build on the work of the session and in this respect they can be set as the session progresses and agenda items are tackled rather than leaving this to the end of the session. Collaboration is also important here. A patient who has actively shared in the process of reviewing and agreeing further homework is going to have greater investment in its

completion than when it has been imposed by the clinician with little input from the patient.

- *Using handouts, audiotapes and written summaries.* This aspect relates to the psycho-educational component of the CBT model. Handouts that describe skills that have been practised in session (e.g. how to identify NATs; monitoring activity levels) are vital to the successful completion of homework assignments and need to be used routinely. Similarly audiotapes of session that the patient can take away, with the contents of the session (including the negotiated homework tasks) are a further way of maximizing the chances of homework completion.
- *Modelling the skills required for homework completion in the treatment session.* A commonly cited reason for not completing homework is that the patient was not clear what they had to do. The impact of this can be reduced by modelling in the session the skills required to complete the task, especially if it involves completing a diary. A useful rule of thumb is to ensure the patient has had an opportunity to practise in the session the skill required to successfully complete the agreed homework before attempting to apply the skill outside of the session.

Non-completion of homework assignments is common and there are a number of reasons for this which include both patient and clinician factors. These are described below and examined in greater depth in Garland and Scott (2005):

Patient factors:
- the patient did not understand how to carry out the homework assignment
- the patient did not see the assignment as useful and relevant
- the patient experienced NATs or practical obstacles that interfered with the completion of the homework

Clinician factors:
- the clinician is too prescriptive and the process has a feel of 'teacher collecting homework from pupil', which is experienced as anxiety provoking, especially if the patient has concerns about failure, or being judged and humiliated
- the clinician sets too much homework and the patient is overwhelmed and does nothing
- the clinician fails to review homework that has been completed, which will reduce motivation to complete future homework tasks
- the clinician's own NATs (rules for living and core beliefs) regarding the reasons the patient has not completed the homework, which can be less than helpful. For example: 'the patient is not trying', 'the patient is not psychologically minded' 'the patient does not listen to me'. The clinician needs to recognize what contribution her own thoughts, feelings and behaviour may play in the process of agreeing and reviewing homework, which may exert a beneficial or detrimental effect on the process of homework completion. What is required is a compassionate stance toward the patient and their plight combined with a problem-solving approach aimed at understanding obstacles to homework completion.

PROBLEM AND GOAL SETTING IN CBT

Purpose of problem and goal setting

The chief mechanism for maintaining a structured and focused intervention in CBT is the use of a problem list to define in precise terms what difficulties are to be addressed in treatment and relevant goals that when reached would indicate the problem had been resolved. This process is usually referred to as problem and goal setting and its purpose within a CBT intervention is as follows:

- It makes explicit to the patient what to expect in treatment by clearly defining with the patient what problems are going to be addressed and what goals are going to be worked towards.
- It fosters hope for the patient by providing the possibility of change, focusing the patient on the future rather than on current difficulties.
- It reinforces the idea that the patient has responsibilities within the treatment contract, and is an active participant in the change process rather than a passive recipient of care.
- It gives structure to the treatment process and allows presenting problems to be prioritized and addressed.
- It prepares the patient for discharge from the outset of treatment by making it explicit that treatment will end when treatment goals are reached or discontinued if progress towards the goals is not made.
- It allows for evaluation of the outcome of the intervention as measured by the patient's progress toward the goals of treatment.

Key features of problem and goal setting

Given the problem-solving focus within CBT it is in keeping with the model that problems and goals are defined in precise terms. Ideally, problem statements and goals:

- *Are generated by the patient in collaboration with the clinician who is guided by the theoretical models that underpin the CBT intervention.* What is important for both patient and clinician to recognize here is that most CBT interventions involve the patient engaging with high levels of emotional distress. Many patients, perhaps understandably, attempt to introduce their avoidant coping into the goals that they set themselves for treatment. Equally, many clinicians collude with this avoidance. Most CBT interventions require patients to face their feared consequence and the clinician needs to have sufficient theoretical knowledge and practical skill to enable the patient to do this. Thus a patient who presents with panic disorder and agoraphobia who is unable to go out alone further than the end of the street may want to set a goal of being able to go out with a trusted other, but not want to go out alone. Within CBT theory, wanting to go out only with a trusted other (but to continue to avoid going out alone) would constitute a safety behaviour and would not be advocated as a goal. Equally, the same patient may agree a goal to go out alone but only do so on one occasion. Again within the CBT model this would theoretically be formulated as avoidance and again the clinician would not advocate this as a goal. Appropriate goals for the end of treatment would address the usual avoidances those patients with panic disorder and agoraphobia describe. For example:

1   to visit the town centre alone every Saturday, between 12 noon and 4.00 pm, visiting two department stores, staying in each for 30 minutes and to walk down the main shopping precinct staying for 40–60 minutes

2   to be able to visit the local superstore at the busiest time and complete my weekly shopping, joining the longest checkout queue.

These are just two examples of myriad goals that can be set which aim to enable patients to gain the most benefit from CBT interventions, which involves facing up to avoidances. However, one note of caution: making a problem list and setting goals follows a comprehensive assessment and the more complex a presentation is then a more sophisticated level of theory may be needed to understand which CBT interventions are going to be most appropriate. For example, Jane and Angela were both referred for CBT with the presenting problem of panic disorder and agoraphobia. Jane's problems had an onset of 6 months following a stressful time at work where she had been taking on more responsibility, working long hours and not taken any holidays for a year. She experienced her first panic attack in a supermarket one evening after an especially hectic day. Jane had continued to go to work but had started to avoid certain meetings and was having difficulty going to the shops and driving.

Meanwhile, Angela had a 3-year history of panic attacks. The onset had occurred following an assault by an ex-partner. Angela avoids going out as much as possible for fear of encountering her ex-partner. The onset of her difficulties occurred 2 months after the assault when she was out shopping and saw a man who looked like her ex-partner and she experienced memories of the assault. She had been avoiding going out since that time.

While both women seem to present with the same problem (panic disorder and agoraphobia) the circumstances leading to the onset are very different and it would be important in the case of Angela to assess for the presence of symptoms of post-traumatic stress and possibly generalized anxiety disorder for which the CBT treatment is very different from that of panic disorder with agoraphobia and therefore the problem statements and treatment goals would be different. It is for this reason that the authors would advise clinicians reading this book who are interested in developing CBT skills to access clinical supervision from an appropriately qualified CBT clinician, so that the skills necessary to discern these important differences can be developed from the outset.

- *Are realistic and achievable within the patient's presentation and the negotiated treatment contract.* Many patients and the clinicians who seek to help them have high standards. These high standards are often reflected in their expectations of what CBT can achieve within a time-limited treatment contract. It is therefore important to be explicitly realistic with the patient in terms of what problems can be addressed in treatment, and what goals are realistic for the timeframe of treatment. Thus, if you work in a primary care setting and have an upper limit of 6–12 sessions, realistically you are going to be most effective in working with mild problems and some more straightforward moderate problems (e.g. mild depression, recent onset panic disorder without agoraphobia, specific phobias, mild grief problems, stress-induced illness), more longstanding problems with possible comorbidity such as chronic depression, chronic obsessive compulsive disorder, generalized anxiety disorder, health anxiety and social phobia usually require anything between 15–20 sessions for a moderate presentation and 25 plus for more chronic and comorbid presentations. Equally for some patients CBT is going to be about helping them manage longstanding problems more effectively and the outcome is going to be less clear-cut. This needs to be reflected in the problems that are placed on the problem list and the goals that are negotiated as part of treatment. Thus something such as low self-esteem needs to be viewed as something which the patient will need to address on a long-term basis and cannot be completely resolved even in a 25 sessions plus treatment contract.

This reality needs to be reflected in the goals that are set with patients so the patient is not set up for disappointment because the goals are unrealistic in terms of the patient's capacity for change and the treatment contract available.

- *Are specific, concrete and detailed in terms of how they are described and are measurable in that change can be quantified.* It is always helpful to operationalize problem and goal statements so that there is clarity regarding what precisely the problem being addressed is and what exactly is the goal the patient is working toward. Thus, for example, when writing a problem list with a patient who is anxious about his health consider the following ways of writing the problem statement:

> *'Health anxiety'* versus *'Worry about my health on a daily basis, which leads me to check my body for signs of illness, log on to the internet to check out symptoms and visit my GP/ accident and emergency once a week for reassurance that I don't have something seriously wrong with me.'*

It is possible to see how the second statement captures the problem in terms of how it impacts on the patient's functioning on a day-to-day basis. In addition the problem statement naturally suggests some excellent treatment goals as follows:

> *'To make psychological sense of my worry about my health and understand what behaviours I engage in keep the problem going.'*
> *'When I notice a bodily sensation and start to worry to resist the urge to seek reassurance (e.g. internet and visit GP/accident and emergency) and to try and deal with my worry in a more helpful way (i.e. use my CBT skills).'*
> *'To stop visiting my GP/accident and emergency on a weekly basis to seek reassurance about my health.'*
> *'To stop logging onto the internet to check out the meaning of certain bodily sensations.'*

These operationalized goals clearly identify the expectations within the CBT model for treatment health anxiety and are concrete observable behaviours that if the patient were able to engage in would indicate a significant improvement in the problem. These can also be measured as treatment progresses. For example, the patient could keep a daily log of how often he logs on to the internet to check symptoms or a weekly log of his visits to the GP/accident and emergency.

How to develop a problem and goal list with the patient

There are four basic steps as follows to developing a problem and goal list:

Step 1: define each problem in precise operationalized terms (see earlier).

Step 2: make a written list of the problem statements (usually 3–5).

Step 3: develop 1–3 treatment goals for each problem statement, which are achievable and measurable. Make a written list of the treatment goals.

Step 4: prioritize the order in which the problems are going to be addressed in treatment.

Some sheets follow, which can be photocopied, specifically designed for writing problem and goal statements. These sheets contain a built in subjective measure of progress in treatment. The patient is asked to make ratings of each problem statement on a scale of 0–8 of how much the problem interferes with normal daily activities (where 0 is not at all and 8 is significantly) and the patient is asked to rate how much success they currently have in reaching the goal. Again this is measured on a 0–8 scale where 0 is no success and 8 is complete success. (Pages 34 and 35).

How to prioritize a problem list

There are a number of factors the clinician and patient need to consider in deciding which problem to tackle first in treatment. At face value the most pressing problem often seems a reasonable place to start provided the patient and clinician can agree on what this is. There are a few questions the clinician can use to guide the decision-making process:

- *Is the person or their relatives at risk as a result of a particular problem?* The most commonly occurring issue here is hopelessness and suicidal thoughts. If the patient is feeling hopeless and experiencing suicidal thoughts then this becomes the first problem to be tackled in treatment using CBT interventions. If the person is experiencing thoughts of harming others (and the healthcare context is ouside a forensic mental health setting) then these would also be prioritized as needing addressing but would be done so outside of the CBT contract as this would generally not be something addressed within standard CBT for anxiety and depression. Some disorders that are amenable to CBT may put others at risk; the most commonly experienced example is the patient with chronic obsessive compulsive disorder who may, for example, be so concerned about dirt and contamination that they are bathing children in water with bleach added to it. This obviously needs to be addressed as a priority within the CBT model.
- *Which problem is primary in the presentation?* Many patients present with comorbid problems, particularly an anxiety disorder with depressive symptoms. Often the depressive symptoms are low grade and secondary to the anxiety disorder; this is often the case in obsessive compulsive disorder and panic disorder with agoraphobia. Frequently when the primary problem is addressed the depressive symptoms remit of their own accord so identifying the primary problem is important to how the CBT intervention is delivered. Where there is true comorbidity between disorders, for example it is common for an anxiety disorder such as social phobia or health anxiety to co-occur with generalized anxiety disorder or depression, then problems are best defined in terms of symptom focus, e.g. worry, intrusive thoughts, rumination or avoidance as these can be manifestations of both disorders.
- *What is the most disruptive or distressing problem?* While this may seem the reasonable place to start treatment it is not necessarily viable. A good example is relationship discord, which usually exerts a detrimental effect on an individual's mental health.

However the discord may be a product of the presenting problem. For example irritability, social withdrawal and loss of libido are common experiences for men who become depressed. These symptoms can give rise to conflict in a relationship because they have an impact on the couple's social life and sexual relationship. Treating the depressive symptoms will often resolve the conflict and therefore the symptoms should be the target for treatment. Also, many women experience depression in the context of emotionally abusive relationships and yet find themselves unable to leave the relationship. Placing the relationship at the top of the problem list is likely to render individual CBT ineffective because in order to address relationship difficulties both parties need to acknowledge a problem and solve it together. Therefore a more appropriate problem to focus on may be the patient's low self-esteem and her view of herself that keeps her in an emotionally abusive relationship. Another example of a problem that is often prioritized by the patient but is usually a red herring is weight gain and a desire for weight loss. While it is tempting to believe that if the patient could lose x amount of weight their mental health problems would recede, that is unlikely. Weight gain and the attendant distress it causes are likely to be a manifestation of longstanding self-esteem issues. Seeking to address weight loss while grappling with a mental health problem is likely to set the patient up to fail. It is better to consider a desire for weight loss in the context of self-esteem and encourage the patient to see this as a long-term goal once the CBT intervention has been completed. This is not to say the patient cannot try his or her own methods outside the session but that weight gain will not be a prioritized problem and weight loss will not be a goal in treatment.

- *What is the easiest problem to tackle in terms of reducing symptoms?* The most important first step in any CBT intervention is to instill hope, as this is the best way of engaging the patient in treatment. The easiest way of instilling hope is to choose a problem that can be resolved relatively easily or in which you will see an improvement in the first three sessions. Resolution of a relatively straightforward problem can instill hope that CBT interventions are effective and enable the patient to engage in more difficult aspects of treatment and resolve more distressing problems. Useful items to consider here are specific symptoms, e.g. poor concentration or sleep disturbance or withdrawal from specific activities, which can have a major impact in terms of improving day-to-day functioning.

- *What is most difficult/risky to tackle?* For some patients, their problems serve a protective function in that they keep their distress at a tolerable level and enable them to function to some degree. Sometimes it is risky to address certain problems as this may lead to deterioration in the patient's mental health problems. Nearly always this manifests itself in the context of complex problems with comorbid features. For example, it is not uncommon for excessive cleaning rituals to be an avoidant coping strategy used by the patient for managing high levels of emotional and cognitive arousal, which would be potentially overwhelming if engaged with by the patient. Similarly, self-harming behaviours (cutting, burning) can have adaptive purposes and, in both examples, childhood trauma may be a factor that needs to be considered.

  Engaging the patient in tackling these behaviours without mechanisms for managing the thoughts and feelings that will be accessed is likely to exert a detrimental effect on their well-being.

Problems and goals

Problem A □

Problem B □

Problem C □

Rating key

This problem upsets me/or interferes with my normal activities

| 0 | 1 | 2 | 3 | 4 | 5 | 6 | 7 | 8 |

Not at all   Significantly

Goal A1 ☐

Goal A2 ☐

Goal A3 ☐

Goal B1 ☐

Goal B2 ☐

Goal B3 ☐

Goal C1 ☐

Goal C2 ☐

Goal C3 ☐

Rating key

My progress towards achieving this goal regularly without difficulty

0	1	2	3	4	5	6	7	8

Complete success   No success

MATERIALS

A fundamental principle in CBT is that it is a self-help model, the aim being to equip the patient with a set of skills they can use to tackle their problems outside the session. Enshrined within this is the concept of psycho-education and this is articulated within the CBT model in the form of handouts, reading materials and CBT self-help literature with the discrete aim of supporting specific CBT interventions, as well as the overall treatment process, and thus enabling the patient to translate what is learned in the treatment session into their every day lives. In this respect an appropriate handout should accompany every intervention that is used with a patient from the treatment rationale given at the start of the intervention to the relapse prevention strategy at the end. How to choose handouts needs to be guided by the CBT training and clinical supervision you receive. There are myriad CBT handouts and self-help materials and careful judgement is required when choosing which to use with the patient, as its content needs to be concordant with the treatment rationale you have shared with them. Throughout this book some guidance is given on handouts that are available to support core CBT interventions and where these can be accessed. It is advisable to develop your own library of CBT handouts and self-help materials for use in your clinical practice, but it is advised that these are going to be most beneficial to the patient when they are used judiciously in the context of an ongoing programme of CBT training and clinical supervision.

There is a wealth of CBT self-help literature available. Here are some texts the authors have found helpful when working with patients within a CBT framework:

- Burns, 1990
- Butler and Hope, 1995
- Fennell, 1999
- Gilbert, 2000b
- Greenberger and Padesky, 1995
- Kennerley, 1997
- Padesky and Greenberger, 1995
- Veale and Willson, 2005
- Williams, 2003
- Williams, 2006

It goes without saying that whatever handouts and self-help literature the clinician chooses to use within treatment, then he or she should be very familiar with the content and able to use it in a way that enables the patient to engage with the written materials in meaningful and productive fashion. It is all too easy to quickly recommend a CBT hand-out or self-help book without the clinician being familiar with its content only to discover it is unhelpful to the patient or even counterproductive in terms of how they have understood its content. The clinician needs to endorse the contents of handouts and self-help literature in terms of relating it to the specific problems the patient is describing and making it relevant to his treatment goals. This can only be achieved if the clinician is familiar with the materials and confident in endorsing and using their contents effectively.

A further aspect of CBT structure is the tape recording of treatment sessions. This is standard in the treatment of acute depression where concentration and memory deficits may inhibit the recall of the content of sessions. However, in the authors' experience this is a strategy worth considering with all patients. It serves two purposes: one to aid recall, which is important given how much material may be covered in a single 60-minute CBT session. Second, it provides the patient opportunity to observe themselves in the treatment session from a third-person observer perspective rather than immersed in the interaction with the clinician. This can provide a unique opportunity for self-refection on problems and self, which clinical experience tells us can reap important benefits in treatment. The patient can be asked at the beginning of treatment whether he wants the sessions taped and the rationale for this is shared with him. Patients are actively encouraged to try this but it is not a prerequisite of treatment. Clinical experience would suggest patients who decline to audiotape sessions and listen to them in between appointments are, overall, more avoidant in their coping style, which usually makes treatment more protracted and with less clear-cut positive outcomes. The patient is asked to provide the tape and the same tape is used each session.

Measurement of change

This is a key component of CBT and its use as an integral aspect of treatment sets it apart from other psychotherapies. The authors would encourage the clinician to become familiar with a few well-validated questionnaires for disorder-specific problems (e.g. depression, panic disorder with and without agoraphobia, obsessive compulsive disorder) and to learn to administer these and interpret their scores.

There is also scope within the model for measurement of patient-specific problems and the main tool here is the use of measures specifically designed to assess a particular problem the patient is describing. Once more the clinician is encouraged to develop this as a core CBT skill during their CBT training and clinical supervision experiences.

Exercise

Experiment with:

- being more structured in your interactions with patients
- using handouts
- agreeing session agendas
- using a more Socratic style.

Try and reflect on these experiments by making a written record of what went well. What didn't work as intended? What can you learn from these experiments and how can you apply these in future clinical situations?

Also consider how the impact on the session could be measured:

- patient satisfaction or dissatisfaction
- your satisfaction or dissatisfaction
- clinical outcome.

In CBT, the style is active and problem focused. The patient is helped to engage in a process of discovery through Socratic questioning. The structure of therapy involves a set amount of sessions that can be estimated in advance, the agreement of clear and measurable 'problem-and-goal' statements, the setting of an agenda for each session and the use of homework. The taping of sessions and use of reading material facilitates the use of CBT interventions.

Making sense of the patient's problems

FORMULATION IN CBT

Case formulation-driven CBT interventions versus protocol-driven CBT interventions

Within the CBT literature, formulation is described in two ways, a protocol-driven intervention and a case formulation-driven intervention. The concept of a protocol-driven intervention comes directly from the evidence base on which the CBT model is based. What this means is that when a CBT treatment is tested in a randomized controlled trial the intervention is delivered following a protocol. The protocol is written before the trial begins and basically identifies which CBT interventions will be used in what order and how each one will be delivered. This means that the CBT treatment is broken down into a series of individual interventions and each patient receives each intervention in a stepwise way in a specified order over a predetermined number of sessions. No other interventions are offered apart from those described in the protocol. This method is adopted in order to ensure the reliability and validity of the intervention and to be able to draw conclusions from the results, based on the principle that each patient has received the same CBT intervention. This protocol method of treatment originally used in research trials has been translated into treatment packages for the anxiety disorders and depression. The CBT literature referred to in this book describes many of these (see Hawton et al., 1989: Wells,

1997) and clinical experience tell us these are highly effective with many patients, particularly when they present with mild to moderate problems with no or low levels of comorbidity. This method is closely aligned to the concept of making a diagnosis of a patient's problem, and typically protocols are described as the 'CBT protocol for panic disorder' or the 'CBT protocol for acute depression'. This originates from the fact that all randomized controlled trials traditionally use inclusion and exclusion criteria and diagnosis is the method for guiding this decision-making process.

In contrast, the CBT literature also describes a case formulation approach to CBT treatment. This case formulation approach originates from the profession of clinical psychology and can be used in the context of any psychological theory (e.g. psychodynamic psychotherapy; systemic therapy). In a CBT case formulation approach the clinician chooses which CBT interventions to use (usually drawn directly or adapted from the CBT treatment protocols) according to the presenting problem that is described and applies them as needed rather than in a stepwise order. In this sense treatment is tailored to the individual symptoms the patient is describing. This method is especially useful for patients who present comorbid and complex problems (e.g. GAD, chronic depression, borderline personality disorder) and patients who present with sub-clinical psychiatric symptoms who do not meet diagnostic criteria.

Each of these approaches to formulation will now be considered in turn.

Protocol-driven CBT interventions

While some professionals view protocol-driven interventions as inherently inferior to case formulation-driven interventions the authors would strongly encourage the reader to become familiar with these for the following reasons:

- Protocol-driven interventions are the basis of the CBT evidence base and as such it is good practice to develop skills in delivering these.
- Protocol-driven interventions lend themselves well to short-term focused CBT interventions (6–18 sessions).
- For certain patient presentations protocol-driven interventions are highly effective.
- Protocol-driven interventions supervised by an appropriately qualified CBT practitioner are a good starting point from which to develop robust CBT skills.

The following is an example of a CBT protocol for acute depression and would be delivered once a CBT assessment had been carried out. This protocol could be used to treat John, described in Chapter 1. Typically a CBT assessment is between 1–3 sessions each of 60-minutes duration. The content of this assessment phase is described in Chapter 5.

CBT protocol for acute depression

Total number of sessions is 18, each of 60 minutes' duration delivered at the following intervals:

2 sessions per week for 2 weeks

1 session per week for 10 weeks
1 session per fortnight for a month
1 session a month for 2 months.

Content of CBT sessions:

Sessions 1–2: problem and goal setting
Sessions 2–4: activity scheduling and graded task assignment
Sessions 4–10: identifying and modifying NATs using behavioural experiments
Sessions 10–14: identifying and modifying rules for living using behavioural experiments
Sessions 14–18: relapse prevention.

The delivery of the protocol is guided by a treatment manual which describes each step of the intervention. Each session is supported by patient handouts for each step of the specified intervention on how to use it, and the relevant diary sheets.

It is intended that the steps in the protocol build on each other. Thus it is envisaged that the patient continues to use the skills he or she learns at each step but learns to do so independently of the clinician.

CBT treatment protocols currently exist for the following disorders. Next to each disorder are examples of research trials that have used a specific protocol. This list is not exhaustive and there exists a range of CBT-based treatment protocols for each of the disorders described:

Panic disorder with and without agoraphobia (Clark, 1986; Marks, 1987)
Obsessive compulsive disorder (Marks, 1987; Salkovskis and Kirk, 1997)
Social phobia (Clark and Wells, 1995)
Generalized anxiety disorder (Butler et al., 1991; Borkovec and Costello, 1993)
Health anxiety (Salkovskis and Warwick, 1986)
Acute depression (Beck et al., 1979)
Chronic depression (Paykel et al., 1999)
Eating disorders (Fairburn et al., 2003).

Due to the complexities of demonstrating the efficacy of a psychological intervention, there is varying agreement among researchers and clinicians regarding the strength of the evidence base supporting these protocols. To view this debate within the CBT literature, see Barlow (2004) and Williams et al. (1997).

Exercise

Consider your own practice and taking a piece of paper and a pen try and write down what the advantages and disadvantages of using a protocol-driven CBT intervention might be. Consider the protocol just presented and ask how it might help you and the patient and what obstacles it may display.

Case formulation-driven interventions

Butler (1998) defines case formulation as the tool used by clinicians to build a bridge between CBT theory and practice and should, she advises, be as simple as possible. The clinician, through his or her understanding of disorder-specific CBT models of anxiety disorders and depression and the patient's presentation, will work in collaboration with the patient to develop a proposed cognitive behavioural explanation (sometimes referred to as a hypothesis) to make sense of the information gathered during the CBT assessment. This explanation is then tested during the course of treatment either to confirm or disprove the initial theoretical explanation or hypothesis. This is done through the process of what is referred to in the CBT literature as behavioural experiments (see Bennett-Levy et al., 2004) to collect further information as a basis for testing out new ways of viewing self and situations and trying out new behaviours.

Persons (1989) offers a similar definition of the CBT case formulation as follows. The CBT case formulation is the assessor's hypothesis about the inter-relationship between the patient's presenting problems and the psychological mechanism underlying these. Within the CBT model the presenting problems are those identified on the problem list as described in Chapter 2. Meanwhile, the psychological mechanisms within the CBT model are the rules for living and core beliefs described in Chapter 1. For example, returning to the case example of Julie in Chapter 1, she described her main problem as panic attacks. A CBT case formulation may propose that Julie's panic attacks and the related cognitive and behavioural strategies she uses to prevent herself from having a panic attack, are being maintained by her rule for living 'If I am not in control I will be overwhelmed' and her core belief 'I am vulnerable'.

Value of CBT interventions based on a case formulation

In certain clinical circumstances, there are clear advantages to using a case formulation-based CBT intervention. Most notably these are when patients present with complex longstanding problems and where there are high levels of comorbidity. In our view the CBT case formulation approach is of value in a number of ways as follows:

- It helps the clinician understand patients' presenting problems in terms of symptom description that is problematic thoughts, feelings and behaviours and difficulties in their environment.
- As the case formulation represents a description of the idiosyncratic aspects of the patient's problems, this can help the patient feel understood. This in turn can greatly enhance engagement in treatment and inspire a degree of confidence in the clinician and the CBT model.
- The case formulation provides a treatment rationale giving the patient a sense of what can be done to tackle their current problems and it guides the clinician in deciding where to focus CBT interventions.
- Importantly, the case formulation can potentially predict obstacles to treatment and potential future situations that may leave the patient vulnerable to relapse.
- The case formulation can help the clinician understand behaviour such as non-attendance or non-concordance with treatment, as a part of the problem rather than something to be frustrated by.

- It can help make sense of experiences within the therapeutic relationship, in that the patient's interactions with the clinician will be similar to those he or she has outside of the session.

Exercise

Consider your own practice, and taking a piece of paper and a pen try and write down what the advantages and disadvantages of using a case formulation-driven CBT intervention might be. Consider the case formulation just made for Julie and ask how it might help you and the patient and what obstacles it may present.

Maintenance formulation and longitudinal formulation

Within a CBT framework it is also possible to make a distinction between what is termed a maintenance formulation and a longitudinal formulation. A maintenance formulation focuses on the environmental factors, thoughts, feelings, physical sensations and behaviours that keep a problem going in the here and now. In Chapter 1, we refer to this as a 'vicious circle' which is a common metaphor used in CBT to try and present a basic formulation to a patient. In Chapter 1, the Padesky and Greenberger (1995) model is presented and this is an example of a maintenance formulation. Several of the disorder-specific models described later in this chapter are examples of maintenance formulations for which there is a specific diagrammatic vicious circle representation (see Wells, 1997, for the common anxiety disorders). The content of thinking, information processing biases and associated behaviours discussed in Chapter 1 are viewed as the key factors in disorder-specific CBT models that keep a problem going – hence the term maintenance formulation.

Meanwhile a longitudinal formulation aims to make links between what is keeping problems going in the here and now (the maintenance formulation) and the environmental factors in childhood and adolescence that predispose the individual to mental health problems (within the CBT model this would be the rules for living and core beliefs described in Chapter 1), and how these influence the patient in the here and now. As a general rule of thumb some of the most effective protocol-driven interventions (e.g. panic disorder with and without agoraphobia (Clark, 1986)) place most emphasis on the maintenance formulation, while the case formulation-driven intervention places more emphasis on the longitudinal formulation. However, there is within the literature some blurring of these two distinctions depending on which texts the reader consults.

While, as described earlier, the maintenance and longitudinal levels of formulation are connected, they can be separated in terms of a decision being made whether to work with the patient at a problem maintenance level or to develop a full longitudinal formulation. A variety of factors may influence which method you use but as a rule of thumb short-term interventions for mild to moderate mental health problems (6–10 sessions) are best approached with a maintenance formulation based on a protocol-driven intervention. Longitudinal formulations need to be built collaboratively with the patient and take time to develop. They are often most useful in chronic or complex problems where increasing psychological understanding may be necessary before the patient can even begin to con-template making changes in their life. However, like all things this is not a definitive guideline. Some patients who take readily to CBT and like to reflect on their previous experiences will start the process of a longitudinal formulation of their own accord, and in these circumstances this would be encouraged.

Frequently both methods are used as part of treatment, particularly if the treatment contract is between 12–18 sessions. Thus the maintenance formulation is used in the early stages of treatment (e.g. sessions 1–6) and this is expanded to incorporate a longitudinal formulation as is deemed necessary and useful. This latter point is important because CBT is underpinned by the philosophy of pragmatism and in this respect the formulation needs to be useful in terms of generating an explanation for the patient's current problems that forms the basis for action to tackle those problems, hence Butler's (1998) observation that the formulation needs to be simple. Formulations that are complex and unwieldy run the risk of overwhelming the patient and clinician leading to much intellectual debate and behavioural paralysis.

Beckian model of longitudinal formulation

The main approach that will be focused on here is the Beckian model of longitudinal formulation (Beck, 1976, 1985; Beck, 1995). This approach is based on a normalization model in which mental health problems are seen to exist on a continuum with the normal emotional responses that we all experience. The Beckian model proposes that experiences in childhood and adolescence shape our sense of who we are and how we exist in the world. These experiences, (which may be, but are not necessarily, negative or traumatic) lead to the development of rules for living and core beliefs (see Chapter 1 for definitions), which form the basis of our self-esteem, and sense of safety and security in the world. Further, Beck proposes that within the longitudinal formulation these rules for living and core beliefs represent the psychological vulnerability factors to mental health problems, which arise when a critical incident in a person's life activates these rules for living and/or core beliefs. Within the longitudinal formulation Beck describes these as the precipitating factors to mental health problems. A critical incident is often a life event such as divorce, redundancy or bereavement. These may also include positive events such as starting a family, retirement or entering a new relationship. The activation of the rules for living and core beliefs in turn gives rise to NATs, feelings, physical sensations and behaviours. This represents the maintenance factors within the longitudinal formulation and reflects the metaphor of a vicious circle described earlier. As outlined in Chapter 1, a Beckian approach to CBT would always intervene at the maintenance level in the first instance. The amount of emphasis placed on tackling rules for living and core beliefs would vary accord-ing to the length of the treatment contract, the complexity of the presenting problem(s) and the patient's ability to tolerate working at this level; and also the clinician's CBT training, skill and experience in working at this level.

As a guiding principle, formulation should, as Beck has said, be done 'early but often'. By that he means that it is important to begin to share this explicitly with the patient as part of the assessment process but it will then usually need to be developed and modified accordingly as treatment progresses and more information about the problem is revealed.

A basic guideline for developing a longitudinal formulation is the connection between the following areas. Some information regarding these areas will have been gathered as part of the CBT assessment (see Chapter 5):

- problem list or main presenting problem (s)
- interconnection between events in the environment and NATs, feelings, physical sensations, behaviour (maintenance formulation) either in the form of a generic vicious circle (i.e. Greenberger and Padesky, 1995) or ideally as a disorder-specific CBT model (e.g. Wells 1997)
- factors associated with the onset of the most recent episode of mental health problems (precipitating factors or critical incident)
- an account of the individual's childhood and adolescence and identification of possible themes (see Chapter 1) in the rules for living and core beliefs (predisposing psychological and environmental vulnerability factors)
- information from psychometric and idiographic measures (these are discussed in detail in Chapter 5).

The following box gives a clinical example of a Beckian longitudinal formulation. Other examples in the literature can be found in Blackburn and Twaddle (1996) and Moore and Garland (2003).

Patient example

Alex had been brought up in an environment (both at home and at school) in which great emphasis was placed on achievement and success and these were the criteria by which she measured her worth and formed the basis of her self-esteem. Alex received considerable criticism from her parents if she did not achieve highly in any activity and at school disappointment was expressed if she did not come top of the class. Her teachers in particular encouraged her to strive hard in all her endeavours. Alex and the treating clinician identified two rules for living:

> 'Unless I am completely successful I am worthless.'
> 'If I work very hard I can achieve anything.'

Through most of her life Alex had been able to live by her rules and had been successful academically, as well as in sport and music. As a result her self-esteem had been maintained. However, while at university despite working hard, Alex received by her standards poor marks for a particular module and became anxious and low in mood. Thus her rules for living were compromised and her self-esteem challenged. Alex became preoccupied with the idea of failure and began to worry she may fail this and other modules, exaggerating the likelihood of that happening. She reported NATs as follows: 'I'm bound to fail the course', 'my work's not up to scratch', 'the tutors have no confidence in me'; 'I'm letting my parents down'. She began to experience herself as worthless. Her behavioural response to the anxiety was a degree of procrastination in doing her work, coupled with working excessively long hours when she did start working, plus a self-focus on her anxieties rather than on the task at hand. Her depression led her to withdraw from friends who had been a good source of counsel and encouragement. The effect of this was to impede her progress towards her goal of passing her course.

This formulation is represented in diagrammatic form in Figure 3.1.

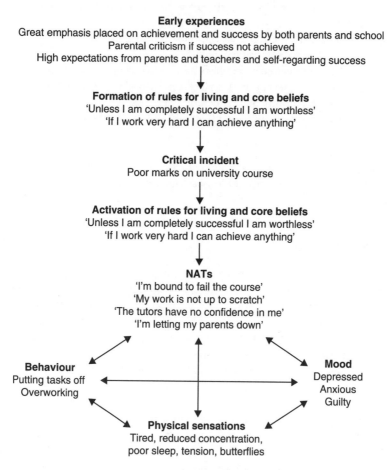

Early experiences
Great emphasis placed on achievement and success by both parents and school
Parental criticism if success not achieved
High expectations from parents and teachers and self-regarding success

Formation of rules for living and core beliefs
'Unless I am completely successful I am worthless'
'If I work very hard I can achieve anything'

Critical incident
Poor marks on university course

Activation of rules for living and core beliefs
'Unless I am completely successful I am worthless'
'If I work very hard I can achieve anything'

NATs
'I'm bound to fail the course'
'My work is not up to scratch'
'The tutors have no confidence in me'
'I'm letting my parents down'

Behaviour
Putting tasks off
Overworking

Mood
Depressed
Anxious
Guilty

Physical sensations
Tired, reduced concentration,
poor sleep, tension, butterflies

Figure 3.1 Beckian longitudinal formulation for Alexandra

MAINTENANCE FORMULATION OF COMMON MENTAL HEATH PROBLEMS USING DISORDER-SPECIFIC CBT MODELS

Introduction

Within the CBT literature there are a range of disorder-specific CBT models for anxiety disorders and for acute and chronic depression. In order to develop a maintenance formulation of the patient's presenting problem, the clinician needs to be familiar with these disorder-specific models. It is also useful to be aware of the diagnostic criteria for each of the common mental health problems the models represent. Familiarity with these models helps during the CBT assessment, as during the process of information gathering the clinician can begin to consider whether the person's problem as described, fits with a particular disorder-specific model and diagnostic criteria, for example obsessive compulsive disorder (OCD). However it is important to keep your questions open and consider a range of possibilities until you have, by a process of systematic assessment, settled on which disorder-specific model best describes the patient's current problems. An initial hypothesis regarding the presenting problem on the part of the clinician will shape the specific questions that will be asked. It can be unwise to blindly follow your initial hunch and not consider that an alternative diagnosis may be more likely.

For example, the patient's initial description of his current problems may be worrying thoughts, anxiety and checking. Your initial hunch may be that this could be a problem of OCD, however more focused questioning could lead you to see that the focus of his anxiety is on his health and this could lead you to speculate that this is a problem of health anxiety. Further questioning, with these two hunches in mind, would, by a process of elimination, lead the clinician to accept one hunch over the other. It is clear from this example that this process of testing out your clinical hunches and reaching a conclusion can only occur if you have a clear grasp of both the diagnostic criteria and the CBT models of OCD and health anxiety.

One problem with this disorder-specific approach as with the idea of diagnosis approach is that some problems that patients describe do not fit very easily into a diagnostic category or a disorder-specific CBT model. This is often the case for complex, comorbid presentations.

Diagnosis and formulation

The idea of diagnosis is a medical one and it means defining the disorder in terms of the presenting signs and symptoms. There are internationally recognized systems for diagnosing mental health problems, notably, ICD-10 in Europe (American Medical Association, 2006) and DSM-IV in North America (American Psychiatric Association, 2005). Obviously in using the concept of diagnosis it is important to guard against the effect of labelling the patient, and the reader will be aware, the use of diagnostic labels can be a point of controversy in mental health work. This can lead to an inconsistency between the medical and non-medical approach to working with patients, with the medical staff applying a diagnosis and other clinicians declining to do this. From a CBT perspective a further problem with diagnosis is that many patients' problems do not readily fit with diagnostic criteria. In this sense the CBT formulation approach used in CBT has advantages over diagnosis in that it can account more readily for mixed anxiety and depression presentations and other forms of comorbidity.

The view of the authors is that it is useful to consider what diagnosis the patient has been given and to discuss their views regarding the diagnosis with them. However, as stated previously we would see the CBT formulation as being more useful than diagnosis as it is the formulation that guides the CBT intervention.

Anxiety disorders

The generic CBT theory of anxiety disorders will be described which is derived in its origin from the work of Beck et al. (1985a). Wells (1997) summarizes the basic CBT theory of anxiety as follows: anxiety occurs as a result of the individual making negative predictions of future events as being dangerous in some way. Some people are more likely to perceive certain situations as dangerous because they hold particular rules for living and core beliefs about the perceived threatening meanings in situations and their perceived lack of ability to deal with this threat. To put this in simple terms, the anxious person frequently believes that something dangerous is about to happen and they have neither the internal nor external resources to deal with it. As a result of these perceptions the person experiences anxiety and develops a range of unhelpful behaviours as a means of managing these exaggerated perceptions of danger and threat. These types of behaviour are discussed extensively in this book and fall into three broad categories: escape/avoidance, safety behaviours and reassurance seeking. Descriptions of these are given later in this chapter and their clinical manifestations are discussed in more detail in Chapter 8. In Chapter 1, a distinction was made between the content of thinking (*what we think* i.e. NATs, rules for living and core beliefs) and the process of thinking (*how we think* i.e. information processing biases). In considering this in relation to the anxiety disorders then the following themes are important.

Common themes to what we think in anxiety disorders

We will consider the common themes in *what we think* (content) in the anxiety disorders, with reference to the three levels of thinking we described in Chapter 1 as follows: NATs, rules for living and core beliefs. It may be helpful at this stage to return to Chapter 1 and refresh your memory as to the definitions of these different levels of thinking. Given that there is a theoretical assumption that core beliefs are the mechanism that drives emotion then we will first look at this level of thinking. As you progress through the chapter you will see that the authors give examples of typical cognitive themes for both the *content* and *process* of thinking that arise in patients who present with anxiety disorders. These are only examples and while they are useful as a general guide, it is vital when working with patients to make psychological sense of their specific problems. This is so that the idiosyncratic meaning of the patient's perceptions is captured and the clinician does not impose the language of a textbook on them.

CORE BELIEFS

There is an extensive amount of research evidence examining the cognitive features of anxiety disorders. One of the leading scientist–practitioners in this field is David Barlow (see Barlow, 2004) who describes the following three themes in core beliefs as being central to anxiety disorders:

1   uncertainty
2   unpredictability
3   uncontrollability

People with anxiety disorders thus strive for certainty, predictability and control in their everyday lives. In keeping with the normalization rationale on which CBT is based these would seem not only reasonable things to strive for, but will be adaptive in terms of maintaining a sense of security and safety in the world. However for the person experiencing a problem with anxiety this perception of uncertainty, unpredictability and uncontrollability is heightened and the striving for certainty, predictability and control is exaggerated and extreme, or the individual has a low threshold for tolerance of uncertainty, unpredictably and lack of control. This often arises when the environment in which the individual was raised (or currently lives) was marked by uncertainty or unpredictable and uncontrollable events. From a clinical perspective when trying to make psychological sense of the anxious patient's problems using a CBT formulation common themes that emerge in the core beliefs are:

'I am weak/vulnerable/out of control/powerless.'
'Others are unreliable/let you down/not to be trusted/controlling.'
'The world is dangerous/unpredictable/uncontrollable.'

RULES FOR LIVING

Three common themes emerge in the rules for living:

1   *Control*: 'If I'm not in control at all times something bad will happen.' 'If I'm not in control people take advantage.'
2   *Responsibility*: 'If I think a bad thought I must want it to happen.'
3   *Approval*: 'If I don't do what others want they will reject me.'

THOUGHTS

The content of thinking in these disorders can be experienced as images or words. Imagery consists of the pictures the individual experiences in their mind's eye when they become anxious. Imagery is frequently neglected when assessing and treating anxiety disorders and yet research would suggest (e.g. Borkovec and Inz, 1990) that imagery is central to the maintenance of anxiety problems. The specific content of thinking, both verbal and images, relevant to specific anxiety disorders, are described below and in Chapter 8:

1   *Panic disorder*: catastrophic misinterpretation of bodily sensations where threat is imminent, e.g. 'I'm going to faint/die/have a heart attack', image of self collapsed on floor clutching chest.
2   *Social phobia*: fear of negative evaluation of self by others e.g. 'I will look foolish' 'people will think I'm stupid', image of people laughing and ridiculing them.
3   *Health anxiety*: catastrophic misinterpretation of bodily sensations where threat is in the medium to long term future e.g. 'I have cancer', 'I have multiple sclerosis', image of self lying in a hospital bed dying a slow and painful death.
4   *Obsessive compulsive disorder*: appraisal of intrusions where there is an inflated sense of responsibility for harm to self or others.
5   *Generalized anxiety disorder*: worry in the form of negative predictions about future events e.g. 'what if . . . what if . . . what if . . .'. Images of accidents etc.

Common themes in how we think in anxiety disorders: information processing biases

Increasingly, in CBT for anxiety disorders greater attention is being paid to how information is processed when anxious (*how we think*). In the CBT literature (Barlow, 2004; Harvey et al., 2004; Wells, 1997; Williams et al., 1997) these are usually described as information processing biases. As described in Chapter 1, processing biases refer to the way in which information the individual takes in becomes distorted in a specific way due to feeling anxious or depressed.

The common information processing biases in the anxiety disorders are:

1　*Worry*: as described previously a central cognitive theme in anxiety disorders is negative predictions about future events commonly termed worry. Importantly within CBT theory, worry is defined as a cognitive phenomenon where both the content and process of thinking need to be considered; and the related feeling is one of anxiety; formulating and tackling the *worry process* is a key aspect of CBT treatments.

2　*Thought suppression*: this involves deliberately trying not to think a thought that is upsetting by pushing it out of conscious awareness and occurs frequently in response to intrusions. This deliberate thought suppression has the paradoxical effect of creating a rebound effect so that the more a particular thought is suppressed the more frequently it re-intrudes each time with greater intensity and emotional resonance. A typical example of such thought suppression and rebound effect occurs when we get a song stuck in our heads. The more we try and not sing the song to ourselves and push it out of our minds the more it re-intrudes on our conscious thought each time with greater degrees of irritation. In anxiety disorders this is common in OCD and GAD.

3　*Threat cue detection*: the individual more quickly notices or pays attention to and notes concern about things that they perceive to be potentially threatening, e.g. patients who experience panic attacks more readily detect slight changes in bodily sensations

Specific problematic behaviours in anxiety disorders

AVOIDANCE

This is almost always a feature of anxiety disorders and can be formulated as behavioural avoidance, cognitive avoidance (thought suppression is an example of this) and emotional avoidance. If we accept that much of anxious thinking is focused on negative predictions about future events then it is easy to see that avoidance is a problem because it stops the person finding out that the predicted negative future catastrophe does not occur, is not as awful as predicted, or can be coped with. It is also a problem because it has a significant impact in that it interferes with the person's day-to-day functioning. For example, they may not be able to pick their children up from school, visit certain places, enter crowded situations or even leave the house.

ESCAPE

People will frequently wish to escape from situations when they are anxious. The reason for wanting to escape will be informed by the idiosyncratic NATs they are experiencing in the anxiety-provoking situation. People usually wish to escape in order to avert a predicted feared consequence such as being overwhelmed by their anxiety, losing control or making a fool of themselves. They usually wish to escape to somewhere safe like home or hospital, into fresh air or towards a trusted person. Escape behaviour is a problem in that the person is not learning that this predicted feared consequence is unlikely to occur.

REASSURANCE SEEKING

Patients with anxiety will frequently seek verbal reassurance, and this usually involves using tactics aimed at getting others to tell them that nothing terrible will happen when they are feeling anxious. This reassurance is usually sought from close family members or friends, but sometimes from their general practitioner or mental health clinician. Sometimes this reassurance seeking is overt, for example the patient says 'please tell me I'm not going to die' or it can be quite subtle, especially if it has been longstanding; it may be a comforting look or touch, sought from or given by the other person. The patient may not even have to ask for it as the reassuring person is so used to the scenario that they reassure automatically.

Sometimes the desire to be reassured is very great. If the reassurance is sought in medical settings, it may mean frequent trips to casualty or the GP and possible requests for medical investigations. Obviously reassurance in life is normal and the difference here would be that while the non-anxious person is likely to accept the reassurance, a patient experiencing an anxiety disorder will ask for frequent reassurance and receive only limited or short-lived relief from having done so. In anxiety, reassurance seeking is problematic because as it brings relief from anxiety in the short term this can reinforce the behaviour and will invariably lead to repeated seeking of reassurance, which can often escalate over time. Also, the person seeking reassurance often has an inflated sense of responsibility for the safety and security of others and in seeking reassurance they are shifting responsibility for potential harm to the person from whom the reassurance is being sought. Finally the act of seeking reassurance keeps the patient focused on the fear and potential risk, which is usually exaggerated and extreme.

SAFETY BEHAVIOURS

These are idiosyncratic behaviours that the person believes will reduce the likelihood of the feared catastrophe occurring. Again what the specific safety behaviour is will depend on what the feared catastrophe is and examples would include: sitting down, taking one's pulse, taking deep breaths, carrying water etc. There is a detailed table of these in Chapter 8.

Further details about the formulation and treatment of specific anxiety disorders are in Chapter 8 and a full description of formulating and creating depression in Chapter 9.

Patients may be treated by employing a protocol intervention for a particular disorder, which has been shown to be effective in research studies. The advantage of it is that it can be easier to follow for the clinician and there is a confidence in its efficacy. A formulation intervention uses the idea of understanding the patient's problems and symptoms in terms of CBT theory. This may be better for complex cases that do not fit into a category; it may engage the patient if they feel the formulation is correct and it can allow for predictions of the patient's reactions. The formulation could be a 'problem formulation' with the emphasis on a vicious circle of thoughts, feelings and behaviour, or it could be a full case formulation which tries to understand how early experiences have shaped core beliefs and rules and how they are activated because of various experiences and how they lead to the problematic vicious circle. Thought content, process, emotional and behavioural response are all important here.

The therapeutic relationship in CBT

Chapter contents

- CBT has always paid attention to the therapeutic relationship
- The evidence base is undeveloped regarding the mechanism of change in psychotherapy, namely the therapeutic relationship versus specific interventions
- Bordin's (1979) ideas of tasks, bonds and goals can be helpful in understanding the therapeutic relationship
- Difficulties in the therapeutic bond can occur and should be addressed promptly
- These difficulties can occur because of issues with the clinician, the patient or some dynamic involving both

INTRODUCTION

In this chapter, the intention is to describe key strategies that allow the clinician to develop a productive therapeutic alliance with the patient. In keeping with the book, a detailed review of the very large and comprehensive literature regarding the therapeutic relationship in helping professions will not be attempted. Instead, emphasis will be put on describing the particular elements of the therapeutic relationship that are important for mental health professionals using a CBT approach with straightforward anxiety and depressive disorders.

In the early days of CBT the therapeutic relationship was viewed as simply a means to get the patient to carry out the technical CBT interventions. Beck articulated one of the fundamental principles of the CBT model, namely that the mechanism of change lies in the CBT interventions themselves and the therapeutic relationship, while important, is considered secondary to the interventions themselves as a mechanism of change. At times this assertion has led some to believe that CBT as a treatment is cold, technical and even inhumane. The authors would advocate that this is clearly a misrepresentation of the model and if you consider some of the interventions CBT clinicians successfully engage patients in using, most of which involve engaging with high levels of emotional arousal, this is indeed a testimony to the strong therapeutic bonds that need to exist in order for treatment to be successful.

Exercise

Imagine you are working with Angela who has phobia of spiders (arachnophobia). The CBT treatment of choice would be graded exposure in vivo (Marks, 1987). This intervention is discussed in more detail in Chapter 10. This would involve encouraging Angela to face her fear of spiders in a graded way, using a hierarchy; this would start with the least anxiety-provoking stimulus, for example a dead spider in a jar, and work towards the most anxiety provoking, for example a live spider crawling on her body. What personal qualities and skills would you need to establish a therapeutic relationship that enabled you and the patient to successfully work your way to the top of the hierarchy?

In terms of the evidence base investigating the importance of the therapeutic relationship in comparison to the technical CBT intervention, it is clear that there has been much less research done in this area. The majority of CBT research focuses on treatment outcomes where the technical intervention has been tested with little or no consideration of therapist factors within this. In terms of the research that has been done, Mathews (1976) found that agoraphobic patients (to their surprise), rated therapists' encouragement and sympathy as more important than the practical component of therapy. Persons and Burns (1985) found that patients' ratings of the quality of the therapeutic relationship were significantly related to mood changes. This research is in line with the current CBT perspective that the therapeutic relationship is important in terms of facilitating a beneficial treatment outcome. There is an ongoing debate in the CBT literature about the relative importance of the therapeutic relationship over the technical CBT interventions and vice versa. One perspective, articulated by Safran and Segal (1996), is that it is meaningless to attempt to separate them. An often cited clinical argument is that the more complex the patient's problems are (for example, chronic depression, personality difficulties) then the more attention needs to be paid to the therapeutic relationship. For more detailed discussion, see Moore and Garland (2003) and Young et al. (2003).

TASKS, GOALS AND BONDS

The authors are influenced by the important paper of Bordin (1979), who divided the therapeutic alliance into the three components of *tasks*, *bonds* and *goals*. He argued that the strength of the therapeutic alliance depends on the amount of agreement between the therapist and his patient on these elements. The goals are defined as the general objectives of the treatment (for example, in CBT that may be 'to repeatedly face up to socially avoided situations without significant anxiety'). The tasks are the particular activities that the patient has to engage in to reach the goals (for example, in CBT that the individual completes a thought record and engages in behavioural experiments). It would be CBT practice to discuss the goals and tasks at an early stage and if there were a significant disagreement, then that could be addressed at that point. In terms of bonds, Bordin argues that different types of therapy make different demands of the relationship. Different types of problem are also likely to make different demands of the therapeutic alliance.

In terms of how the bond can best be formed, as stated previously, Beck (Beck et al., 1979) emphasizes that the core conditions of warmth, accurate empathy and genuineness are necessary (but not sufficient) to conduct CBT. Warmth can be conveyed through the clinician being open and receptive, showing genuine interest and concern in the patient's problems and demonstrating warmth in both their verbal and non-verbal interactions. The clinician demonstrating a real understanding of the person's problems is central to being able to convey accurate empathy. In a CBT model, this can be ably demonstrated through the use of the collaboratively developed formulation of the patient's current problems (see Chapter 3 for further discussion of this method). The clinician being professional, competent and honest can demonstrate genuineness. CBT interventions are conducted in the spirit of 'collaborative empiricism' (Beck et al., 1979). This means working together and learning from mutual experience as to the best way to help the patient solve their own problems. Ideally the patient should be thinking 'I can trust this person and get along with them: he knows what he is doing and he understands me'. At an emotional level the patient should be feeling fairly relaxed and behaviourally should be focusing on the specifics of treatment. Clinical impression would be that with more straightforward problems, when showing warmth, empathy and genuineness, it is reasonably easy to develop a productive therapeutic alliance very quickly (i.e. first two sessions). With more complex and comorbid problems and personality difficulties, establishing a productive therapeutic alliance may take weeks or even months. For example, if a patient has a core belief, 'people cannot be trusted', then plainly from the start, the therapeutic relationship will require careful building and tending in order to minimize the occurrence of ruptures.

It would be expected that the clinician demonstrating the core conditions would be sufficient to develop the alliance. However if the patient had been given a diagnosis of personality disorder, has suffered from a longstanding problem or had ongoing mental healthcare, it would be wise to pay more attention to the dynamics of the relationship from the start. Useful references in this domain are Safran and Segal (1996) and Young et al. (2003).

DIFFICULTIES THAT CAN OCCUR IN THE RELATIONSHIP

Difficulties can still arise in the alliance, even with patients who do not have complex problems. These can be understood and shared with the patient by using the standard CBT formulation in order to make sense of the difficulties. This involves identifying the triggering situation or environment, the emotional response, the NATs/rules for living and core beliefs and the related behavioural responses.

The difficulty in the therapeutic relationship may arise in the clinician or the patient; or in the interaction between the two. When assessing obstacles that arise from the patient, one should look out for significant changes in emotion, e.g. anxiety, hurt, shame or embarrassment, that arise from something in the interpersonal encounter, rather than something about the presenting problem. It is likely that these are quite delicate issues and simply saying 'what's going through your mind?' may be a bit too direct. It may be better here to be gentler by saying 'you looked a bit embarrassed when I said that'. One could comment on the patient's behaviour, 'you seem to be having difficulty making eye contact at the moment' and see if there is a response from the patient that allows you to go forward. It may be better to use an empathic response, such as 'I can see this is a difficult topic between us . . . what should we do . . . what would be helpful?' It is likely that the patient finds something difficult about what the clinician has said or done and he is going to find it difficult to directly say to her what the problem is. It is a clinical judgement as to whether one should try to discover what the problem is at that time or postpone this to another occasion. Sometimes it is difficult for both patient and clinician to talk about a particularly difficult interaction at the time it occurs. As a guiding principle the clinician should try and discuss it to some extent at the time. Some patients may drop out of treatment on the basis of such an interaction and this needs to be avoided at all costs as it would be potentially psychologically damaging for the patient. The authors would recommend that a review of any difficult interactions be placed on the agenda for the next session and that clinician and patient work together to try and understand the incident using the CBT vicious circle maintenance formulation described in Chapters 1 and 2. A note of caution: even with straightforward patients such discussions require tact and sensitivity and adequate time allowed for their resolution. With complex patients, unless such discussions are handled carefully and anchored in a robust CBT formulation then there is danger that addressing the issue may further entrench the difficulty. Our recommendation would be that such issues are taken to CBT clinical supervision and a specific plan developed for tackling the issue in the next session with the patient. In such situations the clinician needs to be mindful that their own rules for living and core beliefs may be activated and this may need to be considered as part of the CBT clinical supervision.

Patient issues

Some common rules for living and core beliefs held by patients that may impede CBT are now described. Obviously it is useful to formulate these with the patient whenever practicable:

1   'The clinician should always support me.'
     Patient actions: at a behavioural level the patient may verbally seek support and validation for anything that he does. He may show anxiety, anger or disappointment if it is not always forthcoming.
     Helpful response: the core conditions are essential to CBT, but it is important for the therapist to explain that CBT is about supporting the patient in his tasks and goals and this may involve a degree of challenge.
2   'It is more important that the clinician understands, empathizes and cares for me rather than that we address problems' (Leahy, 2001).
     Patient actions: he frequently asks for a nurturing and caring response, emphasizes the awfulness of his predicament and frequently describes it. He seeks validation that his situation is terrible and he may feel hurt if the clinician does not give validation as much as is desired.
     Helpful response: it is part of the clinician's role to allow validation and it may be important to allow the patient to spend some time on this. It may be possible to help the person understand why he has this need, and possibly to look at the pros and cons

of spending time seeking validation. One approach (Leahy, 2001) would be to acknowledge, if appropriate, that the situation is truly awful and CBT may indeed struggle to help. An alternative approach (Ellis, 1985) would be to say that nothing is truly awful as something worse could possibly happen and the person has managed to survive the awful event. This approach would not spend a lot of time on validation.

3 'CBT is about rationalizing my problems with the clinician.'

Patient actions: he may be quite emotionally avoidant in the session, not displaying anxiety, sadness or tears and putting emphasis on being logical about his problems. He will over-emphasize the element of CBT that is concerned with using rational thinking, and downplay the elements of emotional processing and integration.

Helpful response: the clinician could explain that CBT is not about rationalizing but about emotional regulation. Treatment sessions will encourage the appropriate expression of emotion and develop behavioural experiments to allow this.

4 'It is up to the clinician to get me better.'

Patient actions: in the session, he does not show initiative, seeks excessive reassurance, and frequently asks for solutions and suggestions. He will try to get the clinician to do most of the work in and out of the session.

Helpful response: emphasize the importance of collaborative empiricism; the clinician and patient work together, the clinician providing structure and guidance but the patient doing most of the therapeutic work between sessions. The clinician should resist automatically making suggestions to the patient and work with him or her to pick up the responsibility for themselves.

5 'I cannot talk to the clinician about this because it is so awful.'

Patient actions: in session, the person may be evasive, embarrassed and ashamed about some aspect of the problem though this may become less so as the relationship develops.

Helpful response: it may be that the patient requires a number of sessions to get to know the clinician and this should be respected. If the person seems unable to talk about it a strategy may be to ask what the most shameful part of the revelation is and what he thinks may happen. There may be fears about how shocked the clinician will be or an issue of confidentiality may have arisen; or it may be about the patient suffering particular legal consequences. If the last is realistically the case, it is important to explain what the organization's policy would be.

6 'I need the clinician to be my friend.'

Patient actions: in session, he may be too friendly, perhaps overfamiliar, talking and asking about personal issues such as social events, children and likes and dislikes. The person may believe that it is a requisite of treatment to be friendly, he may have an excessive need to be liked or he may be lacking friends and looking for new ones.

Helpful response: the clinician, while politely acknowledging his overfriendliness, can gently point it out and perhaps consider addressing it as a problem, particularly if is blocking therapeutic change.

Therapist issues

Some of the clinician's rules for living and core beliefs (from Garland and Scott, 2005; Padesky, 1996) that can impede CBT are now described. It is useful to try and identify how your own rules for living and core beliefs may impact both helpfully and unhelpfully on the therapeutic alliance. Increasingly, attention is being given to the impact of clinicians' rules for living and core beliefs as a part of both CBT training and clinical supervision The authors would endorse this perspective but encourage the clinician to seek CBT clinical supervision from a colleague who has undertaken specific CBT training and is a recognized clinical supervisor of CBT practice. This is discussed more fully in Chapter 12.

Therapist beliefs

1   'If the patient is talking I shouldn't interrupt.' This may lead the clinician to be inadequately structured, to not ask enough questions and to allow the patient to digress onto CBT-irrelevant topics.
2   'If I'm structured I'll miss important information or appear unfeeling.' This may lead the clinician to minimize structure and maximize empathy.
3   'If my client is emotional I can't let them leave the room until they feel better.' While this may be the humane response it can lead to an inability to finish the sessions on time.
4   'This patient is boring.' This can lead to a lack of concentration on the person's problem and various implicit strategies to bring the session or the treatment contract to a speedier conclusion.

Interaction between clinician and patient issues

There are other clinicians' rules for living and core beliefs that could damage the therapeutic bond. It is important to recognize that these rules and beliefs elicit certain types of behaviour in the clinician that can trigger off a particular set of patient rules and beliefs that will affect the therapeutic bond. A well trained, thoughtful and reflective clinician would notice if she was experiencing negative feelings toward a patient and take action to manage this appropriately both in and outside the session. In such circumstances, provided the clinician had established a safe and trusting bond with their supervisor then clinical supervision would potentially be an appropriate place to bring issues of this nature with the aim of addressing them effectively within a CBT framework.

Further reading

Chapter 3 in *Cognitive Therapy: Transforming the Image*, Wills and Sanders (1997).
Interpersonal Processes in Cognitive Therapy, J Safran and Segal (1996).
Chapter 2 in *Cognitive Therapy for Chronic and Persistent Depression*, Moore and Garland (2003).
Overcoming Resistance in Cognitive Therapy, Leahy (2001) is a sophisticated book looking at blocks to change in CBT including difficulties in the therapeutic relationship.

Chapter summary

CBT has been criticized for ignoring the therapeutic relationship. This has never been the case and the relationship issues have attracted more attention recently. Clinical opinion is that more complex cases require more work in this area, but it is acknowledged that the research evidence does not give a clear answer about the emphasis that should be put on the relationship as well as the more technical aspects of therapy. Bordin's (1979) model of considering tasks, bonds and goals in any clinical encounter is a helpful framework from which to consider the nature of the therapeutic relationship. In terms of problems with the therapeutic relationship, the problem may lie with the patient, the clinician or the dynamic between the two. A patient issue could be that they demand too much support and validation and a clinician issue may be that they avoid structure or interrupting the patient, because they believe they will appear insensitive or miss something important.

Assessment

THE ASSESSMENT PROCESS

The aim of this chapter is to provide clinicians with a template for carrying out a cognitive behavioural assessment of the patient's problems. This model can be used to assess not only mental health problems but also physical illness, social functioning and spiritual needs. If it is clear following assessment that cognitive behavioural interventions are not going to be used then the clinician will still have gathered valuable and detailed information that will be helpful in developing an alternative treatment plan.

When discussing cognitive behavioural assessment an area of debate is which type of language to use to describe the patient's problems. Traditionally, the medical model uses diagnostic criteria to describe, categorize and define these problems e.g. 'Mrs. Brown has a diagnosis of depression'. Meanwhile, nursing models use the language of symptom description e.g. 'Mrs. Brown complains of feeling tired, sad and guilty. Her sleep and appetite are disturbed and she complains of a loss of interest and motivation'. From the perspective of a psychological model such as CBT the patient's presentation is usually summarized in terms of problem definition e.g. 'Mrs. Brown is low in mood, she has stopped engaging in activities of daily living and has withdrawn from her social network'.

In this book, the authors will attempt to integrate the most helpful aspects of each of these models. This is generally referred to as a psycho-bio-social understanding of the patient's difficulties. Therefore consideration will be given to the relationship between cognition (negative automatic negative thoughts, rules for living and core beliefs), physical/biological symptoms, feelings behaviour and environmental factors in the patient's presentation. The cognitive behavioural model will be used as a foundation stone for making links between these elements in the context of individual patient presentations. These will be integrated into a coherent formulation of the patient's problems that goes on to form the basis of the treatment intervention.

Exercise

Spend a moment considering these questions:

- What are the differences between a diagnostic medical model and a CBT model?
- What are the advantages and disadvantages of each?
- Can they complement one another?

PLANNING THE ASSESSMENT INTERVIEW

Sources and settings

The referral letter is usually the patient's first point of contact with the mental health professional. Referral sources can be wide and varied and most clinicians work within a system where patient contact is managed via a referral process. Cognitive behavioural treatments can be found at each service level. For instance, primary care mental health services are often the first point of contact with services for patients presenting with anxiety disorders and depression. In this setting, cognitive behavioural interventions may be one of a range of psychological therapies that is available to the patient within a brief intervention framework, i.e. 6–8 sessions. Referrals generally originate from primary healthcare workers such as general practitioners (GPs), health visitors, practice nurses and the like.

Meanwhile, in a community mental health team (CMHT) setting there may be clinicians with specialist CBT training who deliver medium term interventions of 12–25 sessions to patients who present with anxiety and mood disorders and in some services schizophrenia, psychosis and bipolar disorder. Often this is delivered within a psychotherapy framework or a psychosocial intervention model. In addition, many clinicians in this setting may integrate cognitive behavioural interventions into their generic work with patients who present with more complex mixed presentations and/or personality factors. Referrals in this setting may originate from outside the team via GPs or primary care workers or may be from within the team.

Cognitive behavioural psychotherapy is often available in specialist service settings such as a psychotherapy unit or psychological therapies services, child and adolescent mental health services, psychological medicine and drug and alcohol services to name a few. Here, typically, referrals are received from primary care and CMHT settings as well as other specialist services. Clinicians in a specialist service setting usually apply some form of inclusion criteria in order for a patient to access that particular service. A wide range of patients are also treated in private practice.

The referral process may occasionally be verbal but is usually written. The description of the patient's problems can vary from a one-line letter to a comprehensive assessment report. If it is a written referral from a health professional it is likely to describe some details of the problem and what help is being requested.

How long does a cognitive behavioural assessment take?

The assessment session is usually the first point of contact for patient and clinician.

It is important to consider how long to allocate to the assessment. A full CBT assessment usually takes around 2 hours, if the presentation seems straightforward. This may be carried out over one 2-hour period or broken down into two 1-hour sessions. It is not uncommon for the assessment to be extended to a third hour in which case it is best to ask the patient to return on a future occasion. The stages of the assessment are:

- The patient's current problems and mental state assessment including an assessment of risk (1–2 hours).
- The development and maintenance of these problems (30–60 minutes).
- Social and environmental factors from childhood to present day (1 hour).

This is generally completed within one 2-hour session or two 60-minute sessions. Most cognitive behavioural training courses will teach clinicians to consider carrying out between 1–4 further sessions for the following reasons:

- The complexity of the patient's presentation may dictate an extended assessment period.
- As a direct result of concentration and memory impairment caused by the patient's current problems it may be better to have shorter sessions (e.g. 30–60 minutes).
- The patient may need to collect further information about their problem in order to help with problem definition. For example, a sufferer of obsessive compulsive disorder may be asked to complete a diary between appointments; this would be in order to collect information regarding specific triggers to their intrusive thoughts and their appraisal of these in the form of NATs, their emotional response to these and the impact of these on their subsequent behaviour.
- It is generally helpful to ask the patient to complete validated questionnaires (usually referred to as psychometric measures) such as the Beck Depression Inventory (Beck et al., 1961). These can be helpful on a number of fronts during the assessment process and are discussed later in this chapter.
- At its heart CBT is a self-help model. In this respect the patient's active participation in the treatment process is vital. After the first assessment session the patient may need time to consider what has been discussed in the interview and to reflect on the initial CBT formulation of their problem and the proposed treatment. This allows the patient to consider whether a CBT approach is right for him.
- The clinician may decide to set a 'behavioural experiment' to be completed in between

assessment sessions. This is usually a specific task that asks the patient to begin to address their problems in a small way. The purpose of a behavioural experiment in this context is for the patient to collect information as to whether he will be able to work within a CBT treatment model. Examples of behavioural experiments might include negotiating with a patient who has obsessive compulsive disorder to stop using disinfectant every time they wash their hands. Behavioural experiments need to be devised in collaboration with the patient, directly linked to the treatment rationale and realistic and achievable for the individual concerned.

An accurate and comprehensive assessment is the key to making an effective CBT intervention. In this respect allowing time for the assessment process can lead to significant payoffs once treatment begins. Of course, some service settings, e.g. primary care, do not allow clinicians the luxury of several hours of assessment time. With this in mind a shortened assessment procedure may have to be followed, but service settings that only allow shorter assessment periods need to consider the types of referral received by the service and recognize the limitations created by capping assessment time. Incomplete assessment can lead to inaccurate formulation of the patient's presenting problems. This, in turn, can give rise to the application of an inappropriate treatment intervention. Common examples include: failure to distinguish the subtle differences between panic disorder, health anxiety and generalized anxiety disorder, all of which have different treatment rationales; or patients who present with a mixture of depressive symptoms and anxiety symptoms where it is important from a CBT perspective to determine which symptoms relate to which problem. Incomplete assessment can therefore lead to:

- extended treatment contracts beyond the remit of the service. Not only is this not cost effective, but it also is demoralizing to the patient, running the risk of compromising their potential to benefit from CBT
- use of inappropriate CBT interventions that are ineffective
- exacerbation rather than alleviation of the patient's presenting problem
- patient and clinician becoming demoralized when there is a poor response to treatment, leading to early termination of treatment by either or both parties
- referral of the patient to other services for further work, which for the patient is often experienced as 'starting from scratch'. Clinical experience would suggest that the longer a problem continues, the more hopeless an individual becomes regarding an effective treatment. Continuous referral on to other services is demoralizing and frustrating. In an ideal world health services should be structured so the patient is able to access appropriate services for his problem in the first instance.

Setting the scene

Imagine that a person is in the situation of waiting for a mental health assessment. Howe (1993) stated that he is likely to have three concerns:

'Will the clinician accept me?'
'Will the clinician understand me?'
'Will the clinician and I get on?'

It is important for the clinician to be aware of these patient anxieties when he invites the patient into his room. How the patient responds to the initial meeting and the conclusions that the patient arrives at regarding these questions will affect the therapeutic bond (see Chapter 4 for further discussion). One of the overall aims for the clinician during their first session is to form a productive therapeutic alliance and instil confidence in the patient that she knows what she is doing and understands the presenting problems.

In setting the scene for the initial assessment session, the following behaviours are helpful in terms of projecting this confidence and establishing the collaborative therapeutic stance, which is at the heart of the CBT model:

- When collecting the patient from the waiting room introduce yourself using your preferred designation, e.g. Emily Jones, Dr. Edgar etc. It is useful to always use your second name as well as your first name/title. All these behaviours impart to the patient that they are dealing with a confident and professional clinician.

- Once settled in the room where the assessment will take place it is helpful to reintroduce yourself and invite them to address you by your preferred designation. It is also respectful to enquire as to the patient's preferred form of address. For example the clinician may say: 'As I said downstairs my name is Emily Jones; please feel free to call me Emily. What do you prefer I call you?' Clinical experience tells us that many patients appreciate this type of consideration and it can play an important role in engagement and the confiding of problems. Often patients in their relationships with others are not called by the name that is written on their case notes. On asking this question of one patient she replied: 'My name is Monica but everyone calls me Sue, which is my middle name. I prefer this and in the 5 years I've been receiving treatment no one has ever before asked me this.'

- Next, it is helpful to provide the patient with information regarding your professional background and if appropriate your training in CBT. This is respectful of the patient's right to know with whom they are sharing highly personal information. One would also say: 'Today we are going to discuss whether this treatment could be helpful in dealing with your current problems.'

- It is also important to ask permission to take notes during the assessment and to give an indication of what happens to those notes, including who will receive copies of assessment reports. It is also useful to give the patient the opportunity to discuss any concerns regarding this. Similarly, it is necessary to explain the parameters of confidentiality including the limitations of this and the duty, if necessary, to break confidentiality. For example, if there is an issue that the patient wants to talk about that suggests that he or other people are at significant risk, then it may be necessary to discuss that risk with other health professionals and it would be necessary to inform the patient of this. The disadvantage of this statement is that it may inhibit discussion about certain issues that are important to the patient. Sometimes, during the interview, the patient will signal that she wants to tell you something that is worrying her or related to abuse; the assessor at that point may feel that she needs to remind the patient of the boundaries of confidentiality while not stopping the patient from talking about an important issue. This is a difficult problem and an example of the ethical dilemmas faced by health professionals in their daily practice. Finally, it can be useful to inform patients that they can have access to their notes and indeed if appropriate a copy of their assessment report.

- In the collaborative spirit of CBT the final question before beginning the assessment process is to ask the patient if there are specific things they wish to get out of the session. This is important as it sets the collaborative tone and imparts the message that the patient is not a passive recipient of care but an active and involved participant in the treatment process.

Structure

As CBT is a highly structured intervention that requires detailed information in order to make a CBT formulation and deliver treatment interventions based on this formulation, it is wise to take notes, as it is not possible to hold all the details of the interview in memory.

The clinician must ensure that they remain structured and, as stated earlier, this is an essential element of CBT. Structure includes:

- a focus on the goals of the assessment session
- creation of an agenda of topics to be addressed that is systematically worked through during the session
- effective management of time during the session
- systematic gathering of information pertinent to the patient's problems using the CBT model
- clarity in the clinician and patient's mind about any work that needs to be done at home prior to any further assessment session.

Clinical experience tells us that developing a structured assessment style enables the rapid collection of detailed information. It also conveys to the patient that the clinician knows what he is doing and has an understanding of the problems. This is vital for encouraging hope and optimism in the patient. Development of this style dictates that the clinician continually focuses the patient on discussion of a particular area and actively takes steps to prevent the patient straying from the topic at hand. This highly structured method of assessment can seem harsh and insensitive to clinicians who are schooled in other approaches. However, experience tells us that patients respond favourably to such a structure when used in conjunction with good interpersonal skills. Common concerns that clinicians have about structure are that it is too directive, it does not allow the patient to tell their story and it can be insensitive or non-empathic, but experience would suggest that this is not the case. It is certainly the case that it is difficult to be structured in one's approach and is a behaviour that needs to be learned and practised. For anyone who wishes to develop CBT skills then this structured intervention is a core competency.

Introducing the assessment

It is important at the beginning of the interview for the clinician and patient to define the goals of the session. A typical spoken introduction would be:

'Thank you for coming today. Elaine Parker has referred you to this service in order to discuss the possibility of using CBT in order to treat your current difficulties. The session will give you the opportunity to describe your problems as you see them. You will find that I ask a lot of questions. Some of these you may have been asked by other health professionals in the past. If you can bear with me this helps me to understand the problems you are experiencing. We will probably spend between 1–2 hours talking and the purpose of this is for me to try and understand your problems and for us to decide together whether a cognitive behavioural therapy approach would be helpful [or more neutrally "whether we can help you here"]. Is there anything you would like to say before we do that?'

It is sometimes the case that the clinician and patient will not arrive at the session with agreed goals. Patients' comments have included 'I did not know this was about my psychological health', 'I just want medication', 'I want to see a doctor' or 'I've just got 10 minutes for this'. The approach to this is a common sense one of allowing the patient to express what their goals are, trying to incorporate them or rearrange that they come back on another occasion.

Use of language

It is obviously important for the clinician and patient to be 'speaking the same language'. In other words an agreed vocabulary is used to describe the person's problems. Ideally, the clinician should listen to the words the person is using and try to share them: in other words, if a patient is talking about her 'moods' and the clinician is using the term 'affect' then there is scope for miscommunication; if it is difficult to use the patient's language then at very least the clinician should express himself clearly and avoid psychotherapy jargon. In CBT for example (as discussed earlier) there are various words used in different schools of CBT that probably mean a similar thing e.g. beliefs, schema, core beliefs etc. and various adjectives attached to them namely dysfunctional, unhealthy, irrational, unhelpful, untrue and it is rather easy to start using them interchangeably with the patient which can lead not only to confusion but also to disengagement.

Questioning style

In the CBT assessment, the clinician should begin by asking open questions and then move to closed questions, in order to get the specific information that will aid the formulation. For example:

C [clinician]: 'Tell me about the anxiety you describe.'
P [patient]: 'I feel churned up inside if I can't check and I'm constantly cleaning.'
C 'Tell me about the checking.'
P 'I've got to do it every day.'
C 'How many times a day do you check?'
P 'I'm not sure, around five or six.'
C 'What do you check?'
P 'Locks on the house and car, electric sockets and the cooker.'
C 'What makes it important to check these things?'
P 'Safety in case anything bad happens such as a burglary or fire.'

The assessor's style should always move from the general to the specific.

It is very useful, periodically, to summarize the patient's history as he is giving it you. For example after further discussion with this patient experiencing obsessional difficulties, a summary could be given as follows:

'What you're telling me is that your main problem is that you become anxious when you think you have neglected to do something such as locking the car or turning the gas cooker off. This anxiety you experience as a churning in your stomach and you repeatedly check the gas knobs on the cooker or the car doors to ensure there is no risk of theft or fire. Have I understood you correctly?'

It is quite common for patients not to give information in the level of detail that is required for a comprehensive CBT assessment that will allow adequate formulation of the problem. Therefore, the clinician needs to be persistent in seeking to obtain the information and may need to ask the patient certain questions again or rephrase the same question in a way that elicits the information that is required.

INTERVIEW STRUCTURE AND PROCESS

The goal of the CBT assessment is to formulate the patient's problems within the CBT model, assess the suitability of the patient's problems for treatment using CBT interventions and to develop a treatment plan if appropriate.

The CBT assessment format is now described. The aim of the format is to enable the clinician to understand the development and maintenance of the patient's problems within the CBT format described earlier. This is as follows:

1 Brief description of the main current problem(s).
2 Description of a particular instance of the main current problem using the Greenberger and Padesky (1995) vicious circle CBT maintenance formulation (as described in Chapters 1 and 2), environment, feelings, thoughts, physical sensations and behaviours.
3 Formulation of a basic treatment goal in terms of the current problem as described.
4 Points 1–3 related to any additional current problems identified.
5 Onset of current difficulties and their development including history of previous episodes.
6 Use of prescription drugs, alcohol and caffeine consumption and any use of illicit drugs.
7 Personal life history.
8 Mental state examination.
9 Initial CBT maintenance formulation (see Chapter 3).
10 Explanation, discussion of suitability of CBT for patient's problems and consent.

The session should start off by asking the patient to give a description of the main problem (or problems) he wants help with. This will hopefully build on the referral letter. Questions should be open at this stage, 'tell me a bit more about that' and 'describe the difficulties you are having'. Sometimes the patient may describe a variety of problems in his opening sentence, for example, 'oh, I'm tired all the time, I feel low, I'm really worried about my job and I get splitting headaches'. It is the clinician's task to make sense of this information and help the patient organize it. Here this would be best done by either asking the patient to state which of the four problems he wishes to talk about first or the clinician could focus on the mood described, namely 'feeling low', as this would more directly lead on to the next part of the assessment process.

Assessment of presenting problem: the Greenberger and Padesky five areas model

The clinician then starts to use the five areas assessment format to understand the problem fully.

Identifying triggering events

The first consideration is examples of triggering events to feeling anxious/depressed/angry etc. These can be situations in the person's environment where the problem occurs or bodily sensations the person is experiencing at a given time. Thus in the case of panic disorder, going to the supermarket or getting on a bus may activate specific feelings, physical sensations, NATs (and related rules for living and core beliefs) and behaviours. Other triggers to panic attacks may be noticing a fluttering of the heart, or contemplating travelling by bus. Using this format the clinician asks the patient to recall a specific and recent (ideally in the last week) concrete example of a problem situation e.g. feeling low or a panic attack. Thus the clinician would ask:

C   'Thinking back over the past week can you recall a situation where you experienced particularly high levels of anxiety?'
P   'Yesterday when I was standing in the checkout queue at the supermarket.'
C   'Okay, I would like you to imagine yourself back in that situation now and I would like you to describe it to me as if it is happening including as much detail as you can.'
P   'I am walking around the supermarket and it is about 10.00 a.m. It isn't too busy but I feel a bit on edge, I have butterflies in my stomach. I get to the checkout, I have about 20 items in my trolley and there are two people in front of me. The cashier is talking a lot and I'm feeling really restless, I wish she would hurry up. I feel hot and a bit light headed. The woman in front only has six or seven items so it doesn't seem so bad and then as she is going through the checkout she says "Oh no, I've forgotten my milk" and dashes off to get it. I am starting to feel really panicky, I am sweating and I feel sick and really dizzy.'

The instructions that the clinician gives to the patient are very important and patients should always be asked to describe an upsetting situation in the first person present tense as if it is happening right now. The reason for this is that being able to identify the different elements of the vicious circle is dependent on the patient experiencing and engaging with reasonably high levels of emotion. Therefore asking him or her to recount the situation as if it is occurring maximizes the chances of them engaging with relevant feelings.

Identifying feelings

The next area for consideration is feelings. The main feelings to look out for are anxiety, sadness, depression, anger, embarrassment, shame, guilt, humiliation and jealousy. A CBT approach would say essentially that there is a reciprocal relationship between how we feel and how we think and once a negative mood state arises then there is a change in both the content of our thinking (*what we think*) and the process of our thinking (*how we think*) (see Chapter 1 for a review). As such the CBT model makes links between specific types of NATs (and related rules for living and core beliefs) and specific feelings, and ascribes cognitive themes to particular feeling states. In the anxiety disorders and depression these themes are articulated as part of disorder-specific CBT models. These are described in more detail in Chapters 3, 8 and 9.

In terms of helping the patient identify and describe relevant feelings and continuing with the concrete and recent example of a problem situation as just described the standard format is as follows:

C   'Yesterday when you were standing in the queue at the supermarket checkout at what point did you feel at your worst?'
P   'When the woman in front said she had forgotten the milk and went off to get it leaving us all waiting in the queue.'
C   'At that point as the woman left how did you feel?'
P   'Really anxious.'
C   'If I asked you to rate how anxious you felt on a scale of 0–100 where 0 means you were perfectly calm and 100 the most anxious you have ever felt how anxious did you feel at that point?'
P   '95 per cent'

Identifying physical sensations

The CBT model makes a distinction between feelings (an emotional state) and physical sensations in the body. This distinction is as follows: feelings have a physical component that can be expressed in terms of bodily sensations, thus when we feel *anxious* then we experience physical sensations such as dizziness, racing heart, butterflies in the stomach, sweating and the like. Again continuing with the example this information can be elicited as follows:

C   'At that point in the supermarket queue when the woman in front went to get the milk she had forgotten you felt anxious 95 per cent. At that point did you notice any strong physical sensations in your body?'
P   'Oh yes. My legs turned to jelly, I felt light headed, my stomach was churning and I was burning up.'

Identifying NATs and related rules for living and core beliefs

The most effective method for identifying NATs is to ask the question: 'What is going through your mind?' There are a number of important factors to take into consideration when identifying NATs that are crucial both as part of CBT assessment and treatment. These are discussed in detail in Chapter 6. We would particularly draw the reader's attention to the importance of learning to recognize what Greenberger and Padesky (1995) refers to as 'hot' thoughts, which are the thoughts driving the emotional distress. One method CBT uses to try and identify these is taking ratings of how strong a particular feeling is (as illustrated in the earlier example) and how much the patient believes a particular NAT. The clinician can be guided by the themes to feelings and NATs described earlier and elsewhere in the book. To continue with the clinical example:

C   'So you felt anxious 95 per cent and your legs turned to jelly, you felt light headed, your stomach was churning and you were burning up. At that point in time what was going though your mind?'
P   'I'm going to be sick and pass out.'
C   'And at that time, when you were feeling like that how much did you believe that thought on a scale of 0–100 where 0 you didn't believe it at all and 100 you believed it absolutely?'
P   '100 per cent.'
C   'Did any particular images come into your mind at that time?'
P   'Yes, I saw myself lying on the floor in a pool of vomit and people looking disgusted and turning away.'
C   'And using the same 0–100 scale at that time in the supermarket queue how much did you believe you were going to end up lying on the floor in a pool of vomit and people looking disgusted and turning away?'
P   [very tearful] '100 per cent.'

It may take several attempts to elicit the 'hot' NATs and this is essentially achieved by persisting with a particular line of questioning until there is a strong emotion experienced and it is at this point that the hot thought will be most readily identified. If the patient is becoming overtly distressed, finding it difficult to discuss a particular incident or is evasive in their answers this is usually a sign that you are probing in the right area. It is important at this point to persist in your line of questioning, even if the patient is becoming upset. This is obviously carried out in a sensitive manner and empathic statements are used frequently to assist the process. Such statements might include: 'I understand this is really difficult for you to talk about and it is upsetting to think about. However, if you can try and bear with me for a few minutes it helps me understand your problems more fully and this is going to be important in terms of making decisions about how your problems are best treated.'

It is vital that the clinician does not collude with the patient's avoidance and works with the patient to try and engage with their emotional distress in a contained way. The ability to do so is fundamental to the patient being able to use any CBT intervention.

It is helpful, but not always easy at this stage to try and begin to make psychological sense of the patient's presenting problem by trying to make distinctions between the different levels of thinking, which are NATs, rules for living and core beliefs. The first stage is to elicit the NATs using the method already described. The next step is to use Socratic questioning to try and explore the themes in the patient's rules for living and core beliefs. Continuing with our example the clinician may ask the following:

C   'Can you say what it is about the panic attack in the supermarket that you found so
    upsetting?'
P   'I'm not really sure it just feels so frightening.'
C   [warm voice tone] 'I see. Can you say what the most frightening aspect of the panic
    attack is?'
P   'The feeling dizzy and jelly legs, I feel so out of control.'
C   'That sounds very important. What is it about that out of control feeling that you
    dislike?'
P   'It feels really dangerous.'
C   'When you say the out of control feeling feels really dangerous, what is the worst thing
    you can imagine happening?'
P   'Something terrible will happen.'
C   'Okay, so you have a sense that if you are not in control then something terrible will
    happen.' [possible rule for living]
P   [fidgeting in her seat] 'Mm . . . yes, I guess.'
C   'Can I ask would you say it is important for you to have control in other areas of
    your life?'
P   'I'm not sure.'
C   'How about for example do you like going on fairground rides?'
P   'Definitely not.'
C   'What are your reasons for not liking them?'
P   [smiling] 'I'm not in control – that's really interesting I have never thought about that
    before.'
C   'Okay, it seems that the need to be in control might be an important theme for us to
    come back to in terms of understanding your panic attacks. Is it okay if we talk about
    this theme of control a little longer?'
P   'Sure.'
C   'What is it about not being in control that you find difficult?'
P   'It is frightening; you don't know what is going to happen.'
C   'Okay, these seem important themes too. You described an image that came into
    your mind in the supermarket of yourself lying on the floor in a pool of vomit
    and people turning away in disgust. How does this fit with your need to be in
    control?'
P   [becoming tearful] 'Well, I would look really foolish and no one would help. That is
    really scary, the idea no one would help.'
C   'You are doing really well to talk about this. It seems really close to your heart and
    upsetting to think and talk about. Just a couple more questions and then we can reflect
    on what we have found out about your problems. Can I ask why you think people
    wouldn't help you?'
P   [crying] 'It is because I'm weak and pathetic and don't deserve help.'
C   'So you experience yourself as weak and pathetic. [possible theme for core belief
    about self] How do you experience other people in this situation?'
P   'People would judge you, wouldn't they? [possible theme for core belief about others]
    They might think I was drunk or something.'
C   'Okay, so if I can just summarize there in this particular situation you feel it's import-
    ant to stay in control in terms of your panic symptoms otherwise something terrible
    will happen. And that something terrible seems to be related to a sense that others

would judge you negatively in some way and that you and possibly others would see you as weak and pathetic.'

P   [crying again] 'Yes.'

C   'Thank you for sharing that with me. I know it was not easy but it has enabled us to identify some important themes in terms of making sense of your panic attacks. Let's take a few minutes to help you feel a little calmer before we go on.'

Thus, to summarize, this example identifies the theme of control within the patient's rules for living (e.g. 'If I am not I control something terrible will happen'). In addition, the theme of self as weak and pathetic and other as judgemental may also be important. At this stage these areas should be labelled as themes and established as a hypothesis for what is keeping the problem going (maintenance formulation). As part of the ongoing assessment and treatment, further examples of situations where the patient has panic attacks can be analysed using the same method as a means to verifying or modifying the hypothesis as necessary. This in essence is an example of the collaborative empiricism that is essential to CBT as described in Chapter 1.

Tips for identifying rules for living and core beliefs

A full discussion of rules for living and core beliefs is outlined in Chapter 6. The following offers a brief preview of this in terms of considering rules for living and core beliefs within the CBT assessment process. The defining feature of rules for living is that they guide behaviour. Therefore looking out for repeated patterns of behaviour is often a useful way of highlighting themes to rules for living. This is illustrated in the following example:

P   'I'm exhausted because I always seem to be running after people.'

C   'What do you mean there?'

P   'I always say "yes" to people's requests even when I sometimes don't want to or don't have time to.'

C   'What in your mind would happen if you didn't always say "yes" to people?'

P   'I'm frightened they won't like me, particularly my friends.'

C   'So you seem to be describing a sense in which you believe "If I say no to people they won't like me"?'

P   'I suppose I do, I've never really thought about it closely, but I do agree that I find it impossible to say no to people.'

C   'This seems like a potentially important theme we need to look out for in other situations.'

Other potentially problematic behaviours that are key to identifying rules for living are:

- always putting other people before self
- not getting close to people or not letting others get close
- always showing deference to others, excessive politeness and self-apology
- avoiding taking responsibility or making decisions
- avoiding giving an opinion or expressing a preference
- keeping the home excessively tidy

- doing things to a high standard
- working excessively to the exclusion of family or leisure activities
- avoiding anything that is upsetting, distressing or anxiety provoking. This could be a situation or event or it could be their own thoughts and feelings.

Another way of identifying rules for living is to listen out for the patient's use of the words 'must', 'should' and 'got to'. Of course, not all uses of these words are an indication of a rule for living and the clinician can establish this by asking the patient whether such demands help the person reach their goal in a given situation or whether they lead to behaviours on the part of the person that are constructive. For example:

P 'I need to work very, very hard.'
C 'What is it about working very, very hard that is important for you?'
P 'I don't know what you mean.'
C 'What does working hard give you?'
P 'A sense of purpose and meaning to life.'
C 'Okay, does your work take over other areas of your life?'
P 'No, but I enjoy my work and I'm doing well at it.'
C 'Do you take work home in the evenings?'
P 'Only usually one night per week. But I am very strict with myself in that I leave work on time at 5.30 every day and I never work at weekends'.
C 'Okay, that sounds good. Do you have a social life and hobbies?'
P 'Well I spend a lot of time doing things with my kids and I help run the local football club at my daughter's school.'
C 'Do you feel you have time to relax and take it easy?'
P 'Oh yes, my wife and I make time for this most evenings; we might read or watch a film or just sit and talk.'

This reply would suggest that the rule is sufficiently flexible that the individual has a balance between his commitment to paid work and other areas in his life. However, there may be cause for concern if he believed it was important to be active at all times and this was part of this definition of work, with no time for himself, his family and his own interests.

More general questions can be used to try and establish the patient's core beliefs. For example:

Core beliefs about self:
- 'What are the words you would use to sum yourself up as a person?'
- 'What do you like about yourself as a person?'
- 'What do you dislike about yourself as a person?'
- 'How would you see yourself in comparison to others?'
- 'How would you describe your personality?'

Core beliefs about others:
- 'How would you say you experience other people?'
- 'How do you anticipate other will treat you?'
- 'How easy do you find it to trust other people?'

Core beliefs about the world:
- 'What is your view of the world as a place?'
- 'How do you feel when you are out in the world?'

Eliciting behaviours

Once the person's thinking has been fully understood then it is important to discover the other element of the vicious circle maintenance formulation, namely the behaviours. To continue with our earlier example:

C 'At that point where you felt light headed, hot and believed you were going to be sick and faint did you do anything specific to try and prevent that happening?'

P 'Oh yes. I always carry water with me so I had some sips of that. I held on very tightly to my trolley for support and I started to recite my times tables to try and distract myself.'

C 'How effective were these strategies on this occasion?'

P 'The water helped a great deal it always does.'

C 'I take it on this occasion your worst fear was not realized and you were not sick and you didn't faint.'

P 'No that's right.'

C 'How do you make sense of the fact you didn't faint?'

P 'Well, as I say the water helped.'

C 'Did anything else occur that helped alleviate the situation?'

P 'Well, yes as I got to the front of the queue my partner turned up and she packed the shopping and paid and I went and waited outside.'

C 'So, just to check I have understood you correctly. Your partner arrived and she packed the shopping and paid while you waited outside?'

P 'Yes.'

C 'If your partner had not turned up allowing you to leave the situation quickly what do you think would have happened?'

P 'I would have done what I have done in the past and just abandoned the shopping. There are several supermarkets I no longer visit because I have had to leave the shopping because I was going to faint.'

Dryden (1999) describes a variety of reasons why we engage in particular behaviours – to bring about a change in our emotions, to bring about a change in our physical or interpersonal environment and to act in accordance with our values, standards and goals. It is often necessary to ask about specific behaviours that you think the person could be carrying out on the basis of the information the person has given you thus far. Typical counterproductive behaviours to look out for are avoidance, reassurance seeking and safety seeking behaviours (anxiety problems); withdrawal, reduction of pleasurable and valuable activities and suicidal behaviour (depression), outbursts, physical assaults on persons or objects (anger). It is essential to understand the purpose of the behaviour in the context of the other elements of the vicious circle formulation and to discuss each in detail with the patient and help them to make connections between them as illustrated in our example.

Generalizing

Once you have collected a specific example of the patient's problem using the Greenberger and Padesky (1995) model then the next stage is to attempt to 'generalize' it, in other words to understand how it affects other areas of the person's life. The first question is to ask about other environmental activating events, and to make a list of these: 'Are there any other situations (or experiences or triggers) other than the supermarket queue where you experience panic attacks?' One would also generalize the list of behaviours by asking, as appropriate, whether the patient engages in any other avoidance, escape, withdrawal, safety, reassurance seeking or other problematic behaviours. Try to ensure that this list is comprehensive.

What you are seeking to establish is a measure of the following:

Frequency: how often something occurs e.g. 'How often do you have a panic attack?'
Intensity: how strong the emotional response is in an upsetting situation e.g. 'On a scale of
    0–100 where 0 is not at all distressed and 100 is the most distressed you have ever been
    how distressed do you become when you have a panic attack?'
Duration: how long the distressing feelings last e.g. 'How long did the panic feelings last on
    this occasion?'

This information is important in terms of establishing the severity of a problem. Thus, if the patient is experiencing a panic attack once a month, at an intensity rating of 10 and it lasts 2 minutes this is a very different picture to a patient experiencing two panic attacks per day, at an intensity of 70–80 and each lasting 5–10 minutes.

Establishing goals

When the previous step has been completed, the next is to enquire about what the patient's goal is in tackling the presenting problem. When establishing a goal with the patient it is important that the goal is realistic, achievable and indeed measurable. For example, it would be unlikely to be a realistic goal for a chronic pain patient never to have pain again. Patients often describe their goals in vague terms such as 'feeling better' or 'being happier' so it is important to help them think of their goals in terms of the problem e.g. one could ask: 'Thinking back to the problem that we have been talking about, how would you like to be feeling differently or what would you like to be doing differently?' Many clinicians frame goals in a behavioural way because this is most specific and easiest to measure. If the patient is unable to think of a goal then asking the patient what their dream is may help stimulate ideas. However, in order to work from a CBT perspective it would be necessary at some point to ask what their first step is towards fulfilling this dream and setting that as a goal. Chapter 2 discusses the process of establishing a problem and goal list as part of a CBT intervention. In the assessment phase, the purpose of probing for goals is to gain some understanding of whether the patient is being realistic in terms of what CBT can achieve. If it is impossible for you and the patient to agree on a realistic and achievable treatment goal, then this is likely to indicate that a CBT approach would not be suitable.

Eliciting further problems

When a clear understanding of the person's main problem has been obtained, then if appropriate it is necessary to ask about further problems. A question such as 'have you any other problems you wish to discuss?' will prompt the person to describe it. The same approach just outlined for the first problem is used to assess any remaining problems and this process may have to be repeated several times. With regard to the number of problems the patient brings they are likely to interlink in some way and the clinician has to make sense of these links through the process of formulation.

Onset and history

The next stage of the assessment is to trace the history of the problem. It is possible to ask separately for the history of all described problems, but is probably most helpful to ask for one history. The purpose of obtaining the history is to understand how long the person has had the problem(s) they have described and what factors are associated with their onset and maintenance and the patient's reasons for seeking help (Hawton et al., 1989). It is also an opportunity to ask about previous help that they have had and the nature of this help, whether it was practical, psychological or medication based and how useful they found this help. If they have had a previous CBT approach then it is important to enquire as to what they gained from this and whether they are still using the skills they developed from this intervention. If previous CBT was not effective and you were considering a further CBT intervention then it is vital to consider the reasons why the previous intervention was not of benefit. This may be for various reasons: the person may not have properly engaged with CBT or completed homework exercises or the clinician may not have been experienced enough to conduct it optimally or certain problems may not have been addressed or different problems have emerged. The patient should be asked about these in some detail.

Modifiers

Modifiers are strategies that either exacerbate or reduce symptoms. These can be behaviours (e.g. safety behaviours, reassurance seeking and avoidance) or substances such as prescribed medication, illicit drugs, alcohol and caffeine. Any prescribed medications that the patient is taking need to be noted, recording the proper name of the drug, the dosage of each, how long they have been taking it, how concordant they are with taking it as prescribed and how helpful they find medication as a treatment. The assessor then needs to find out if the person drinks alcohol and how many units a week they drink. It is best to ask about units as people may answer this question in a vague way, particularly if they have a problem with alcohol. If it is suspected that a person has previously had a problem with alcohol then this should be asked about. Any use of illicit drugs should be enquired into, although, for obvious reasons, they may not give an entirely truthful answer. The level of the patient's caffeine consumption (as contained in tea, coffee, fizzy drinks and chocolate) should be established. Excessive consumption of caffeine can mimic anxiety symptoms in general, exacerbate the frequency of panic attacks and contribute to disturbed sleep patterns and irritability in anxiety disorders and depression. It is also relevant to ask about the person's diet particularly where there may be disturbance in eating such as in depression, or where eating problems may be the primary presenting problem such as in bulimia nervosa, anorexia nervosa or clinical obesity.

Life history assessment

We then move on to considering the person's 'life history', which refers to their experiences during childhood, adolescence and adulthood with the aim of trying to make connections between events and experiences in their life and the problems for which they are seeking help.

The areas to cover are as follows and it would typically take at least one 60-minute session to collect this information:

- where the person was born and raised
- relationships with parents and siblings, family atmosphere and quality of parents' relationship
- how the person would describe themselves as a child (e.g. shy, outgoing, made friends easily etc.)
- what the quality of their friendships with others was, episodes of bullying etc.
- significant losses in childhood e.g. death of a family member, divorce, illness
- experiences at school and educational achievement, relationships with peers and teachers
- religious faith or spirituality
- sexuality, sexual relationships and any unwanted sexual experiences
- current relationships, children
- work history
- current living circumstances, debt
- current hobbies and interests
- past and current medical, psychiatric and, where relevant, forensic history.

When starting to ask about life history it is useful to explain to the person the purpose of this phase of the assessment. The aim being to gain a sense of the person's life experiences in order to understand them better and to explore connections between past experiences and current problems as well as to collect information to help make psychological sense of the patient's current problems.

Mental state examination

It is recommended that a brief mental state examination be conducted with particular emphasis on assessment of risk of harm to self or others, the assessment of depressed mood (when this is not the primary problem) and looking out for symptoms that may be indicative of psychosis or dementia. In conducting a mental state examination, then the first thing to do is to observe the person's appearance, voice and demeanour. The task then is to collect detailed information regarding the areas as listed:

- low mood
- concentration
- memory
- energy and activity levels
- appetite
- sleep
- libido
- hopelessness and suicidal thoughts (including previous suicide attempts)
- self-harming behaviour (cutting, burning, hitting self)
- thoughts of harming others.

Within a CBT framework, when assessing these areas it is important to collect information on the frequency, intensity and duration of these problems, what makes them better or worse (modifiers) and what the consequences of each of them are in terms of the person's day-to-day functioning. For example, it is insufficient to know that concentration is impaired. The clinician needs to know at what time of day concentration is at its best and worst; how long is the patient's concentration span at its best or worst; what activities does the reduced concentration interfere with; can the patient read a newspaper article or watch a 30-minute TV programme/3-hour film and retain the information; follow written instructions if necessary; and, finally how does the patient make sense of this reduced concentration. As you can see, this is much more comprehensive than a normal psychiatric assessment and this level of detail is vital in terms of being able to target CBT interventions in a way that is most effective and to use CBT interventions to ameliorate these symptoms.

Concluding the assessment

We have now reached the end of the assessment and it is good practice to ask: 'Is there is anything that we have not covered or anything that it is important for me to know?' This occasionally reveals important information. At this stage the clinician is in possession of a considerable amount of information and it is from this that he needs to give the patient an understanding of their current problems within a CBT framework and discuss the suitability of CBT in tackling the problems described and share a treatment rationale with the patient.

This process can be aided by the use of measures and questionnaires and this important issue will now be considered.

MEASURES AND QUESTIONNAIRES

It is very important to use self-monitoring tools to complete the assessment process (Hawton et al., 1989). The use of psychometric measures and diaries during the assessment phase provides a baseline measure of the severity of the problem from which improvement can be monitored. Measures also help with the assessment of the problem itself. The patient should be provided with simple and clear diaries and the information collected should be relevant to the patient's current problems. The patient should understand the reasons for collecting the information and be given instructions on how to collect it. For example an obsessional patient could be asked to keep a daily record of her hand washing, recording the trigger to hand washing, how anxious she felt (rated on a 0–100 scale), the frequency and duration of the hand washing and the amount of soap used. This level of detail would provide a baseline of the severity of the problem, would be useful in setting goals for treatment that can be objectively measured and could be repeated as a means to measure change in the problem area as treatment progresses. There are a number of standard psychometric measures that are of use in assessing patients' problems and measuring change, such as the Beck Depression Inventory (Beck et al., 1961), Beck Hopelessness Scale (Beck et al., 1974), Maudsley Obsessive Compulsive Checklist (Hodgson and Rachman, 1977), Beck Anxiety Inventory (Beck and Steer, 1990).

Psychometric measures are not diagnostic. They measure symptoms at a given point in time and are used as an adjunct to the CBT assessment process. A major issue in using several of the measures just described is copyright and before using any measure it is important to check out whether it is copyrighted and to decide with your service manager which psychometric measures the service is able to use within copyright guidance. There are a number of CBT texts that contain useful symptom measures, one particularly useful source being Wells (1997).

Exercise

Take 5–10 minutes to consider these questions:

- What are the essential elements of the CBT assessment?
- What's the best way to keep structured?
- What can go wrong?
- Are there ways it could be improved?

PROMPT SHEET

When initially conducting CBT-type assessments it is wise to use a prompt sheet, in order that important parts of the assessment are not omitted. We have provided a prompt sheet for you to photocopy and make notes in.

Example of prompt sheet

1 Consider the information provided in the original referral and use that to consider your hypothesis regarding the patient's current problems and how you may make psychological sense of these potential formulations and how the therapeutic relationship can be initially developed.

2 Explain the purpose of the assessment interview, the duration and ask what the patient wishes to gain from the assessment process. (See earlier fuller discussion.)

3 Ask for a general description of the main problems. Ask for a specific example and question the patient about this using the Greenberger and Padesky (1995) vicious circle CBT maintenance formulation. The following questions will guide you:

- Can you recall a situation in the past week where you have felt particularly anxious/depressed?
- Can you imagine yourself in the situation; describe it to me as if it is happening right now?
- At what point in the situation did you feel most anxious/depressed?
- How anxious/depressed did you feel on a scale of 0–100 where 0 is not at all anxious/depressed and 100 the most anxious/depressed you have ever felt?
- At that point what was going through your mind?
- What was the worst thing you could imagine happening?
- Did you see any pictures in your mind's eye? What is the worst thing you can imagine happening?
- On that same scale of 0–100 (where 0 is you do not believe it at all and 100 you believe it with certainty) at the time in that situation how much did you believe what was going through your mind?
- How did you act/what did you do as a result? How did you manage the situation? What do you think would have happened if you hadn't taken that action?

4 Try to consider what themes to the rules for living/core beliefs may typically be present in this problem situation.

5 Establish what the person's goal is in terms of the presenting problem.

6 Identify further trigger situations where the person may feel anxious/depressed, and further problematic behaviours.

7 Ask about other problems the patient may be experiencing using the same format as just given.

8 Ask about the onset and history of the patient's problems.

9 Find out the patient's reasons for coming for help at this time.

10 Ask about prescribed medication, use of alcohol, illicit drug use and caffeine consumption.

11 Complete a mental state examination covering the following (consider frequency, intensity, duration and impact on current day-to-day functioning):

low mood
concentration
memory
energy and activity levels
appetite
sleep
libido
suicidal thoughts (including previous suicide attempts)
self-harming behaviour (cutting, burning, hitting self)
thoughts of harming others.

12 Collect information regarding childhood, adolescence and adult life experiences as follows:

- where the person was born and raised
- relationships with parents and siblings, family atmosphere and quality of parents' relationship
- how the person would describe themselves as a child (e.g. shy, outgoing, made friends easily etc.)
- what the quality of their friendships with others was, episodes of bullying etc.
- significant losses in childhood e.g. death of a family member, divorce, illness
- experiences at school and educational achievement, relationships with peers and teachers
- religious faith or spirituality
- sexuality, sexual relationships and any unwanted sexual experiences
- current relationships, children
- work history
- current living circumstances, debt
- current hobbies and interests
- past and current medical, psychiatric and, where relevant, forensic history.

TYPICAL PROBLEMS IN USING THE CBT ASSESSMENT AND POSSIBLE SOLUTIONS

A range of problems can arise in trying to complete a CBT assessment. As with most skills, repeated practice guided by good quality clinical supervision is the key to developing high-level CBT assessment skills. Here we have chosen to discuss two of the common problems that arise when carrying out a CBT assessment and we suggest some possible solutions.

Maintaining structure and focus

Keeping structured and collecting information within the CBT model as described in this chapter are key skills to develop. Many novices to CBT grapple with this for a number of months before feeling confident, so this is normal. The patient obviously does not understand the structure that the clinician wishes to follow and may have her own way of wanting to tell their story. She may wish to start at the beginning, whereas the CBT approach is to initially focus on the current problem. It is very important to keep the patient to the structure. You may say something like this: 'I would like to hear about the issue you are describing, but it would help me if we can go back to it after discussing x . . . Is that alright?' It will, in actual fact, be revisited if the comprehensive structure described is followed. Occasionally a patient may be adamant about providing some information outside the structure and in these circumstances flexibility on the part of the clinician is to be encouraged provided the information is made sense of within the CBT framework. Occasionally a problem can get lost in too much detail. Patients want to give details that they feel are pertinent but which are not really necessary for the assessor to know. Again, one could say: 'These details are important but it would help me if we could focus on . . .' Many clinicians have concerns about interrupting the patient and we would encourage you to view these concerns as NATs that can be tested out as a behavioural experiment (see Chapter 7). In the authors' experience provided this is done with sensitivity most patients are amenable to the structure.

Clinician and patient reluctance regarding questions

Another problem can be the reluctance of the clinician to ask certain questions and the patient to answer them. This problem typically arises in two areas: when discussing either emotionally powerful material or information relevant to taking a sexual history. As a clinician it is quite reasonable to have a degree of caution and a high degree of sensitivity around these areas. How much the clinician and patient explore this material together is a matter of common sense. A collaborative approach is vital and asking permission to explore these issues and giving the patient time to prepare and permission to stop at any time enables them to have a sense of investment in and control over the process, which will facilitate the establishment of a strong and productive therapeutic bond. If the patient finds the material overwhelming then the clinician can try to discover what is going through their mind at the time that is making it difficult for them to explore the relevant issues. Typical answers would be 'it's overwhelming', 'I don't know you well enough' and 'talking makes it too real' or 'if I talk about bad things they're more likely to happen'. Most people can address these issues even in the first interview. Issues that it may not be possible to explore at this stage are ones of physical and sexual traumas; it would be wise to say to the patient, in a sensitive way, that they would likely have to discuss them at some point if they wanted to work with a CBT approach. Regarding non-traumatic sexual information, then if this is asked about in a professional way then most patients expect such questions and answer them freely. If answers were refused then the authors' response would be: 'We understand why it's difficult to answer this question and it is your choice, but if you do not do so it may be difficult for me to fully understand the problem.' This is not said to intimidate the person into answering but to explain the situation and allow the patient to make a decision.

As a clinician it is vital that you develop the capacity to tolerate and deal with both your own and the patient's discomfort when asking questions in these domains. Avoidance of discussing emotionally powerful subjects or sexual issues is likely to operate to the detriment of the patients you are seeking to help. If you are able to recognize this difficulty then addressing it as part of your CBT clinical supervision is going to be vital. Again this can be approached as a behavioural experiment and in a safe way you could test out with your CBT clinical supervisor, a plan for tackling this difficulty.

Further reading

The chapter on assessment in *CBT for Psychiatric Problems* (Hawton et al., 1989) is detailed and comprehensive. Likewise the assessment section in *Cognitive Therapy: Basics and Beyond* (Beck, 1995) is very clearly written. *Cognitive Therapy: Transforming the Image* (Wills and Sanders, 1997) has sections on assessment and formulation as does *Cognitive Therapy for Chronic and Persistent Depression* (Moore and Garland, 2003).

Chapter summary

Patients who may potentially benefit from CBT can come from a variety of sources and can be seen in a variety of settings, including GP practices and specialist psychological therapies services. In assessing the patient it is important to have a shared language and to avoid jargon. A CBT assessment usually takes about 2 hours, but further time may be needed to address complexity. In that time one would be considering the goals of the session, the agenda, time management, and relevant information gathering. Open questions are usually asked, closing in on detail when necessary, with the clinician frequently summarizing. The format of the interview is to ask about problem areas using the Greenberger and Padesky (1995) vicious circle maintenance formulation or a relevant disorder-specific CBT model (e.g. panic disorder; social phobia) and then to move on to issues of development and maintenance of these problems. The difficulties that can arise in the interview include dealing with very emotional experiences and sensitive material such as taking a sexual history.

Identifying and modifying thoughts using cognitive and behavioural methods

Most people believe they see the world as it is. However, we really see the world as we are.

Anonymous

Chapter contents

- When to work with automatic thoughts
- Helping the patient understand the best way of working with them
- Distinguishing thoughts and feelings
- Working with both thinking content and process
- Troubleshooting problems using the diary
- Using behavioural experiments to evaluate thoughts

INTRODUCTION

As described in Chapter 1, there are three levels of thinking acknowledged in CBT theory and practice, namely NATs, rules for living and core beliefs. It may be helpful at this point in your reading to return to Chapter 1 and re-familiarize yourself with the distinctions between these three levels of thinking. This chapter will focus on the process of identifying and modifying NATs and setting behavioural experiments to test the validity of NATs, which is a key intervention in CBT. This is a complex skill for both clinician and patient to master and there are a range of factors that make the effective use of this intervention trickier than it seems at first. These factors are discussed in this chapter.

Given that CBT is intrinsically a self-help model a key aspect of the clinician's role is to enable the patient to develop his own strategies for dealing effectively with problems. A central aspect of this role of enabling is teaching the patient how to use CBT interventions effectively. In order to do so, the clinician has to have a sound understanding of the theoretical principles that underlie the intervention and the practical skill of being able to teach the patient to use the intervention for himself.

WHEN TO WORK WITH NATs

As stated previously, when using a CBT model a key task for the clinician is to help patients recognise the inter-relationship between events in the environment, NATs, physical sensations, feelings and behaviours. This is the Greenberger and Padesky (1995) generic vicious circle CBT formulation discussed in Chapter 1. When working with NATs the following steps can be usefully separated out and introduced to the patient one at a time:

- identifying the link between feelings and NATs
- identifying processing biases
- verbal methods for modifying NATs
- behavioural experiments to test the validity of NATs.

HOW DO WE DISTINGUISH BETWEEN THOUGHTS AND FEELINGS?

A quirk of the English language is that we do not automatically distinguish between thoughts and feelings when we speak. Thus we may say, 'I feel sad' and 'I feel you don't like me' both of which are grammatically correct. However, while the first phrase reports a feeling, that of sadness, the second phrase is actually reporting a thought or perception. This automatic lack of distinction causes problems for the practice of CBT. Further, the ability to accurately distinguish between thoughts and feelings within the CBT model is a key clinical skill if the clinician is to use CBT interventions effectively. The clinician also needs to be able to teach this distinction to the patient.

Theories of emotion (Power and Dalgleish, 1997) identify five basic emotional (feeling) states of which all others are considered to be derivatives. These five emotional states are fear, anger, sadness, happiness and disgust. The common derivatives of these are anxiety, depression, guilt, shame, humiliation and jealousy. When working with patients the authors tend to use only these terms when referring to feelings. There are, however, a number of terms that are frequently used to describe emotional states, which within a CBT framework are more helpfully considered as being related to thinking and these are 'helpless', 'hopeless' and 'suicidal'. The reason they are best understood as being related to thinking is that the specific types of NAT that go with each of these themes can be usefully targeted as part of treatment.

A further consideration here is the fact that this lack of distinction between thoughts and feelings means we often report our response to a painful event using terms such as 'I feel bad' or 'I feel such a failure'. Within CBT theory such reports would be considered to be perceptions (cognitions) open for exploration using Socratic questioning rather than feeling states.

A useful rule of thumb in trying to make these distinctions is if you can insert the word 'that' into the sentence and it still makes sense, then it is usefully considered as a NAT. For example 'I feel *that* you don't like me'.

WHAT ARE NATs?

As described in Chapter 1, NATs are defined as *our appraisal of an event or situation*. In this respect they represent our stream of consciousness thinking or what is going through our minds at any given time. These can be associated with pleasant feelings such as happiness or excitement or unpleasant feelings such as anxiety, guilt, shame and sadness. As described in Chapters 1 and 3, there are two aspects to NATs; their *content*, that is *what we think*, and their *processes*, which is *how* we think. In addition, there are a number of characteristics of NATs that it is helpful to consider. First, NATs are habitual and recurring. What this means is that most people will describe the same two or three recurring content and process themes within their NATs that are problematic in a variety of situations. For example, Jane, who was anxious and depressed recognized that whenever she mixed with people at work or socially she always experienced NATs (what she thinks) around the theme of others not liking her as follows: 'they only asked me out to be polite', 'I bet they will talk about me when I go to the toilet' and 'they think I'm boring'. She also paid more attention (how she thinks) to times when people were not actively talking to her and discounted those when they were and readily picked up on cues that suggested she was not liked (e.g. two people sharing a joke or planning a trip out and not inviting her).

Second, NATs are often rapid and fleeting, in others words, they pass through our minds at great speed; this is especially true when we are anxious. As a result it takes time and practice to capture the content of thoughts and identify their meanings. A related idea here is that thoughts can occur in abbreviated form and it may be necessary to unpack the meaning. Thus Andrew became anxious in any situation where he thought he might have upset someone. He found it particularly difficult to tolerate others people's anger and would simply leave a situation if someone became angry. During the early stages of treatment, John was pretty sure he did not have any NATs in situations where others got angry other than the phrase 'time to leave' running through his mind. However, he worked with the clinician to examine in detail two recent situations where someone had raised their voice and he had left the situation. Using Socratic questioning (Padesky, 1993), he identified a fleeting image of himself as a small boy being shouted at by his mother and told that it was his fault she was angry, at which point he would run and hide in his wardrobe. From this an accompanying thought was identified: 'It's my fault, I'm going to get told off.' This last example also nicely illustrates an important aspect of NATs, which is that while there are common themes to NATs across disorders (see later) every person's experience of them is unique and it is this unique description that needs to be identified and worked with. This uniqueness comes from the fact that we are shaped by our experiences, which are ours alone combined with our individual personality differences, which also make a contribution to the unique perspective we have on our experiences.

The CBT model distinguishes between different types of NAT as follows:

- NATs that are *facts*
- NATs that are a *response to* an emotional state
- NATs that are *driving the emotion* the patient is experiencing ('hot' thoughts).

For example, a patient with panic disorder may report the following NATs: 'I feel awful', 'I'm going to panic', 'something terrible is going to happen' and 'I'm going to have a heart attack.'

The first thought, 'I feel awful', is probably a fact; panic sensations are rarely pleasant. The second thought 'I'm going to panic' is an appraisal that is made on the basis of the patient's subjective experience of their emotional state and therefore is a response to the feeling of high levels of anxiety. This is therefore a response to his or her emotional state. The thought 'something terrible is going to happen' is also a response thought to the individual's subjective sense of anxiety, but is also a negative prediction. The final thought 'I'm going to have a heart attack' is the thought that is driving the patient's anxiety and is usually described as the patient's feared consequence or the worst thing they can imagine happening when a panic attack occurs. In this respect, 95 per cent of NATs that are either facts or response thoughts are irrelevant and not worth pursing. Therefore, a key skill for clinicians is to be able to recognize for themselves and to help the patient accurately identify the 5 per cent of thoughts that are driving the patient's distress and that are key to the maintenance of the patient's problems. These NATs are referred to as *driving thoughts*, which can usefully be described to the patient as *hot thoughts* (Greenberger and Padesky, 1995).

As described previously, NATs occur in both words ('people think I'm boring') and images (image of audience yawning and falling asleep while I give a presentation). As stated in Chapter 3, imagery is especially important in anxiety disorders and research shows (for a discussion, see Barlow, 2004) it is strongly associated with high levels of emotion. Imagery is very common in anxiety disorders but clinicians often overlook its occurrence. Equally, because it is often related to high levels of emotion, patients avoid thinking about or discussing images. It is therefore important to identify imagery when it occurs as overlooking this can mean the difference between problem resolution and getting stuck.

It is also worth noting that depressed individuals more readily recall negative memories of past events and these can be important in terms of the maintenance of depressed mood. Therefore it is useful to try and identify these with the patient where relevant.

Many clinicians ask how they can begin to identify common themes in patients' thinking processes. A starting point are the disorder-specific cognitive models described in Chapter 3 and elsewhere (e.g. Simos, 2002) as a guide to identifying the patient's strong feelings and the related driving or hot thoughts. However, the clinician is trying to work with the patient's own idiosyncratic interpretation of their experiences and it is vital this is captured in full. Thus when recording the patient's NATs it is important to write them down word for word as the patient says them. Do not translate them into your own or psychological language.

IDENTIFYING THE LINK BETWEEN EMOTIONS AND NATs

Patients frequently come to treatment quite understandably, having never considered the distinction between thoughts and feelings. Sometimes they are not quite aware what feeling(s) they are experiencing. Thus patients may, when asked about this, describe themselves as upset, distressed or feeling bad and it is the clinician's task to help them be more specific about what actual feelings they are experiencing. The majority of patients are able to do this with some help.

A crucial ability in the patient in order to use any psychological therapy, including CBT is that of being able to identify, describe, label and experience and regulate their feelings. Patients and clinicians who struggle with this are likely to find CBT difficult. Many patients who have experienced emotional, sexual or physical abuse in childhood use emotional avoidance as a coping strategy. For these individuals identifying, describing, experiencing and regulating feelings both in and outside of treatment sessions may be potentially destabilizing and the clinician should tread with caution if resistance to this process occurs. Emotional avoidance may be highly adaptive and serve a protective function for the individual and they should not be drawn into treatment without explicit discussion of the potential adverse effects that may result.

The feelings and physical sensations we experience in any given situation is the key to identifying driving NATs and it should be these, as described already, that are identified first when teaching the skill of identifying NATs. In order to do this effectively the clinician should always focus on a *specific, concrete, recent upsetting event or situation that is located in time, place and person*. An example of this would be: 'Last week, in the supermarket when I had a panic attack at the checkout.' Ideally this should have occurred as close to the time you are seeing the patient e.g. that day or the day before and preferably in the last week. Also, choosing an experience which is still upsetting to the patient will be more effective than one that no longer causes any or only partial emotional arousal. Once a concrete, specific situation has been identified then the clinician should ask the patient to recall this in the first person present tense as if it is happening right now. Then the patient should be guided to focus on the point in the situation where they felt most upset.

An example that is vague and over-general, e.g., 'I'm upset whenever I think I'm a failure', will lead to an unfocused discussion that will quickly degenerate into unproductive debate. In disorders such as depression where thought processes are by definition global and over-general, then focusing on a specific event is vital. Failure to do so will feed straight into this over-general processing which will not only seriously undermine the effectiveness of the intervention but may confuse and demoralize the patient leading them to disengage.

The following process using Socratic questions forms a template for how to identify NATs. The steps are as follows:

- Focus on a *specific, concrete, recent, upsetting event located in time, place and person* and ask the person to describe it in the first person present tense as if it is happening right now.
- Once you and the patient have a good grasp of the situation ask the patient to describe the point at which he or she felt most distressed.
- Identify bodily sensations.
- Identify feelings.
- Rate the strength of the feelings on a 0–100 scale (where 0 is the low end and 100 is the high end of the scale).
- Elicit the driving or hot NATs by asking: 'What was going through your mind?' This question can be followed up with further questions such as:

  'What are you saying to yourself?'
  'What is the worst thing you can imagine happening?'
  'What does this situation say about you as a person/partner/parent etc.?'
  'Can you describe any pictures in your mind's eye?'

- Once you have identified the NAT(s) rate each one on a scale of 0–100 where 0 means the person does not believe the NAT and 100 they believe it with certainty.

This process is now illustrated with a clinical example of Socratic dialogue for identifying NATs:

C   'Can you describe a situation over the last couple of days where you have felt anxious?'
P   'Yesterday when I was on the bus going to work.'
C   'Okay, that sounds good. Can you describe it to me now as if you were in the situation again? You could even close your eyes and imagine you were back there if that would help.'
P   'I'm getting on the bus at the usual time, 8.30 a.m. It is busier than usual and I have to sit at the back, which is a bit uncomfortable.'
C   'How long is the journey?'
P   'About 20 minutes.'
C   'Okay, how anxious are you feeling when you first sit on the bus on a scale of 0–100 where 0 is not at all anxious and 100 the most anxious you have ever been?'
P   'About 30.'
C   'And can you notice any strong physical sensations your body as you are sitting on the bus?'
P   'I feel a bit tight in my chest.'
C   'Okay what happens next?'
P   'At the next two stops about 10 people get on and I am surrounded on all sides, including people standing up. Now the bus is stuck in traffic, there is an accident.'
C   'Right, so you are sitting at the back of the bus, surrounded by people and the bus is stuck in traffic. How anxious do you feel at this point?'
P   'About 70.'
C   'Is there any change in your bodily sensations?'
P   'Yes, I feel hot, breathless and dizzy and I feel sick.'
C   'Okay, at this point, where you feel hot, breathless, dizzy and sick and anxious 70, what is going through your mind?'
P   'I am going to keel over.'
C   'At this point in time how much do you believe you are going to keel over on a scale of 0–100?'
P   '80.'
C   'So you believed the thought "I'm going to keel over" 80. At this point are there any pictures come into your mind?'
P   'Yes, I can see myself falling onto the lap of the person sitting next to me and vomiting all over her.'
C   'Thinking back to how you were feeling at the time, on that same scale of 0–100 how likely do you think that would happen at that time?'
P   '95.'
C   'What happens next?'
P   'I take a sip of water and then get off the bus at the next stop and walk the rest of the way.'
C   'If you had not got off the bus what do you think would have happened?'
P   'I would have keeled over and made a complete fool of myself.'
C   'And on that same 0–100 scale how much do you believe that?'
P   '100.'
C   'That sounds like quite a distressing experience. With your permission I'd like to

discuss this further and consider how CBT might make sense of your experience. Before we do that do you have any questions or observations about the exercise we just did?'

P   'Well, I do feel a bit anxious just retelling the story.'

C   'That's not an uncommon experience for people with panic disorder to describe; let's try and see how we might make sense of that.'

In this example, the clinician has used Socratic questioning to determine the actual bodily sensations and feelings the patient is experiencing in the situation. Ratings of the strength of these were taken and the question 'What is going through your mind'? was used to elicit NATs in both verbal and imagery form.

The key emotion in the example is anxiety rated at 70. The key physical sensations are hot, breathless, dizzy and feeling sick. The driving NATs in the example are verbal: 'I'm going to keel over' rated at 80, image of self 'falling on to the lap of the person sitting next to me and vomiting all over her' rated at 95 and a further verbal NAT: 'I will make a complete fool of myself' rated at 100. The ratings of the intensity of emotions and believability of thoughts are crucial to the intervention of identifying and modifying NATs. During the process of identifying NATs accessing driving or hot thoughts is essential. Therefore the clinician needs to help the client focus on strong feelings they are experiencing and to identify the most upsetting thoughts. There also needs to be a matching between the strength of the feeling reported and how much the patient believes the NAT. Thus if the patient in this example had rated her anxiety at 70 and 'I'm going to scream' as a NAT which she rated at 20 then this mismatch between the reported level of anxiety and the believability of the NAT is an indication that the driving or hot thought has not been identified and further questioning is required.

Exercise

Consider the following questions:

How many emotions are there?
What are they?
Why is it important from a CBT point of view to be able to distinguish between thoughts and feelings?
Are the following thoughts or feelings?

- I'm feeling out of control.
- I'm having a nervous breakdown.
- You're making me angry.
- I feel a failure.
- I'm anxious.

The first step in identifying NATs is to help the patient to identify links between feelings and NATs that occur in problem situations. The best way of achieving this is through the use of a thought diary. This consists of three columns the first column labelled feelings, the second situation and the third NATs. Looking at the thought diary in this form it may seem odd to have feelings as the first column followed by situation. However, tuning into feelings is key to identifying NATs and so in the first stages of teaching this skill it is to help the patient to recognize changes to how they are feeling and link these to situations and their NATs. CBT interventions are only effective if they are taught in relation to concrete experiences in the patient's everyday life and teaching of CBT skills should always be carried out in relation to a concrete and specific situation pertinent to the patient's current life circumstances.

USING THE NEGATIVE THOUGHT DIARY

It is important when introducing the patient to the negative thought diary, to consider:

- At what point in treatment should this be done.
- How best to help the patient understand the rationale for using the diary and use it effectively.
- How to deal with the person's concerns and difficulties when using the diary.

Regarding the issue of when the diary should be introduced we would suggest that this be done at an early stage, probably in session two or three, after the assessment, questionnaires, the defining and measurement of problems and goals and the beginning of developing the therapeutic relationship. However, in some circumstances, for example when treating acute depression (see Chapter 10) interventions such as activity scheduling and graded task assignment are often the best starting point. Generally speaking, cognitive interventions work most effectively with mild to moderate depressive symptoms. In more severe cases of depression where biological symptoms such as poor concentration and memory are very pervasive, then thinking will be very negative, black and white, and rigid. In such instances, cognitive interventions are often ineffective and behavioural strategies are best used, often in combination with antidepressant medication as a means to reducing the severity of such symptoms. Thus, in these circumstances, thought diaries might not be introduced until session eight onwards.

The best way of introducing the thought diary is to focus on a currently upsetting situation or experience in the patient's life and use the format just described to identify the driving or hot thoughts. Once this has been completed the relevant feelings, description of the situation and NATs with ratings can be transcribed onto a thought record for the patient to take away to use as a guide for recording their NATs outside of the treatment session. In addition, the patient will be given an instruction sheet on how to identify NATs.

At this point the patient would be shown the diary. There are a variety of diaries in different books and a photocopyable one is provided here.

Negative thoughts diary

Situation	Feeling	Negative automatic thoughts
Write a brief description of the situation that triggered your thoughts and feelings.	Use one word to describe the mood you had (e.g. anxiety, depression, guilt, shame, anger etc.). Rate it on a scale of 0–100 where 0 is not at all anxious/depressed/guilty etc. and 100 the most anxious/depressed/guilty you have ever felt.	Write down what was going through your mind when you were feeling this way. Try to find the hot thought that is upsetting you the most. Rate how much you believe each thought on a scale of 0–100 where 0 is you do not believe it at all and 100 you believe it with certainty.

Additional questions

What does this thought say about myself, others or the future?

If this thought is true, what's the worse thing about that?

Do I have distressing visual images linked to this thought?

Evidence that supports the negative thought	Evidence that does not support the negative thought	Balanced thought
Write down evidence that supports the negative thought	Write down the answers to each of the following questions: **1** What evidence does not support the negative thought?	Write down a short statement that counterbalances the original negative thought
	2 What alternative perspective can I take in this situation?	
	3 What type of processing bias is this an example of?	What action can I take to test out this thought?
	4 What is the effect of thinking this way?	
	5 If my best friend said they had been thinking this way what would I say to him/her?	

Patient guide to completing the negative thoughts diary

1 Become aware of a change in your feelings and if this is an upsetting feeling, complete the diary.

2 Write your feelings down alongside the situation.

3 Write down what is going through your mind at the time you notice these upsetting feelings. It would be helpful if you could try to find the hot NATs associated with these upsetting feelings.

Once you understand this part of the diary move on to the next step, which is to question your NATs from a range of perspectives. The following contains questions to apply to each NAT.

How to question NATs

- What evidence do I have to support the thought in this situation?
- What evidence do I have against the thought in this situation?
- What alternative perspectives can I take in this situation?
- If my friend x told me he/she had this NAT what would I say to him/her?
- How would I help him to deal with its effect on him/her?
- What is the effect of thinking this way?
- What action can I take to test out my thought (behavioural experiment)?

What processing bias is at work here?

Use the following information to recognize the themes in your thinking style and record them in the NAT diary.

When mood is depressed and/or anxious how we process information takes on a certain form; these are known as processing biases. When mood is depressed our thought processes are:

- more *negative* and often *focuses on past events*
- more *black and white*.

We have difficulty thinking in *specific* terms and tend to make *over-generalizations*, using one specific incidence to jump to a general usually negative conclusion about ourselves, other people or events in or lives. We more easily *recall negative memories* from the past and it is harder to recall positive memories. Our thinking about *past* events can become *ruminative*, that is, we turn the same thing over and over again in our minds repeatedly and we are *more much sensitive to criticism* and see this where perhaps it is not intended, tending to *take things personally* whether they are meant this way or not.

When mood is anxious our thought processes are:

- more *negative* and often *focused on future events*
- automatically looking out for what is potentially *threatening or dangerous* to us
- *narrow in perspective, only focusing on the threat* at hand and not taking in other information
- *overestimating the risk* in a situation
- *underestimating the likelihood of our dealing* with the situation
- focused on the *worst possible outcome* often stretching weeks, months or years into the future
- dominated by *worry about future events* and we turn the same thing over and over again in our minds.

In introducing the skills of identifying and modifying NATs to the patient it is useful to break it down into two distinct steps. The first step is identifying NATs. The patient needs to recognize and record NATs and this would be taught in the session using a concrete and specific example of a situation located in time place and person of an upsetting event in the patient's life or a time when they noticed their mood was especially low or anxious, ideally in the past week. It needs to be a situation that caused a degree of distress and has emotional meaning for the patient. The aim of treatment is for the patient to emotionally engage in CBT. We would avoid using hypothetical examples, as the use of hypothetical examples can promote disengagement from the process and reinforce avoidant coping by distancing the person from upsetting thoughts and feelings. More importantly, perhaps, the hypothetical example may not seem relevant to the patient and this can not only reduce the understanding they gain from the introduction to the skill but they may also conclude the method is not relevant to their problems. The aim is to go through the situation with the patient in detail and complete the identifying NATs sheet with the patient. It is important while doing this to introduce the information sheet for identifying NATs and to model in the session how the patient is to use this. This would include talking through the sheet with the patient and explaining how to use it. It is also important to indicate to the patient that identifying NATs is a skill, which requires practice. It may be hard at first but through a combination of work in the sessions and homework assignments it will hopefully get easier as time goes on. Teaching the skill of identifying NATs initially takes between 45–60 minutes depending on how readily the patient can engage with their distress and focus on hot thoughts. It is very important to identify *hot NATs* and to teach the patient that it is the *hot NATs* we are interested in dealing with. Many patients can report a raft of NATs but a large proportion of these are response thoughts or thoughts that are facts (see earlier for further discussion of these), which are irrelevant. The patient is often much more reluctant to focus on their *hot NATs* because they are, by their very nature, upsetting. However, this is the goal of treatment. The skill of identifying *hot NATs* and recording these on a diary sheet is then practised for homework.

The next step to teach the patient is how to modify hot NATs. Initially it takes one 1–hour session to introduce this skill to the patient. Subsequently we would spend on average at least 6–8 sessions practising the skill of modifying NATs with the patient in session. It is rarely less than this and usually it is more (8–10). The first session devoted to this would focus on working through an example of how to modify NATs using a NAT recorded as part of the previous week's homework. This would include filling in a blank diary sheet so the patient had a template that could guide them when they practise the skill outside of the session. This would be supported by written information giving instructions on how to modify NATs. It is the clinician's role to teach this skill to the patient. In choosing a *hot NAT* to illustrate the method to the patient the following criteria are key here:

- Ensure the thought chosen is a *hot NAT* and not a rule for living or core belief. If rules for living and/or core beliefs are recorded on the diary sheet it is important to note them for the formulation. However, it is vital you do not attempt to modify these using the method described because it will not work. This will be deskilling to you as a clinician and demotivating and/or distressing to the patient. It is not uncommon that both clinicians new to CBT and patients conclude CBT is ineffective, and often this is because they are not using CBT interventions as intended. At this juncture we would draw your attention to the definitions of the different levels of thinking in the CBT model as discussed in Chapter 1. It is in teaching these skills to the patient that you, the clinician, need to understand the practical differences between the different levels of thinking. Ensuring you are working with a *hot NAT* (as opposed to a rule for living or core belief) is most usefully achieved by establishing the chosen *hot NATs* are a *specific appraisal of that situation or event* (the definition of a NAT) and not generally how the patient experiences him or herself, others or the world in a general sense (failure, worthless, unlovable, better than, dangerous) or a treasured value such as fairness, or imperatives such as should and ought. The skill of making this judgment is one of clinical experience and cannot readily be conveyed in detail in the written form. This is in part because each patient is unique and what is one man's hot NAT is another's core belief and also because clinical experience of CBT is the only way of acquiring this understanding and skill. Taking questions like this to your CBT clinical supervision is one of the best ways of beginning to make sense of the differences between the levels of cognition especially if you can take audiotapes of your sessions and listen to these within supervision. Often the skill of distinguishing between differ-ent levels of thinking is learned through trial and error. You will soon know when you start trying to modify a rule for living or core belief because the method described here does not work with these types of belief. Rules for living are value judgments and therefore are not open to evidential challenge. Such beliefs are derived from cultural and family norms and will be shared by a range of people to varying degrees. Trying to modify these using evidential challenging can often deteriorate into a heated and unproductive debate, which needs to be avoided at all costs. Trying to modify core beliefs using this method quickly descends into the patient saying things like: 'I just know I'm worthless, I've always been this way and it's just is how I am.' Once again core beliefs represent our fundamental sense of self, others and the world and are closely related to self-esteem. This is how we are and this is not open to question, it is experienced as a fact. A further consideration here is the level of distress experienced by the patient and the degree of conviction reflected in their rating of the believability of the thought. This is often an indication that a rule for living or core belief is prominent. If you do start to modify what you think is a *hot NAT* only to realize it is a rule for living or core belief, do not persist. Simply say to the patient: 'This doesn't seem to be working, this happens sometimes with particular types of thoughts. This method is only helpful when working with hot thoughts. I wonder if you have ever noticed this idea of seeing yourself as worthless coming up often. I think we need to look out for it to see if it is a theme. It seems important and upsetting to you, lets add this idea to our formulation and try working with a different *hot NAT* and see what happens.'

- The example of the hot NAT chosen is still upsetting to the patient. If as time has passed the sting has gone from the NAT (which is common) then there is little point in using this to teach the next step, the skill of modifying NATs. The NAT chosen needs to evoke strong feelings and these need to be present to a degree when teaching the method. This said, for the purpose of teaching the skill in the first instance it is often useful to choose an example that carries a moderate amount of emotional resonance so the patient is not so overwhelmed by emotion that they cannot engage with the skill element.

We have given instructions for how to complete the diary, the main points being:

- Noticing a change in feelings should be the trigger to recognizing NATs and making an entry on the thought diary. In CBT, we are most interested in negative feelings (anxiety, anger, sadness, depression, guilt, shame) and patients need to learn to be alert to changes in their mood in order to be able to recognize and label changes in feelings. It may be helpful to discuss with them the first signs that there is a change in their emotions often by recognizing changes in bodily sensations. These exact changes are often unique to individual patients, learning to recognize these and label them as feelings is a key skill in CBT.
- Ideally, the diary should be completed at the time the patient notices a change in their feelings. If it is done later then it is likely the feeling state has changed and it will be much more difficult to identify the most important NATs, namely *hot NATs*. The skill of modifying NATs is only effective when the person is experiencing emotional arousal. Modifying NATs in the absence of emotional arousal at best renders the intervention an intellectual exercise and at worst can lead the patient to disengage from the intervention. This said, it obviously can be more difficult and distressing for both clinician and patient to work with active emotion but this is a key CBT skill for both parties.
- In order to develop the skill of recognizing and modifying *hot NATs* the diary needs to be completed and it is much less desirable for the patient just to do the exercise in their heads. Research into the mechanism of change in cognitive interventions identifies enabling the patient to take a metacognitive position and *seeing thoughts as thoughts not as facts* is a key factor in its effectiveness (Teasdale et al., 2002). The act of writing down *hot NATs* and observing them on paper from a different viewpoint other than the patient's internal reality is an important step in enabling the patient to begin to take the distancing perspective that is so central to developing a metacognitive position. Indeed, a sign that the patient has grasped the skill and is using it effectively is that they cease to work through the questions to modify NATs and simply recognize a NAT for what it is and let go of it e.g. the patient may say 'that is a negative automatic thought' rather than seeing it as a fact or truth about themselves or a situation. Once the patient has reached this position he may naturally stop writing down his NATs, which is permissible.
- It is important to try and convey to the patient that completing the diary it is not a test or exam, and that it will take a lot of practice to 'get the hang of it'.

You need to address any reservations or concerns that the patient has about using the intervention. The typical anxious NATs that the patient would have about doing the diary are as follows:

- '*It's a bit like homework from school.*' Here, it would be emphasized that the most important changes are going to be made in the patient's environment, so it is most important that these between-session tasks are completed. The clinician would try to ensure that the process is very collaborative, as that comment may imply that the task is being imposed. The clinician may choose to abandon the term homework and use a phrase (which may be preferable) such as 'inter-session task' or a phrase of the patient's choosing.

- '*I'll get it wrong/make spelling or grammar mistakes.*' In response to this statement it is useful to consider how this may fit into the overall formulation of the patient's problems, as the patient may have a rule for living around the theme of high standards or perfectionism. It would be useful to observe this with the patient and discuss the impact of the NAT in terms of their approach to the task. A general statement that there is no interest in the grammar or spelling and it will not be judged is also useful, but if you are dealing with a rule for living this is likely to fall on deaf ears unless it is highlighted and discussed. Likewise, there is not an absolutely right way of completing the diary as it is a tool to help the patient and some patients choose to modify it in a way that works for them. There is only one caveat here and that is the diary is not modified in such a way that is becomes an ineffective intervention. For example, some patients ask to monitor positive thoughts, which is likely to be an avoidant tactic. CBT is about engaging with problems actively and solving them and NATs are an example of such a problem and modifying NATs involves much more than using reassuring positive statements, which are meaningless in the face of acute mental health problems. It would be explained that most people take some time to develop a degree of skill in using this intervention but generally do find it very helpful.

- '*If people see me filling it in they'll realize I've got a problem.*' It is important to recognize that this could be a real issue in some patients' lives. One suggested solution here is that the patient transfers the format of the diary to a more inconspicuous format like a Filofax or a notepad. If this were not practical then one would suggest that they take themselves out of the situation for a short time (to another more private room) and record their NATs.

- '*I can't see the point of doing it.*' The rationale of doing the exercise would be explained again, and their concerns dealt with. It is often useful to set up completion of the diary as a behavioural experiment to test out the usefulness or otherwise of engaging in the activity. However, a comment like this may suggest a significant anxiety about the strong emotion that he or she may have to face and may be a sign of an avoidant coping style, or a lack of engagement with the CBT process.

- '*I'm not sure that I've got time to do it.*' There may be some truth in this or it may mask underlying concerns that need to be explored. It is important that the patient makes space in their life for treatment and sets aside time each week to devote specifically to homework assignments. This would be made explicit to the patient. Similarly, if the patient has difficulty with this then considering this as part of the formulation and discussing this openly in a collaborative manner would be vital. Typically, rules for living around the theme of approval and subjugation are key here. Often patients spend so much time meeting others' needs that they have never learned to recognise or prioritize their own needs. This often becomes very apparent when asking patients to prioritize CBT homework assignments. The issue of motivation to change also arises here. The clinician could enquire how much impact the problem was having on his life. It may be that the problem exerts very little impact on the patient's life and therefore the work required in the patient's view represents too much effort.

- '*How many negative thoughts do you want me to write?*' It is important to give clear instructions regarding what you are asking the patient to do. As stated previously, if the patient is very distressed and is experiencing numerous NATs it will be excessively onerous to ask him to complete a diary every day. Given that the patient's mind can be dominated with NATs it is usual to ask them only to collect one or two examples.

When it comes to working on NATs in the next session one may be confronted with either no diary completed because the patient, believing they had to record every NAT, felt overwhelmed and therefore wrote down nothing, or one is presented with 10 completed sheets. Both of these scenarios are going to potentially impact negatively on the session. In the first instance, the patient may be very distressed at not completing the diary sheets and blame themselves or see themselves as failing at CBT. In the second scenario, it will be impossible to review every completed sheet and this can be a demotivating experience for the patient who has worked hard to collect NATs but they are not looked at in the session. When asking the patient to record NATs it is best to ask them to collect one or two examples only. This is manageable for the patient outside of the session and manageable for the clinician and patient at the next session. If the patient returns with several sheets completed it is useful to take a collaborative approach and explain to the patient that within the hour-long session it is likely you can only work together on one NAT and discuss with them which is the best example to work with.

Once the patient has begun to develop the skill of recognizing and modifying hot NATs then practice is key. Therefore, taking the opportunity to practise at least once a day would be encouraged. However, in the context of people's lives this initially can prove difficult, but it is important to emphasize to the patient that practice is key to tackling their problems.

As stated previously, it is best to view identifying hot NATs and modifying hot NATs as two separate skills that are taught in a sequential way in that the clinician and patient do not move on to modifying NATs until the patient has gained a degree of skill in identifying negative feeling states and associated hot NATs. The normal procedure would be that clinician and patient together would first review the patient's examples of hot NATs and if necessary any difficulties or questions dealt with before moving to the next step. As stated previously, the most common problem is that the patient records response NATs and avoids writing down or even thinking the hot NATs. Thus attention needs to be given to working with the patient to write down their hot NATs. If there is avoidance of this then it should be discussed openly with the patient in a collaborative manner and the avoidance made sense of within the overall formulation of the patient's problems. In terms of completing the diary there is not usually a problem with the first column, situation. However patients may write some feelings here or even NATs. It is important to help the patient recognize what belongs in which column. This needs to be done sensitively and the best method is to use Socratic questions to explore how best to differentiate between thoughts and feelings rather than the clinician correcting the patient which may tap straight into rules for living for example about not doing things properly and being open to criticism. Regarding the second column about feelings, patients usually can identify the relevant feeling in a given situation. Sometimes the patient (as we described in an earlier example) has several emotional responses in one situation and it is helpful to try and capture this in the diary. The important thing here is to help the patient recognize that NATs (as described in Chapters 1 and 5) contain different themes and therefore are related to different feeling states. For example the hot NAT 'I'll lose my job and be destitute' is likely to be associated with anxiety and 'I'm a failure' associated with depression. In terms of the format it is important to separate the different hot NATs and related feelings into their individual columns. There is often a lot of difficulty in deciding what the hot NAT is and indeed there may not be just one, there may be two or more thoughts of equal emotionality. Key to the clinician developing competence in this area are:

- CBT training to use the intervention.
- CBT-focused clinical supervision from an appropriately qualified CBT clinician.
- Clinical experience with supervised practice.

As stated previously, imagery is especially important in anxiety disorders (see Chapter 8). Therefore, it is important the patient recognize this and record it in the diary.

It is sometimes the case that patients do not make any attempt at their diaries and it will usually be for one of the reasons outlined above, so the clinician needs to explore the reasons tactfully in a collaborative manner.

Another problem is that of the patient who cannot read or write or who is blind and therefore cannot complete the diary. The solution here is to use a tape recorder with a microphone; it is important that the person follows the format described even when using the tape. The person could listen to the headings on to the tape before they make their verbal entry (e.g. 'triggering situation: the situation is that my boss comes into the room').

Time would be taken in teaching the patient how to modify hot NATs going through the next part of the diary:

1   The first column is *Evidence supporting the NAT* and the evidence that supports the NAT should be placed here. Next a series of questions are applied to the NAT in order to examine it from different perspectives as follows.

2   *What evidence does not support the hot thought?* Here, the patient should write down any specific factual evidence that does not support the thought. Thus, for example, James, who is depressed, was called into his boss's office to discuss a piece of work he had been asked to complete regarding sales figures in which he had made an error of calculation and he reported the hot NAT 'I will be sacked'. Evidence against this NAT may be as follows: 'I'm not likely to lose my job as all my appraisals up to now have been good', 'it's not possible to be sacked on the basis of one small mistake, especially as the report has not gone out yet', 'if my boss wants to discipline me then there is a procedure to go through', 'other people have made this mistake and nothing much has happened to them.'

3   *Is there another perspective I can take on the situation?* The patient should try and look at the situation from another angle. Back to James: 'My boss is only doing his job', 'he may be annoyed at the mistake because he is under pressure from his own boss and is letting off steam.'

4   *What is the effect of thinking like this?* Here we are looking at the effect negative thinking can have on the patient's emotions, behaviour, physical state, interpersonal functioning and so on. 'It's not helping me because I'm feeling anxious, which is leading me to feel dizzy and tired, and this is stopping me completing my work schedules. It also makes me over-check my work to ensure I've not made a mistake, which is also slowing me down. It's making me stop talking to my boss and that isn't helping our relationship.'

5   *Am I thinking in a biased way?* The aim is to review with the patient examples of processing biases. This is encouraging the patient to recognize patterns to how they think by identifying relevant examples of information processing biases when they feel

especially anxious or low in mood. In the example of James, he may identify: 'I'm cata-strophizing–I'm looking for the worst possible outcome which is unlikely to happen.'

6 *What would I say to my best friend who was thinking like this? Or what would my best friend say to me if I reported this NAT to them?* Again, this is to help the patient to step back from his NATs and feelings and look at things from an observer perspective. 'I would tell my friend that getting criticized isn't the end of the world, and we all make mistakes. If he had made a genuine mistake he should try to learn from the experience. If he feels that the criticism is not justified he should discuss his concerns with his boss.' Or 'My best friend Alan would say, you are never going to be sacked. You bring in the most business to the company – which is, in fact, true.'

The next thing to do is to arrive at a 'balanced thought'. This is a perspective that is a counterbalance to the original 'hot thought' that is more realistic and helpful (although occasionally realism may conflict with helpfulness). The patient should write out the statement in a relatively short sentence. Most patients will understand this concept fairly quickly and provide good examples. However, you may need to help them by asking 'could you say, in a sentence, what would be a better thought than the original hot thought?' The patient should then re-rate their strength of belief as a percentage score on a scale of 0–100 per cent. If they give a low rating of believability (perhaps below 40 per cent) then they may need to be explored with the patient. There are two main reasons for this lack of believability. First, the patient is engaging in the 'yes . . . but' phenomenon whereby further NATs are being triggered that discount the alternative perspective. If this is the case these NATs need to be dealt with using the same intervention. The second reason is that the NAT is closely related to a rule for living or core belief. If this is the case then these need to be labelled as such and it explained to the patient that different CBT interventions are used to modify these (see Chapter 7). Once an alternative perspective had been summarized the patient would then be asked to do the following:

- Re-rate the original feeling related to the NAT and how much they believe each NAT now.
- Identify and rate their subsequent feelings having gone through the process of questioning their NATs.

Some patients are tempted to just automatically reduce the percentage when they have completed the exercise, as a clinician-pleasing act. The clinician needs to be mindful of this possibility and discuss it with the patient when necessary.

When the patient has arrived at the balanced thought then there is an issue about how to build on this further. It is not possible to work with all the NATs reported by the patient, particularly as these are likely to be numerous. We would suggest that focus is directed to those NATs that have the greatest emotional meaning for the patient or that have a link to the formulation or where the patient is very obviously engaged with the process of working with the NAT. If the patient expresses few feelings, if the clinician can see little link with the formulation or if the patient seems distracted or 'going through the motions', then it is unhelpful to do any further work with the NAT. 'Further work' means helping someone discover whether the balanced perspective carries weight. This is most readily achieved by conducting a behavioural experiment to test out the validity of the more balanced perspective. This process will now be described. If the person does give weight to the more balanced perspective then it is important that the person is able to access this perspective in any future stressful situation. Behavioural experiments are one of the best ways of internalizing such learning so it can be accessed when necessary in future.

Once the skill has been introduced then the clinician would ask the patient if they could feed it back in their own words so that one can be assured that they understand how to use a NATs diary. It is a fairly complex process that is being taught and the clinician should explain that they are not being tested on it and they should be helped if they are struggling to explain it back. It is also important to model the use of the accompanying handouts and explain that these should be used as a guide to practising the skill outside of the session.

One key element in the process of modifying hot NATs is *changing behaviour*. Simply tackling NATs without testing out new ways of behaving is likely to lead to only moderate gains in treatment. The real key to lasting change is changing the behaviours maintaining a problem. The main intervention here is what is referred to in the CBT literature as behavioural experiments, which are used to test out NATs, rules for living and core beliefs. An invaluable text in this area is the *Oxford Guide to Behavioral Experiments* (Bennett-Levy et al., 2004). We now present a brief outline of the role and purpose of behavioural experiments within the CBT model.

BEHAVIOURAL EXPERIMENTS

What is a behavioural experiment?

Fundamentally cognitive behavioural interventions are action oriented. What this means is that modifying NATs, rules for living and core beliefs is not just an intellectual exercise that is restricted to the confines of the CBT session but that NATs, rules for living and core beliefs are hypotheses that are experimented with in everyday life in order to test their validity experientially, and thus develop new perspectives and different emotional responses in problem situations. The main intervention by which this process is achieved is termed a *behavioural experiment* and this is a key intervention in the process of modifying NATs, rules for living and core beliefs.

In their highly informative text, Bennett-Levy et al. (2004) define behavioural experiments as: 'planned experiential activities, based on experimentation or observation, which are undertaken by patients in or between cognitive therapy sessions'. The authors describe the purpose of behavioural experiments in terms of enabling the patient and clinician to obtain new information that can be useful for three reasons:

- to test the validity of the patient's existing beliefs about themselves, others and the world
- to construct and or test new more adaptive beliefs
- to contribute to the development and verification of the formulation of the patient's problems.

The authors elaborate a basic methodology for designing behavioural experiments that is based on the principle of what they term 'hypothesis-testing experiments'. They note the origins of this type of experimentation in social science research methodology and describe three forms of formal hypotheses testing as follows:

Testing hypothesis A. This can be used to test the validity of a NAT.

Testing hypothesis A vs. *hypothesis* B. This method tests the validity of a NAT (hypothesis A) against a new potentially more balanced perspective (hypothesis B).

Testing hypothesis B. This method is used to test the validity of a new more balanced perspective.

This formal methodology can be contrasted with what Rouf and colleagues (in Bennett-Levy et al. 2004) refer to as the discovery-oriented method of behavioural experiments that are extremely useful in situations where more information is needed in order to understand a problem or where the patient does not have a clear view (hypothesis) of what might be the outcome if he or she were to act in a particular way.

How to design and conduct a behavioural experiment

The most effective behavioural experiments are tailor made to tackle the NATs, rules for living and core beliefs that are identified in the formulation. Fundamentally, the concept of hypotheses testing is reflected in every aspect of CBT. The goal is, rather than tacitly accepting and behaving as if our negative predications (NATs), unhelpful assumptions (rules for living) and global generalizations about self, others and the world (core beliefs) are accurate, we learn to be curious and experiment with them to actively test their validity. There are a number of ways in which experiments can be carried out, the most common being the patient taking a lead role in actively testing out the hypothesis in question. Other methods include experiments in which the patient observes a situation in order to gather new information or the gathering of information from others through methods such as surveys or use of the internet.

In using behavioural experiments the emphasis is not on obtaining a particular result or proving a particular perspective to be true of false; it is more in the spirit of taking a position of inquisitiveness in which the individual becomes open to finding out what happens. The concept of the 'no-lose' experiment is essential. What is meant here is that an experiment is constructed in such a way that whatever the outcome, something can be learned that can help the patient further tackle their problems. There now follows a very basic description of how to design and evaluate a behavioural experiment to test a NAT using the hypothesis A vs. hypothesis B method just described. Rouf and colleagues give a comprehensive account of how to devise effective behavioural experiments and the reader is encouraged to consult this text for further information.

First, the patient and clinician need to choose an appropriate hot NAT around which to devise a behavioural experiment and then the following steps are implemented:

- Write down the specific hot NAT to be tested (hypothesis A).
- Write down the more balanced perspective (hypothesis B derived from completing process of modifying NATs).
- Devise an experiment in order to test the two hypotheses.
- Try to make it a 'no-lose' experiment to ensure that constructive learning can occur.

- Discuss and problem solve significant difficulties that may arise in doing it and write these down.
- After the experiment has been completed write down and evaluate the results with particular attention to answering the questions: 'What have I learned about myself/my problems from this experiment?' and 'How can I apply what I have learned in future situations?'
- Consider what new more balanced perspective emerges from this.
- Devise further behavioural experiments to test this new more balanced perspective (testing hypothesis B method).

To follow on from this example, it was agreed to conduct an experiment to evaluate the hot NAT 'I will be sacked' and this was written down. The more balanced perspective hypothesized was: 'I'm unlikely to be sacked as my appraisals have been generally good, proper procedures would need to be commenced, and also my boss was having bad day.' The experiment was: 'I will ask the boss for some feedback on my work performance, within the next two weeks.' We tried to consider the no-lose element because there was no evidence that the patient was going to lose his job, and getting potentially critical feedback would allow him to improve his performance. In terms of problem solving, we agreed that this experiment should be conducted when the boss was not too busy and not in a 'bad mood'. The patient carried out the behavioural experiment and although his boss identified one or two areas for improvement overall, he was viewed as performing well and there was no chance of his being sacked. This generated a more balanced perspective: 'There is room for improvement in some areas of my work (e.g. keeping to deadlines) but fundamentally my boss is happy with my perform-ance and when he is in a "bad mood" this is not necessarily directed at me.' Future behavioural experiments were designed to build on this more balanced perspective that included:

- asking his boss for monthly supervision to monitor progress with target keeping
- observing his boss closely when he is in a 'bad mood' to try and identify triggers and how others interact with him at these times.

There is a worksheet (pp. 108–9) designed for recording behavioural experiments.

Exercise

There is no doubt that the best way to understand this process of working with hot NATs is to try it on yourself. It is suggested that the reader takes a little time to complete a NATs diary: try and use the intervention on your own hot NATs including if you feel able devising a behavioural experiment in order to test out one of your own hot NATs. The reason why it will be helpful to do it is that it will bring the material alive in an experiential way that will aid your understanding of it. It will help you experience at first hand the benefits and potential practical difficulties in completing a NATs diary, which will greatly assist you when using the method with patients. Finally, the exercise may possibly help you learn something about yourself.

1   Collect one or two examples of your own hot NATs over the coming week following the instructions described earlier.

2   Focus on situations during the week where you notice a strong negative feeling and follow the procedure for completing the diary. Try to choose a situation that is only moderately upsetting.

When you have done that, reflect on the difficulties in doing it and whether it was of any help to yourself. Consider, plan and carry out a behavioural experiment to collect further information about a thought using the behavioural experiment worksheet.

DIFFICULTIES IN WORKING WITH NATs

Patient does not record any NATs or very few and these are not hot NATs

This may be because the patient does not understand technically what is being asked; it may need to be re-explained and several examples worked through in the session. He may be avoiding focusing on his thoughts and feelings (which is not uncommon), believing that doing the diary will be too distressing or overwhelming. One could deal with this by formulating the statement as a rule for living (e.g. 'If I face something that is distressing I will be overwhelmed') and conduct a behavioural experiment in the session to record and modify one hot NAT and test out the prediction in the rule for living. If you decide to do this it will take time, at least a full session, so don't start it with 10 minutes of the session left. Rather put this on the agenda for the next session and do justice to the intervention. In addition, the patient may believe that the technique will not be helpful; again one could work with this negative thought in the session using the task of modifying this NAT as a behavioural experiment. It may be the patient is struggling with committing himself to the work of CBT. This can also be made sense of within the formulation. It is often the case that culturally within the UK patients struggle with the concept of self-help. There is a long tradition of the patient visiting the doctor and the patient being a passive recipient of the doctor's ministering. CBT requires equal amounts of active participation between patient and clinician. It is therefore necessary to be explicit with the patient and to explain that although the work done in the session is important, it is necessary to work proactively on problems as they come up in day-to-day life outside the session. If the person is reluctant to do homework at this stage then this suggests CBT will be less effective. There may be rules for living and core beliefs that interfere with active participation in CBT both in and outside the session. For example, a patient may see herself as vulnerable and other as more capable than herself (core belief) and follow a rule for living: 'If I don't have the help of others I cannot function in life.' Such beliefs are going to impede her ability to take initiative and engage proactively in CBT. It is vital to formulate these but also to recognize when these are present that short-term therapy (12–18 sessions) is unlikely to yield results.

Behavioural experiment worksheet

Planning

'What is the hot NAT to be tested?'

'What is the alternative more balanced perspective?'

'What is the experiment?'

'What problems may arise in doing it?'

Behavioural experiment worksheet

Evaluation

'What was the result of the experiment?'

'What have I learned about myself and my problems from this experiment?'

'How can I apply what I have learned in future situations?'

'What is a more balanced perspective?'

'What further experiments would further test this new perspective?'

Patient produces too many entries on the diary sheet

This, in our experience, does not happen very often. It may mean that the person is overwhelmed with negativity, but is actually using the technique appropriately. It may be that the person is writing down too many NATs that are response NATs rather than hot NATs. If this is the case the clinician would need to work collaboratively with the patient to focus on the relevant hot NATs and focus him or her down on recording only one or two examples. Further, the patient may be operating on a rule for living 'if I make maximum effort I will yield maximum results', the implicit message being the more NATs I record the more quickly I will get better. This can be unhelpful in terms of the patient spending so much time pushing himself or herself that he or she does not fully engage with the intervention in order to use it in a meaningful way. Finally, writing down pages of NATs can be an avoidant coping strategy. This tactic is not uncommon in generalized anxiety disorder as a means of avoiding engaging with feelings for fear of being overwhelmed (e.g. rule for living 'If I don't try and do something I will lose complete control of my mind'). If this is the case this needs to be formulated explicitly with the patient and behavioural experiments carried out both in and out of the session of slowing down and focusing fully on negative feelings and associated hot NATs. This type of work is usually slow and painstaking and again is unlikely to be achieved within a short-term treatment contract.

Patient produces thoughts that are too vague or general or a bit longwinded

For example (in the negative thought column), 'I'm feeling really stressed, I'm getting nowhere; my boss is constantly on my back – I wish he'd give me a break. It makes me feel dreadful about myself, especially if I've made a mistake.' These are likely to be response NATs rather than hot NATs. Here there are vague (probably emotional) words like 'stressed' and 'dreadful'; it is helpful to get the patient to specify what emotion she means, and to put them in the correct column in the diary. Likewise 'my boss is constantly on my back' is a bit general. A specific example of this would be helpful and it should be put in the 'trigger' column. The patient could focus in on the 'hot thought' she had in the situation. In addition, dialogues like these may be a reflection of worry and once more, as in the previous example the tactic is to slow the patient right down and work out the specific hot NATs and relevant emotions using Socratic questioning as well as giving consideration to formulating positive and negative rules for living about worry (see Chapter 8).

The procedure of helping the patient use the negative thought diary was described earlier in the chapter. Describing the procedure and problems in some detail is not to suggest that it is a dry and technical exercise, indeed it must be done in a sensitive and engaging manner with an experiential focus. However, it is important to emphasize that a key role of the clinician is to teach the patient the skill of identifying and modifying their own NATs and constructing relevant behavioural experiments and not simply doing this on the patient's behalf.

WORKING WITH HOT NATs IN SESSION

A lot of the patient's work with hot NATs will be done in external situations, but it is essential that the clinician review this work within the session. Putting this on the agenda at the beginning of the session and ensuring adequate time to go over it, initially often the whole hour-long session and subsequently perhaps 20–40 minutes, would be necessary in order to do this justice. In practice, it is usually one of the major items in the session.

The role of the clinician here is to ensure that the patient is developing the skill of identifying and modifying hot NATs and using behavioural experiments to test these out and obviously to verify that the intervention is proving beneficial. We would normally examine the diaries together and use Socratic questioning and guided discovery to distil learning, reinforce new perspectives and identify and solve problems with the intervention. This would be accompanied by encouragement and support from the clinician, while obviously avoiding reassurance giving (see Chapter 8 for a discussion of the contraindications of reassurance giving in CBT).

Apart from reviewing the diaries, the session is an opportunity to work with hot NATs that come up during the discussion. Again it is very important for the clinician to look out for sudden changes in mood during the session, as that would indicate that the patient is thinking about powerful material. Things to look out for would be the patient becoming tearful, stopping eye contact, having a quivering voice, stopping talking, saying 'I can't talk about this' or 'it's too difficult', making a joke, paying you a compliment out of context, changing the subject, becoming hostile and the like. At this moment you are dealing with a human being at his most vulnerable, who needs the clinician to be compassionate and humane. However, it is also an opportunity to use the treatment in a powerful way. It is important that the clinician identifies the distressing feelings and accompanying hot NATs the patient is experiencing at that time and work with these. One could say 'you seem upset', 'what are you feeling like at the moment?', 'what is going through your mind right now as we speak?' It is a matter of judgement at the time as to how much to encourage them but allowing silence and time to speak is important. Therapeutically, this could be an opportunity for the patient to feel and express intense emotion and the clinician's role may simply be to allow that expression. There can be a danger that the clinician, operating on her own rule for living (e.g. 'If someone is upset it is important for me to make them feel better'), rushes to make the patient feel better by distracting them, giving reassurance or too quickly trying to modify hot NATs, driven by a desire to reduce the person's distress and possibly her own discomfort.

From a CBT perspective, we would put emphasis on improved emotional regulation; sometimes expression of strong feelings is fundamental, on other occasions, there may be too much emotion and it needs to be contained. A simple way of deciding this is whether this expression of strong feelings is helping the person reach their goals. Often the person will himself, instinctively, know that. As stated previously in this chapter a key skill is being able to distinguish between NATs, rules for living and core beliefs. Wherever there is emotion that is strong and the patient feels to some degree overwhelmed this may indicate the activation of a rule for living or core belief. If this is the case this needs to be formulated explicitly with the patient alongside the related hot NATs, feelings and behaviours pertinent to the specific situation under discussion, and drawn out as a vicious circle maintenance formulation. This begins the process of recognizing the activation of rules for living and core beliefs and their impact on functioning in specific situations. An attempt should be made to modify the attendant hot NATs, but depending how pervasive the impact of the rules for living and/or core belief is, then the impact of the intervention may be limited. At this point clinician and patient may need to consider starting to work with rules for living and core beliefs more directly. This requires careful thought. Tackling rules for living and core beliefs usually leads to deterioration in mood initially and is distressing and difficult for the patient. Working with these also requires clinical skill and adequate and appropriate clinical supervision. Therefore within the CBT model the patient needs to have a robust set of skills for managing their anxiety and/or depression before moving on to this type of work. Once again, if you find that rules for living and core beliefs are more prominent than hot NATs, this is likely to indicate the patient's problems are not amenable to working within a short-term treatment contract. It is also important that the patient fully consents to working at this level and they are made aware of the risks involved, which can include a major episode of illness. A key CBT skill is the judicious use of CBT interventions in a way that benefits the patient and does not lead to a destabilizing of mood or exacerbation of problems. The best course of action here is to discuss such considerations as part of CBT clinical supervision in order to develop the necessary clinical decision making skills to maximize the potential for the patient to benefit from CBT.

Further reading

The *Oxford Guide to Behavioural Experiments in Cognitive Therapy* (2004) by Bennet-Levy et al. is the definitive work in this area.
Cognitive Therapy: Basics and Beyond, by Beck (1995).

Chapter summary

Identifying and modifying hot NATs is a key intervention in CBT and it is the clinician's role to teach this skill to the patient. It is important to help the patient understand the importance of thinking content and process. Verbal and written methods of modifying hot NATs using the NATs diary should be used and the most significant thoughts are further evaluated through the use of behavioural experiments. It is important to anticipate the difficulties of using the NATs diary and the behavioural experiment method, and try to address this with the patient.

How to modify rules for living

LEVELS OF THINKING REVISITED

As described in Chapter 1, CBT theory identifies three levels of thinking, namely negative automatic thoughts (NATs), rules for living and core beliefs.

What is the relationship between the three levels of thinking?

A key issue is the relationship between NATs, rules for living and core beliefs. It is generally accepted that the three levels are interdependent as follows: building on the discussion of this in Chapter 1, a starting point is to say that human beings are not passive recipients of information, but rather we continually interact with our environment and actively strive to make sense of our experiences. Thus core beliefs are best thought of as information processing mechanisms by which the individual makes sense of his or her interactions with others and the world. These mechanisms for processing information are developed in early childhood and elaborated as we grow and develop; so environmental factors play a significant part in shaping these. However, as many theorists observe (Gilbert, 2000a), biology also plays a role in terms of personality or temperament.

In contrast, rules for living are seen as the principles that guide individuals' behaviour. Authors such as Fennell (1999) see such rules as being mechanisms for the maintenance of self-esteem, in that provided the conditions or demands of the rule are upheld then self-esteem is not compromised. Thus if for example someone holds the belief 'if I am perfect then I will be loved' then maintaining high standards will be observable in terms of their behaviour across a variety of situations including work and home life, relationships and social activities. For this individual, being accepted and loved by others is dependent on maintaining these high standards and the person may fear that not doing so will lead to criticism, rejection or abandonment. NATs are seen as the products of rules for living and core beliefs and the means by which the person's view of self, world and others is expressed. An important aspect of distinguishing between NATs and rules for living is that NATs are an appraisal of a specific situation, while rules for living by definition operate across situations. A further important difference is that rules for living represent value judgements or attitudes, which are to some degree culturally derived and can be shared by families, communities or whole societies. Thus, rules for living are shaped by our individual upbringing and experiences as well as societal influences, which may include race, creed, culture and class. For this reason, while NATs can be modified by examining the evidence to support or disconfirm them this is not the case for rules for living. Given that they are value judgments, these have to be considered in terms of the degree to which they are helpful or unhelpful. It is also worth noting that it is not necessarily the content of the rule for living that is inherently unhelpful Thus, for example, constructs such as working hard, being liked and approved of by others or striving to achieve are things that most of us would endorse to a degree. What it is important to consider is not just the content of the rule but the rigidity with which it is adhered and how closely aligned the rule is to the preservation of self-esteem, particularly where self-esteem is over-invested in one area.

For example, Graham held two rules for living: 'if I am to be worthwhile then I must always succeed' and 'I must do my best in everything I do.' He had advanced rapidly in his career and earned a high salary. However, he was unsuccessful in an interview at work for a job that would have meant promotion. As a result he was devastated and became depressed, viewing himself as a failure and worthless in the eyes of his family and colleagues. The constructs of worth being measured by achievement are common in western culture. The difficulty for Graham is that his entire self-esteem was invested in his work. So most of his time was spent at work, he prioritized work activities over family and friends; he took work home in the evenings and at weekends and always pushed himself hard to achieve the best results. This over-investment forms part of his vulnerability to becoming depressed in terms of his extreme adherence to his rules for living and their dominance in his life. It is also possible to see how such rules can become a self-fulfilling prophecy. Thus the harder Graham pushed himself the more successful he was, the more praise he was given but also the more responsibility he was given by his boss. It became harder to step back from meeting the demand of his rules, which increased his vulnerability to fall prey to their excesses. As can be seen in the examples, the content of rules for living and core beliefs often exist as contrasts. This can be made sense of in terms of rules serving a compensatory mechanism in the way described previously. Thus, for example people who hold core beliefs about self as a failure often develop rules for living around striving for perfection or maintaining high standards. The following example illustrates this point further and the relationship between core beliefs, rules for living and NATs.

Sandra holds the core belief 'I'm weird and horrible' and a rule for living 'If people get to know me well they'll realize this, therefore I *should* avoid all intimacy.' As a result Sandra feels anxious in the company of others and avoids getting close to people. This has the knock-on effect of interfering with her behaviour in social interaction where she is often viewed as hostile and standoffish. This reduces her ability to make friends and she has frequent NATs 'no one likes me', 'I can't talk to people', 'I'm an outsider'. These NATs and behaviours in social situations reinforce both her rule for living and core belief, maintaining her depression and continued behavioural avoidance.

Common themes in rules for living

In his original theory, Beck argued that rules for living and core beliefs formed the psychological vulnerability to anxiety and depression. The evidence to support this has not been strong and there is recent evidence (Williams et al., 1997) to show that that the themes identified in Beck's original model are a product of low mood. Therefore, these do not represent a personality trait but are a phenomenon of a particular mood state. In this respect it is possible to identify core themes within rules for living and core beliefs which may be common to all human beings should they become anxious and depressed. This suggestion does raise complex issues about the route to psychological vulnerability, which is beyond the scope of this text. The interested reader can consult Barlow (2004) and Ingram et al. (1998). For the purpose of pragmatic clinical practice the following themes can be helpful to consider.

Perfection/high and/or unrelenting standards/doing things properly/ following an ideal

On the face of it, these adjectives chosen to describe this theme may seem to be saying the same thing, but there can be subtle differences in the way patients articulate their rules for living, which makes the choice of adjective important in their formulation. In considering the differences in meaning between these adjectives, what is key is always using the patient's language and trying to identify the specific meanings for each patient. It is this level of specificity and idiosyncratic detail that the clinician needs to access in order to work effectively with rules for living.

For example, many patients recognize a tendency to like to complete a task to a high standard. Indeed this information is often spontaneously offered, closely followed by the statement: 'I'm not a perfectionist you know'. This is often a reflection of the fact the patient recognizes it is not possible to do things perfectly but does not recognize the possibility that they are striving toward an unrealistic cherished ideal of things being perfect. This often results in the patient always perceiving a performance gap between how they complete a task and the cherished ideal. This can lead the individual to avoid or put off certain activities or conversely drive themselves hard to strive to live up to their unrealistic cherished ideal. Similarly with the idea of 'doing something properly' the person may have in their mind a predetermined method and unrealistic set of standards by which a task needs to be completed which if these are not followed leads to frustration and disappointment.

In considering this, reflect on how many times a parent or teacher said to you as a child or you yourself have said to a partner or child 'you are not doing it properly!' What does this actually mean? What is the standard that is being requested? Do you think it is realistic and achievable?

There now follows a brief description of the terms used with examples of how patients may articulate these in rules for living.

PERFECTION

This usually refers to trying to achieve a state where there is no mistake or imperfection. For example, the tidily written symmetrical diary sheet or every room in the house neat and tidy with nothing out of place. Not being able to achieve perfection is often associated with irritable mood. Examples:

'I must be perfect in everything I do.'
'If I'm perfect I will be loved.'
'If I can't do something perfectly there is no point in doing it at all.'
'If I make a mistake I will be criticized.'
'If I make a mistake I am a failure.'

HIGH STANDARDS

This usually involves keeping to a pre-prescribed set of very high standards for carrying out activities or being a parent or partner. Thus, the individual will have criteria for what constitutes a good mother, teacher, child, service in restaurant etc. Examples:

'If I maintain high standards people will think well of me.'
'I must maintain my standards no matter what.'
'If I start something I should finish it.'

The theme of unrelenting standards is especially important to draw out (see Young, 1994; Young et al., 2003). This aspect of the rule for living contains an element of striving in which the person pushes himself or herself excessively hard in order to achieve the desired standard. This is usually at great cost to the individual in terms of the amount of effort, time and attention to detail that is invested in achieving a particular standard. When an individual pushes himself or herself to meet unrelenting standards they can have difficulty recognizing this as a problem, often because the rule has helped them to become very successful people. Such an individual is often continually active, often achieves one goal only to move on to the next without savouring the success of the achievement and any sense of pleasure is often derived from working hard. Their unrelenting standards will be applied to everything they do – work, sporting activities, hobbies and relationships. Such people often appear driven, exacting critics of their own and others' efforts, with an intolerance of mistakes and a low threshold for perceived failure. Clinical experience tells us these themes are common in depression but may also be significant in relation to feelings of frustration, anger and irritability. Examples of rules with a theme of unrelenting standards may include:

'If I don't always strive to do my best then I'm worthless.'
'I should always strive to live up to my potential.'
'If I push myself really hard I can achieve anything.'

DOING THINGS PROPERLY

The individual has criteria for how a task should be carried out. The key here is to fully understand what their highly idiosyncratic way of completing a task usually is. For example, providing an evening meal may involve cooking a dish from scratch or washing the car may mean doing it by hand with water, wax and polish. Examples:

'If I am going to do something then I should do it properly.'
'If I can't do something properly there is no point in doing it at all.'

FOLLOWING AN IDEAL

This generally involves holding in the mind's eye, an all-encompassing cherished ideal regarding how something should be. Enshrined within this may be all of the above, carried to an extreme, accompanied by the constant sense of disappointment the individual experiences, as their activities never, in their view, match the ideal. For example, the ideal birthday party would involve all your friends you invite coming, everyone having a thoroughly enjoyable time, all the food being delicious and well received, the weather being warm and sunny, not running out of alcohol, everyone joining in with the party games you have organized, everyone saying it is the best party they have ever been to etc. Examples:

'I must always strive to do my best.'
'If I live up to my ideals then I am a good person.'
'If I am fair and honest in all my dealings others should/will be fair and honest in return.'

APPROVAL/SUBJUGATION

An approval-based belief usually indicates that an individual recognizes he or she has needs and rights but has difficulty getting these met, or has a tendency to always put others before themselves, keep the peace and do what others ask or want for fear of being disliked or criticized.

Meanwhile, someone with a subjugation-based rule usually is unable to recognize that they have and are entitled to have needs, rights and wants and are unable to say what these are when asked. A subjugation-based belief is much more pernicious in its effect and often the individual will find themselves being systematically taken advantage of, they will go to extensive lengths, at great emotional, practical or indeed financial cost to self in order to please others. Individuals with subjugation-based personal rules see the consequences of not pleasing others as catastrophic, for example they will be abandoned, publicly humiliated or severely punished.

This is usually a result of being raised in environments where their relationships with adults were based on putting the adults' needs first. This may have been in a role as caretaker for a parent or younger siblings. As adults such individuals frequently pursue careers in the caring professions and enter relationships where they take high levels of responsibility for others' well-being. In the case of physical and emotional abuse, subjugating self usually helps the child stay safe from harm and as adults, individuals who have experienced such treatment may have difficulty trusting others anticipating hostility and punishment and they may be highly avoidant of conflict or expressing their own opinion for fear of reprisal. The theme of subjugation is especially important in relation to sexual abuse where the child is usually forced into a position of meeting the sexual needs of adults. This often results in extreme mistrust, passivity and powerlessness. For a detailed discussion of subjugation see Young, 1994; Young et al., 2003.

In considering the distinction between approval and subjugation, this can be useful in terms of offering guidance as to how difficult it may be to work within a short-term (6–18 sessions) framework with a particular rule.

Clinical practice tells us approval and subjugation are associated with depression, high levels of anxiety, shame and guilt. Examples of approval:

'If I don't do what others want they will not like me.'
'If I put myself first I am being selfish.'
'I should put others first.'
'If I don't meet all the requests that are made of me I'm a bad mother/friend/partner.'

Examples of subjugation:

'If I don't do as I'm told I will be criticized and rejected.'
'I must put others' needs before my own otherwise I will be abandoned.'
'If I don't comply with others' demands I will be severely punished.'

CONTROL

This theme is common in the anxiety disorders and anxiety is the most commonly occurring emotional state in relation to this theme. It often arises in more chronic presentations where the symptoms of the illness itself may be experienced as out of control. Examples include generalized anxiety disorder and chronic depression where intrusions, rumination and chronic worry are common features, suicidality, obsessive compulsive disorder where there is a high frequency of intrusive thoughts and borderline personality disorder, psychosis and mania. When this theme is present individuals often put a great deal of mental and behavioural effort into strategies that they perceive help them maintain a sense of being in control. This may include monitoring their thought processes for perceived unacceptable thoughts (GAD, OCD, psychosis), monitoring their bodily sensations for signs of danger (panic disorder, health anxiety), always keeping active in order to avoid focusing on thoughts and feelings (chronic depression) or maintaining a very tidy home environment (OCD, chronic depression).

There are two main ways in which the theme of control manifests itself: either as a desire to gain control over experiences that are perceived as out of control or as a drive to continue to maintain rigid control in order to avoid the feared perceived chaos that would follow from a perceived loss of control. The sense of control or lack of it often manifests itself in the following domains.

Examples of emotions:

'If I'm not in control of my feelings I will be ridiculed and humiliated.'
'If I'm not in control of my emotions it is a sign of weakness.'

Examples of mental events:

'If I don't control my thoughts I will go mad.'
'If I think something bad then I must want to do it.'

Example of interactions with others:

'If I'm not in control other people they will take advantage.'

Example of events themselves:

'If I'm not in control at all times something bad will happen.'

This discussion represents examples to illustrate the common themes in rules for living and these are by no means an exhaustive list but more general guiding principles. It is important to note that for ease of understanding we have presented these as discrete categories. The reality of clinical practice is somewhat different. It is not uncommon for more than one theme to be reflected in a rule for living as in the example 'if I am perfect I will be loved,' 'if I do things well people will like me' both of which contain the themes of perfectionism/high standards and approval. It is also important to recognize that for some patients their rule for living may, in a sense, 'stand alone', without there being a clear related core belief. For example, a person may just believe that he should do things perfectly or help others as this was strongly emphasized to him as a child through parenting and education and he does not believe it has major consequences for him or says anything about him as a person if he is not perfect but more that striving for perfection is 'just the way it is'.

Thus, when working with patients the critical clinical skill is the ability to work with the patient to identify, define and describe rules for living and help the patient to identify a statement that holds emotional resonance and meaning using the patient's own language. Only by doing this will you capture the idiosyncratic meaning of each individual patient's experience. Identifying and working with this idiosyncratic meaning is vital because it is this that taps into the key emotions, which need to be active for CBT strategies to be effective.

Themes in core beliefs

While it is important to capture the idiosyncratic nature of the patient's descriptions of their sense of self, others and the world, there are some common themes that arise, and in this section core beliefs will be discussed considering these three domains. Different core beliefs tend to relate to specific themes within the rules for living and tend to be associated with particular feelings or emotional states. This will also be considered within the following discussion. However, this is only guidance and we cannot emphasize enough the importance of working with the patient's own material, using their own language and not translating this into your own language or that of CBT jargon.

In depression, the common words patients use to describe their sense of self (core beliefs) are failure, unloveability, and worthlessness while others are often experienced as critical, hostile and rejecting and the world cruel, harsh and competitive. The related rules for living are in the theme of high standards/perfectionism/doing things properly/cherished ideals and approval/subjugation.

In anxiety disorders, key descriptors are a sense of self as vulnerable or inadequate, others as unreliable, letting you down or abandoning you and the world as a dangerous, unpredictable, uncontrollable place. The most commonly occurring related rules for living in anxiety disorders are in the theme of control and approval.

Often patients experience a mixture of anxiety and depression or have particularly prominent emotions such as anger, guilt and shame. In a mixed presentation you will likely see a combination of the themes and this mixed picture highlights the importance of developing a shared formulation with the patient that contains core beliefs and rules for living that account for the patient's presenting problems (see Chapter 3). Invariably the presence of anger is associated with beliefs about fairness often articulated as 'others are unfair/unjust' or 'the world is fair/unfair'. This is often closely related to rules for living about doing things properly or maintaining standards and a sense of control. The presence of guilt is often an indication that the person has rules for living in the area of subjugation and this commonly goes hand in hand with a sense of self as bad and deserving punishment, others as punitive, harsh and cruel. The occurrence of shame is often related to sense of self as inadequate or defective or odd/different/weird, others and the world as judgmental, rejecting, humiliating and hostile. Some beliefs are expressed in a way that contains implicit comparison to others for example 'I am not good enough' often stands alongside 'others are better than me' and the 'world is competitive'.

The relationship between rules of living and core beliefs can be sophisticated and subtle. For example, sometimes the rules for living and core beliefs seem to share a very close association and it is difficult to decide what is a rule for living and what is a core belief. For example the rule for living 'if I don't do something perfectly then I have failed' may relate to a core belief of sense of self as a failure. However, it could just as well relate to a sense of self as worthless, the implicit message being failure is indicative of worthlessness. However, this perception can be looked at from a different angle and formulated as success is indicative of worth. This may indicate that the patient's most problematic perception is a rule for living 'in order to be worthwhile I must be successful'. There are no hard-and-fast rules for how to settle on the most helpful formulation of rules for living and core beliefs. However, patients can usually indicate the phrases and statements that have most meaning because they carry an emotional resonance. It is vital the rules for living and core beliefs are developed collaboratively and the patient takes a lead in deciding which words to use and how the statements are phrased.

When to work with rules for living and core beliefs

As stated previously there is a theoretical assumption in CBT that modifying NATs will make rules for living more flexible and modifying rules for living will make core beliefs more flexible. Further it is thought that in short-term CBT (12–18 sessions) patients have only one or two rules for living that are problematic and one core belief that is problematic in discrete situations and has other more adaptive rules for living and core beliefs that on the whole lead a person to have a good level of functioning. On the basis of this within a Beckian model of CBT often no direct work is carried out on core beliefs within a short-term CBT framework. However, it is important to address psychological vulnerability and in short-term interventions this is seen as residing in the rules for living, which govern behaviour and the unhelpful effects of these are often very apparent in the patient's day-to-day functioning. In addition, it takes 8 months of consistent work to modify one rule for living. On this basis, within a short-term CBT treatment contract this work would be started as part of the relapse prevention stage of treatment about half to three-quarters of the way through the treatment contract with a view to the patient continuing work on undermining the influence of the rule for living under their own steam.

With more complex presentations this guidance does not hold but it is safe to say where rules for living and core beliefs are more global and entrenched (as manifest in lack of social functioning) then treatment will take longer, will be more difficult and the outcome less certain. As stated at the end of the previous chapter entering into work on core beliefs (and to a lesser extent some rules for living with some patients) can have a destabilizing effect on the patient's mood and functioning and can, if not executed by a skilled, well trained and well supervised clinician do more harm than good. Work at this level should not be undertaken lightly and the clinician needs to be mindful that he or she is dealing with constructs that are central to person's sense of who they are and how they function in the world. In this respect working with rules for living and core beliefs can lead patients to question fundamental aspects of their social role, their relationships and their value system. Challenges to any of these will elicit high levels of emotion and therefore what is modified and how this is executed needs to be, above all, collaborative and based on informed consent.

Working with rules and beliefs

In Chapter 5 the reader is given an explanation of how to work with the patient to identify their rules for living and core beliefs. To briefly summarize, the basic method with regard to identifying core beliefs is to start with hot NATs experienced in a specific situation and use Socratic questioning to 'inference chain' from these hot NATs to more global judgments regarding self, others and the world. In proceeding with this method the key is to pay close attention to the person's strong emotional experiences and to their endorsement of what a particular experience or situation says about them as a person.

In terms of identifying rules for living the method is to look for particular behavioural patterns and enquire about rules that may drive these; to listen out for rule statements such as 'I must . . .' and 'if that happened then . . .'. These are usually readily observable from the outset of treatment if only because they manifest themselves in sessions and often interfere with the basic tasks of CBT. For example the patient who has difficulty contributing to an agenda may follow a rule for living 'if I express an opinion I will be ridiculed' or the patient who has difficulty completing an activity schedule may follow the rule 'if I can't do something properly there is no point in doing it at all' or 'if I make a mistake I will look foolish'.

Modifying rules for living

Within the overall process of CBT treatment there is a gradual progression from working with problematic behaviours and NATs toward modifying rules for living and core beliefs. Given that it takes 8 months of consistent work to modify one rule for living then beginning direct work on this level of thinking is the beginning of the relapse prevention stage of treatment. As treatment has progressed you and the patient will have collaboratively developed a formulation of the patient's problems. By the time you arrive at the position of working with rules for living these will be formulated and at this stage may just require tweaking in terms of their phraseology. This position will have been reached through a process of careful listening to the patient from the point of first assessment session until now and paying attention to, highlighting and discussing consistent themes that will emerge in the course of working with any patient. It is these themes that guide you and the patient in the process of putting rules for living into words using the process of Socratic questioning and guided discovery. You usually know when you have the most appropriate wording for a rule for living because it captures a meaning that carries emotional resonance for the patient and can be observed in action in the patient's everyday life. Ideally rules for living are best worded as 'if . . . then . . .' statements as these are more readily tested using behavioural experiments, which is a key intervention when working with rules for living. Imperative words such as should, must and ought are more difficult to modify and often the patient has difficulty seeing the unhelpful aspects of these types of rules for living. This is usually because whatever the demand is it has been persistently and consistently reinforced in childhood and often contains a moral quality attached to a sense of duty or social priority. A good example of this is being a member of the guide or scout movement. There is a motto: *Be prepared* and there is a promise that is recited once a week making a salute that is a promise to God which goes: 'I promise that I will do my *best*, to do my *duty* to God, to *serve* the Queen and *help* other people and to *keep* the brownie/guide *law*'. If this is repeated from ages 7 to 18 (the age range for scout and guide movement) and reinforced at home with similar values it is easy to see how this may shape people's rules for living around the themes of high standards and approval and subjugation. Anyone who was not member of this movement may be laughing at the very idea of what seems nonsense but for those who were or perhaps still are involved in this organization then you may be able to see how your experience of this has shaped your sense of who you are and your values.

There are a number of steps involved in modifying rules for living:

STEP 1

The first step is to finalize the most appropriate wording of the rule for living and to write this down. This said it is not unheard of that once you start carrying out behavioural experiments to modify a rule for living further work is carried out on refining the wording of the rule. This is important should it occur and needs to be accommodated.

STEP 2

Look out for the rule in action, which are situations in the patient's everyday life where the rule for living is activated. It is helpful here to encourage the patient to return to the idea of vicious circle maintenance formulations (see Chapter 1) and look for the links between events in the environment, feelings, physical sensations, NATs and behaviours that are driven by the rule for living. Thus Mary had a rule: 'If I don't do things properly I will be criticized.' When working on this step Mary observed a number of examples of vicious circles driven by her rule for living. An example is given in Figure 7.1.

Expressing the rule for living in relation to specific events can bring the reality of the impact of the rule into sharp focus. For some patients this is sufficient for the patient to see their reaction in the situation is disproportionate and thus they are able step back from this and act differently.

Formulating the relationship between rules for living and the vicious circles they drive also helps the patient to see the power the rule exerts over their behaviour and to begin to consider how he or she might test out new ways of behaving as a basis for developing a more helpful rule.

STEP 3

The next step is to operationalize the rule. What this means is defining the parameters of the rule for that particular patient. This is very important as this provides both clinician and patient with a base from which to construct behavioural experiments. Thus to continue with Mary's rule for living 'if I don't do things properly I will be criticized' then in order to operationalize this the patient and clinician need to define what 'properly' means and what 'criticized' means. This can initially be done in general terms but it is also very useful to do in relation to specific situations like the one just described as this will enable you to elicit the finer nuances of the patient's perceptions thus improving the quality of your behavioural experiments. Thus for Mary 'properly' meant:

- no mistakes at all
- following her specific standards for whatever activity she was engaged in
- well presented
- completing on time.

On the occasion Mary had avoided completing a NATs diary this rule for living had got in the way. In this situation, her definition of properly was:

- no mistakes
- typed on her computer at home
- having collected all her NATs for that week
- following the written guidelines to the letter.

Similarly Mary's definition of 'being criticized' was either the person who was criticizing her telling her off sternly, taking the huff and not speaking to her or shouting at her in public and humiliating her in front of others. In the example of the uncompleted NATs diary Mary perceived the treating clinician would be angry at her, tell her off, discharge her from treatment for not trying and write to her GP and tell her this very thing. It is not uncommon to be able to make direct links between childhood experiences of the patient and the meanings that emerge in operationalizing rules for living. Thus for Mary her mother was a critical figure in her life prone to criticizing Mary and taking the huff if she

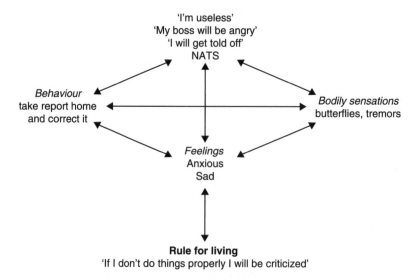

Figure 7.1   Vicious circle maintenance formulation for Mary

did not do things as she should ('properly') and in childhood especially chastizing her publicly which Mary found humiliating.

STEP 4

This step involves developing a flashcard for modifying rules for living and this is described in detail later. A photocopiable workbook format is provided below to help you begin the process of modifying rules for living. The same form can be used when working with core beliefs and the one provided is based on the work of Padesky and Greenberger (1995) and Fennell (1999). Some clinicians use different types of form for rules for living and for core beliefs, but it is reasonable to use one type of form for both. However, it is important to work on rules for living and core beliefs separately and to develop individual flashcards for each and to articulate the differences between these clearly within treatment. Remember work on rules for living may be sufficient to address the patient's problems and is all that is advised when working within a short-term CBT treatment contract (12–18 sessions). However, given that rules for living and core beliefs are related it can be helpful when building the relationship between rules for living and vicious circles to also encompass the core belief as it relates to the rule for living. Thus Mary's core belief was 'I'm a failure' and this could be inserted into the diagram below the rule for living statement. This type of formulation diagram is important in aiding the patient's understanding.

Rule for living/core belief worksheet

I hold the rule for living/ belief that . . .

It is understandable that I hold this rule for living/ belief because . . . (Where did the belief or rule come from and how has it been reinforced over the years? Consider your upbringing and patterns of behaviour.)

Following this rule for living or belief has meant . . . (Consider the advantages and disadvantages of following the rule in the past.)

Advantages

Disadvantages

How do I know that the rule for living or belief is active?

Record an example of a vicious circle formulation that illustrates your rule for living in action.

Record a list of situations from the last month where you have noticed the rule or belief in action.

1

2

3

This rule for living/belief is unhelpful to me because . . . (Consider the effect on your mood, behaviour, current problems, work and relationship.)

1

2

3

4

5

What is a more helpful rule for living or belief?

Why is it better?

Devise behavioural experiments to test out the accuracy and helpfulness of your rule for living/belief (you can use the behavioural experiments sheet from earlier in treatment as a guide).

1

2

3

What other things can you do to help you accept the new rule/belief?

Procedure for using the worksheet illustrated with a clinical example

The worksheet for modifying rules for living builds on and draws together the work already completed in treatment. In working though the worksheet the first task is to write the agreed rule for living at the top of the page.

Explain the rationale for doing this work, by saying, for example: 'In making sense of the problems you describe, you'll remember that we identified rules for living that were contributing to the problem. We have identified between us a rule for living "If I don't do things properly I will be criticized". We have noticed this is problematic in a variety of situations, especially at work, and on the basis of our discussion last session we agreed to begin to do some work on this rule.' It is important for the patient not to feel the clinician is attacking their personality or value system but trying to give a rationale based on the rule for living interfering with the patient overcoming their problems and making progress. It is useful to reiterate the Beckian normalizing rationale here and take the stance that we all have rules for living that are helpful and unhelpful to varying degrees in different situations. However, in terms of tackling problems in treatment it can be useful to recognize how in certain similar situations our rules for living can create, contribute to and maintain the problems the patient is experiencing. It can also be helpful to draw the patient's attention to early experiences that led to the formation and elaboration of the rule for living (as identified in the formulation) and how these may be helpful in some instances but less so in others.

Equally the rules for living may have been vital when the patient was younger to help him or her deal with a situation but they are possibly less relevant now.

The process then involves working together with the patient to complete the workbook, asking the patient to read and respond to the questions and to write the responses in his own words. This has to be a slow and sensitive process, remembering that the patient will have adhered to these rules for a long time and change is going to present challenges.

1   *I hold the belief that . . .?*
P   'I must always do things perfectly.'

2   *It is understandable I hold this belief because . . .?*
P   'My dad was a very successful businessman and had very high expectations of us, in all areas of our life. He was also quite critical, particularly of me, in comparison to my sisters who seemed to be prettier and cleverer. I took his criticisms to heart and it knocked my self-esteem. I felt the only way to get more love and praise from my dad was to be the best in absolutely everything, and I guess I'm still like that.'

It can be quite difficult and emotional for the patient to explore the basis of their rules for living. However, it is important to have a full discussion of key factors. These may be parental attitudes, cultural and religious values, school experiences and relationships, sometimes the patient needs some encouragement in talking about these things. It can also help to explore the way that the rules have been reinforced, which can be a more subtle process. For example, the way that the successful implementation of the rule leads to a reward, the way that the rule stops the person acting in an alternative way and stops them learning that the other way may be better.

3   *Following this rule for living has meant . . .?*

P   'I think when I was younger I used to work very hard at school. It probably helped me get good grades. When I got a job it led me to always want to be the best, to get promotion and so on. More negatively it makes me set fantastic, unrealistic standards for myself. Having to be top saleswoman, never making mistakes . . . it's very tiring. Even if I achieve these things I'm not happy. The main advantage is that in some ways it helps me be successful at work; I've reached quite a senior position. That gives me a good income.'

The clinician should acknowledge the benefits of the rule but, if appropriate, ask if they are genuine benefits. Otherwise, questions should be asked about the historic and current disadvantages of thinking like this. The clinician should acknowledge that the rule may have advantages, but should ask whether the advantages would occur if the person believed a modified version of the rule, for example, instead of believing that she must always do things perfectly, to have believed that she should aim to do her best, but accept that sometimes it will be impossible to achieve. The clinician should always ask what the patient's concerns are about giving up the rule.

4   *How do I know the rule for living or belief is active?*

P   'I feel particularly tired. I also feel stressed if I'm aiming for something like a sales target and possibly not reaching it. I can get a bit irritable with my boyfriend if he's getting in the way of what I want to do.'

It is important to draw out as many factors as possible and relate them specifically to the rule.

5   *This rule or belief is unhelpful to me because . . . ?*

P   'I feel very stressed, anxious. I don't take enough time to rest. Possibly family life suffers a bit because I'm always late at work.'

Again the clinician can ask a range of questions to elicit unhelpful side-effects. For example: 'What adverse effect does the rule have on your mood, your thinking, your behaviour, your relationships, your work etc (at the moment and in the past)?' 'How would you advise your best friend if they always followed this rule?'

The patient should be given repeated homework tasks involving:

- the collecting of evidence on a daily basis that runs contrary to the old rule or belief
- behavioural experiments to test out the old rule or belief.

6   *What is the new rule or belief?*

P   'Perfection is impossible and criticism part of life but open to question.'

At this stage, it is important to discuss with the patient what the new rule should be. It should reflect flexibility, therefore should express a 'preference' rather than a 'must'; it should lead to outcomes that are beneficial to the patient; it should be a statement that the person is happy to try to work on accepting; it should not be a statement that is too long and convoluted; it should reflect that following the rule is not likely to lead to disastrous outcomes.

7   *Why is the new rule/belief better?*
P   'Since I've been trying to follow it I haven't being staying so late. I've been getting slightly behind with my work, but it's manageable. I was spending a lot of time before checking that I've not made mistakes, and it hasn't led to more mistakes.'

8   *Devise behavioural experiments that test or support the new rule or belief.*

This is of fundamental importance and is a process of moving the patient from a lightly held 'intellectual' acceptance of the rule, to a firmly held 'emotional' acceptance of the rule. The key factor here will be devising behavioural experiments, in which the person acts in accordance with the new rule. For example:

> *'I will finish work at 6 p.m. on at least four days out of five.'*
> *'When I am doing a final draft of my essay I will take no longer than 3 hours.'*
> *'When I am studying my university course I will not procrastinate. I will start working within 5 minutes of sitting at the desk.'*
> *'Next month I will aim to be the second top salesperson and not first as I usually do.'*

The construction and testing of these new perspectives would be implemented using behavioural experiments as described in Chapter 6. The person can also use methods such as repeatedly stating the new rule and reminding themselves of the reasons why it is better.

Exercise

Consider these questions:

- What will be the difficulties that this patient will have making these changes?
- Consider a rule that you have that causes you some minor problems and write down ways that you could act against it behaviourally. Try doing this.

When to work with core beliefs

In terms of the format of this book, we would not expect its readers to be working with core beliefs and would encourage the clinician to concentrate on working with rules for living within a short-term CBT treatment contract (12–18 sessions). As stated previously there is an assumption in short-term CBT with more straightforward clinical presentations where rules for living and core beliefs are more flexible and less rigidly held that modifying NATs makes rules for living more flexible and working with rules for living makes core beliefs more flexible. Thus within such short-term treatment contracts there is no need to engage in direct work on core beliefs. However, core beliefs would be identified within the formulation of the patient's problems. On this premise, detailed discussion of how to modify core beliefs is not covered in this text.

In more specialist clinical settings (such as a cognitive behavioural psychotherapy service) working with more complex patients with longer treatment contracts (25–50 sessions) then working with core beliefs would be an important component of the CBT intervention. There is a wealth of CBT literature describing these methods. The main authors are Beck et al., (2004); Padesky and Greenberger (1995); Young et al., (2003).

Further reading

Beck (1995) *Cognitive Therapy: Basics and Beyond*.
Blackburn and Twaddle (1996) *Cognitive Therapy in Action: A Practioners' Guide*.
Fennell (1999) *Overcoming Low Self-esteem*.

Chapter summary

There are three types of thought, namely negative automatic thoughts, rules and (core) beliefs. Rules are ways in which the person acts across a range of issues and are characterized by statements containing 'should' and 'if ... then' phrases. It is often essential when weakening rules to look at the advantages and disadvantages of the rule and then experiment by repeatedly acting against the rule. Core beliefs are fundamental to the person and are unlikely to shift easily; this can be done in a similar way to working with the other thoughts but will need tenacity and effort.

Treating anxiety disorders effectively

Chapter contents

- Information about the treatment of panic, social phobia, OCD, health anxiety, GAD (this builds on the material in Chapter 3).
- Descriptions of treatment strategies
- Clinical examples and solving treatment problems

INTRODUCTION

In this chapter, the CBT treatment of a number of anxiety disorders, will be described, building on the information given in Chapter 3. Each disorder will be described and discussed using the following format:

- description of the disorder within a CBT model
- standard CBT treatment protocol used for each disorder
- troubleshooting the application of the standard CBT protocol for each disorder.

If the clinician is in the position of offering a CBT intervention to the patient, then it is hoped that he or she will have gone through the following stages (described earlier in the book) that are required before proceeding to use CBT interventions. These are:

1   a detailed assessment and formulation of the presenting problem(s) at a maintenance level

2   careful consideration that the problems described by the patient are potentially amenable to change using CBT interventions, and that this is an acceptable treatment to the patient and that he or she consents to it

3   ensuring the delivery of CBT interventions is within the range of competencies of the treating clinician and that he or she has access to regular (weekly to monthly dependent on experience) CBT-focused clinical supervision delivered by a colleague with recognized specialist training in CBT.

When the treatment of disorders is being discussed it will be borne in mind what the evidence base is for treating these disorders and the established protocols that exist. Emphasis will be put on working with a maintenance model of the disorder. However, the authors would encourage every clinician to use the formulation process to develop an understanding of the developmental factors relevant to the maintenance of the problem and the rules for living and core beliefs that are central to the disorder.

ANXIETY DISORDERS

Within the CBT model the basic formulation of anxiety disorders is based on Beck et al's. (1985a) work in which the anxious individual describes an 'increased perception of threat combined with a decreased perception of their ability to cope with this perceived threat'. In other words, something perceived as dangerous is about to happen and the patient believes they have neither the internal nor external resources to deal with this perceived danger. From this generic Beckian model a number of disorder-specific CBT models have been developed. The ones that will be described here are:

- panic disorder
- social phobia
- obsessive compulsive disorder
- health anxiety
- generalized anxiety disorder.

This chapter gives priority to describing the models that see cognitive factors as being the mechanism that maintains the patient's problems and it is, therefore, the *content* of thinking (*what we think*) and the *process* of thinking (*how we think*) which are the target for intervention. This is not to ignore the behavioural aspects of the problem, which would be addressed in the intervention. However, it is important to acknowledge that there is also an evidence base for behavioural interventions based on two main interventions: graded exposure in vivo which has been shown to be effective in the treatment of specific phobias and panic disorder with agoraphobia; and exposure and responses prevention that is effective in the treatment of obsessive compulsive disorder. These behavioural interventions will be described in Chapter 10.

Panic disorder

In the last 15 years the work of Clark and colleagues (Beck et al., 1992; Clark, 1986; Clark et al., 1994) has been the most influential and they have developed a cognitive model of the treatment of panic disorder. This has been elaborated in more recent years by researchers and clinicians such as Simos (2002) and Wells (1997). In the CBT model of panic disorder the central maintenance factor which gives rise to panic attacks is seen as *the catastrophic misinterpretation of bodily sensations*. As stated previously, research evidence demonstrates that individuals with panic disorder more readily detect slight changes in bodily sensations than normal controls and are more likely to interpret these as threatening (Mathews and MacLeod, 1985). Thus, a typical scenario in panic disorder is that the patient may be sitting watching television and suddenly notice their heart fluttering slightly. Most people may not notice such an event in their body (which is quite normal) but for the person pre-disposed to panic attacks this sensation is perceived as dangerous and evidence that some imminent disaster is about to occur. In this example the patient may have the NAT 'I'm having a heart attack'. Other typical NATs are:

'I'm having a stroke.'
'I'm going to faint/collapse.'
'I'm going to die.'
'I'm going crazy.'
'I'm going to lose control.'
'I'm going to be sick.'
'I'm going to wet myself.'

If anyone experiences this type of NAT and believes it to a high degree then they are going to become extremely anxious. This in turn generates further physical symptoms of anxiety (for example breathlessness, palpitations, dizziness, numbness and tingling) that are then taken as further evidence that something catastrophic is about to occur. Certain specific physical symptoms (bodily sensations) tend to generate specific NATs and making these connections with the patient is important in terms of the CBT interventions that are made. These are summarized in Table 8.1.

In order to manage their panic symptoms, the patient may engage in safety-seeking behaviours and specific behaviours are often developed in response to physical symptoms and specific NATs that the patient experiences. The examples of safety behaviours given here are not an exhaustive list. Some safety behaviours are highly idiosyncratic and these need to be comprehensively assessed with the patient in order to ensure the optimum treat-ment outcome. In the patient's mind it is the use of these safety behaviours that prevents the feared catastrophe encapsulated in the NAT from occurring and thus are repeated whenever necessary.

The person prone to experiencing panic attacks usually engages in hypervigilant body scanning behaviours. This involves regular mental scanning of the body to monitor signs of potential panic symptoms, which often in itself is sufficient to trigger a panic attack, hence patients with panic disorder often describe their panic attacks as occurring seem-ingly 'out of the blue'. Indeed, often one of the most distressing aspects of panic attacks for some patients is the fact they occur in situations such as watching TV or while asleep. The triggers to such panic attacks are inevitably detection of small changes in internal bodily sensations that are interpreted as dangerous thus precipitating a panic attack. If the patient is able to work out the typical triggering situations for his panic (e.g. crowds, queues, supermarkets) then he is likely to avoid these situations in the future. This is called agoraphobia and is problematic in that if the person avoids these triggers he fails to learn that his feared catastrophe does not occur, but if he cannot avoid he is immediately feeling anxious at the thought of facing it and therefore more likely to experience a panic attack. This is represented in Figure 8.1.

While situational avoidances are readily detected in panic disorder, it is also important to assess for more subtle avoidances of activities that can trigger panic symptoms. Examples include activities that involve physical exertion such as exercise and sex, avoidance of alco-hol, as the hangover effect the following day can act as a trigger, and caffeine consumption.

Table 8.1 Thoughts, physical symptoms and safety behaviours in panic disorder

NAT	Physical symptom	Typical safety behaviours
'I'm having a stroke'	Numbness and tingling in arms/ legs/head	Calling medical services
'I'm going to faint/collapse'	Light-headedness/dizziness/ blurred vision/nausea	Sitting/lying down/holding on to furniture/carrying water/breathing into paper bag/head between legs
'I'm having a heart attack'	Palpitations/missed heart beats/ numbness and tingling in right arm/sweating/hyperventilation	Checking pulse and BP/ringing medical services, taking beta-blockers/diazepam
'I'm going to die'	Full range of symptoms of autonomic arousal	Listening to iPod
'I'm going crazy'	Racing thoughts/restlessness/ numbness and tingling dizziness/ depersonalization/derealization	Listening to iPod/meditation/ relaxation methods, aromatherapy/ chewing gum
'I'm going to lose control'	Depersonalization/derealization/ hyperventilation	Going out only with trusted other/ listening to iPod/meditation/ chewing gum/relaxation methods/ aromatherapy
'I'm going to vomit'	Feeling sick/hot/sweating	Carrying vomit bags/taking anti-emetics
'I'm going to wet myself'	Urge to urinate	Wearing incontinence pads/always close to toilets/limiting fluid intake

There are various protocols for treating panic disorder: treatment always consists of behavioural experiments to test out the consequences of inducing panic symptoms and dropping safety behaviours to test out the validity of catastrophic misinterpretations of bodily sensations. In addition, avoidance of situations and activities would be addressed. The following protocol is based on Beck's focused cognitive therapy for panic disorder (Beck et al., 1992).

The patient is assessed and if inadequate information is obtained from the initial assessment then he is asked to keep a 'panic diary'. The clinician can construct a diary to record the relevant features of a panic attack. These diary columns should be constructed as follows:

- Date and time.
- Situation in which panic attack occurred
- Duration of the attack (in minutes)
- Severity of symptoms (scale of 0–10)
- Panic symptoms occurring (e.g. palpitations, dizziness, sweating)
- NATs (misinterpretation of symptoms e.g. 'I'm going to faint')
- Whether this was a full blown or limited attack and the patient's explanation as to why this was the case
- What the person did in response to the panic attack.

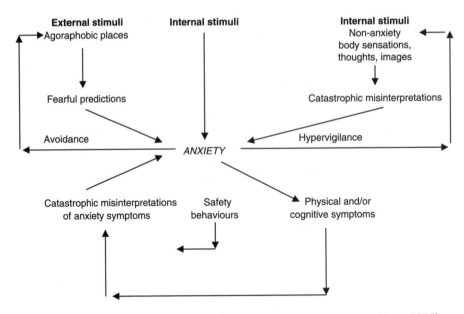

Figure 8.1   Cognitive model of panic disorder (reproduced with permission from Simos, 2002)

A treatment rationale based on a diagrammatic formulation (see Figure 8.1) of a recent panic attack the patient has experienced derived from the diary is shared with the patient. This is based on the metaphor of the problem being maintained by a vicious circle, as illustrated in the diagram, the treatment rationale being to use a series of behavioural experiments to test out the patient's catastrophic misinterpretation of bodily sensations (that is panic-related NATs) while dropping their safety behaviours. It is important that the patient understands and accepts the treatment rationale. The patient's initial response to this treatment rationale may be sceptical and therefore it is important to use Socratic questioning and guided discovery to set up small behavioural experiments to test out the hypothesis proposed in the treatment rationale.

The first method used in session to test out the treatment rationale is a panic induction exercise. This is a fundamental aspect of treatment and is described here.

Panic induction exercise

This is an intervention that is used with patients who have panic attacks. The purpose of the intervention is to deliberately induce bodily symptoms that closely resemble those that occur during a panic attack and work with the patient using Socratic questioning and guided discovery to test out the validity of the patient's catastrophic misinterpretation of bodily sensations (that is their panic-related NATs) by inducing bodily symptoms while dropping safety behaviours. (See Wells, 1997, Chapter 5, for a full discussion of this topic.) This technique has a strong evidence base (Clark et al., 1994). It is also one that the authors would routinely use, having direct experience of its clinical effectiveness.

There is little doubt, however, that the novice clinician new to CBT is often very reluctant to use it for the following reasons:

- She believes that when the patient panics then she, as a clinician, will not be able to control the situation. In reality, the panic will naturally come to an end, as all panics do. If the exercise is set up correctly (as the treatment protocol describes) then the clinician should be able to manage the situation.
- She may believe that it is 'cruel' to get the patient to panic. The patient will become distressed for a short period of time during this procedure; however, the clinician should remind herself that she is helping the patient using a highly effective therapeutic evidence-based intervention that could lead to significant reduction in the patient's distressing and disabling panic symptoms.
- She may believe that the patient will faint or suffer some more serious harm. When panic occurs then the patient's blood pressure will rise and this should preclude them from fainting. There are possible medical contraindications to this procedure, particularly high blood pressure, cardiac problems, asthma and pregnancy. If the patient has these conditions then advice should be sought from the patient's GP.

Clinicians who are unfamiliar with the practicalities of following this procedure should initially practise it on themselves and then practise it with a colleague in the context of clinical supervision from a CBT practioner with a recognized specialist training in CBT.

Clinical procedure

The procedure should be used with a patient who has a diagnosis of panic disorder and where a comprehensive CBT assessment has been completed and where a disorder-specific maintenance formulation of panic disorder has been collaboratively developed. We would suggest that panic induction could readily be used for all patients with a primary problem of panic disorder who do not have medical contraindications. Where the panic attacks are a feature of a more complex presentation such as in the context of anxiety in adulthood related to childhood sexual abuse or domestic violence then caution is needed and careful thought needs to go into when, if at all, this intervention is used in such presentations.

It is advisable to introduce this intervention at an early stage of therapy, in session two or four perhaps. The first issue is to introduce the concept of panic induction, which is usually described to the patient in more simple language such as symptom induction. The introduction of this topic should be linked in to the diagrammatic formulation with its emphasis on catastrophic misinterpretation of bodily sensations. As with all CBT interventions a rationale for using this procedure should be drawn from the patient utilizing Figure 8.1 and based on a recent, concrete and specific example located in time, place and person when the patient has experienced a panic attack which was especially distressing. The rationale would be as follows:

C   'Okay, we agree that the problem when you go to the supermarket is that you feel anxious and in particular you notice you feel hot, dizzy and your legs turn to jelly which you believe means you are going to faint. Indeed, in order to stop yourself fainting in this situation you used a number of safety behaviours which included cooling yourself down by hovering over the freezer section, holding tightly on to your trolley and sitting down.

P   'That's about it.'

C 'What do you think we could do to test out this idea that you believe you are going to faint?'

P 'I'm not sure.'

C 'What would happen if we tried to re-create some of the panic symptoms right now?'

P 'That sounds scary.'

C 'There are a number of things we could do here to bring on some of the symptoms you experience when you panic. The aim in doing this would be for us to work together on making sense of what is happening and trying to see if we could test out this idea you are going to faint by bringing on the symptoms and dropping your safety behaviours.'

P 'I'm not too sure.'

C 'What is your main concern?'

P 'That I will have a panic attack and faint.'

C 'Right, so that would be your prediction. I wonder if this behavioural experiment would let us test this out in a step-by-step way.'

P 'What do you mean?'

C 'Well, your prediction is that you will faint, how much do you believe that right now?'

P 'About 50 per cent.'

C 'Okay, one view here is you will faint [hypothesis A]. What do you think my view is?'

P 'Well, thinking about it I guess you are not really going to ask me to do something that would lead me to faint.'

C 'Okay, so what might my view be of what will happen?'

P 'That it's all in my head!'

C 'Well, that is not quite what I am saying but perhaps what is key to keeping the problem going is this catastrophic misinterpretation of these symptoms [hypothesis B] and if we can examine these further would this help us break the vicious circle and tackle the problem?'

P 'I see what you're saying.'

C 'How about if we have a go and see if we can understand the problem more and work out what our next step needs to be? If you want to stop at any time you can.'

P 'Okay.'

If the patient is unwilling to engage in this exercise then a variety of approaches can be taken. As in standard CBT practice then one can explore what the patient's anxieties are about doing it. The obvious one is that one is asking them to face their ultimate fear, and this is what they have been avoiding. One could try to help the patient challenge these fears but to an extent this may affect the purity of this experiment, as it would push the patient to think 'it'll be alright to do this because the clinician will not let me come to any harm'; this can be problematic because it may be difficult for the patient to induce panic because they are adhering too strongly to this idea. To some extent the clinician is reassuring the patient just by giving them a formulation. The clinician should not just accept the person's reluctance to engage in the intervention, as it is potentially depriving him of a beneficial aspect of treatment. It is possible for this experiment to be graded, in that mild symptoms could be induced initially and the person can learn to de-catastrophize those. However, it is likely that if the patient does not fully face the experience of his worst symptoms then the experiment may not be fully successful.

If the patient does agree to engage with the intervention then it is probably best to start it then and there; if the patient has too much time to contemplate it and get anxious then they may start avoiding coming to sessions. If one is ready to go ahead with the procedure then it is important to set it up as a behavioural experiment. The patient's prediction as to what will happen should be written down and their strength of belief in this prediction should be rated on a scale of 1–100%. An example would be: 'If I start to go dizzy and then have pain in the right side of my head I believe I will have a stroke' (belief 70 per cent).

It is then necessary to consider the best way of helping the patient induce the symptoms and this is aided by having a good list of symptoms from the initial assessment. The standard way of doing this is through a hyperventilation exercise. This is a powerful technique because of its ability to bring on a wide range of symptoms including dizziness, pins and needles, derealization, visual changes, feeling hot, speeded heart rate and paradoxical breathlessness (Wells, 1997).

The induction is usually repeated several times gradually increasing the length of time the hyperventilation is continued in order to increase the range and number of symptoms. Thus the first induction may be for 20 seconds gradually building up to a maximum of 2 minutes adding 30 seconds on each subsequent occasion. This would also be accompanied by the dropping of safety behaviours and deliberately engaging in behaviours that test out the catastrophic misinterpretation further (e.g. if the patient believes they will faint, deliberately standing on one leg while experiencing symptoms).

The first panic induction would instruct the patient, while sitting down, to begin breathing quickly and shallowly and that this will be maintained for 20 seconds (timed on a watch). It is standard practice for the clinician to simultaneously do this with the patient and for the clinician to start 20 seconds ahead of the patient. The rationale for the clinician starting first is to test the hypothesis that if fainting is going to be the outcome then the clinician will faint before the patient and therefore the patient can stop. This would be shared explicitly with the patient. Once the 20 seconds is completed the symptoms induced would be noted and the patient's response explored using Socratic questioning and guided discovery. Ideally the results would be drawn out on the diagram as described in Figure 8.1. It may be the case that after only 20 seconds of overbreathing very few symptoms are induced. Having elicited the patient's response to this it can then be repeated for a longer period. On each occasion conclusions would be drawn from the experiment. As successive repetitions occur it is usual to add extra manoeuvres in order to try and further disconfirm the patient's fears. These include:

- Inducing symptoms while standing up and dropping safety behaviours.
- Inducing symptoms then standing on one leg and hopping to test out predictions about falling while dropping safety behaviours.
- Staring at a spot on the wall or a bright light while inducing symptoms in order to test out predictions based on visual disturbances while dropping safety behaviours.
- Spinning round rapidly in order to induce dizziness while dropping safety behaviours.

During the hyperventilation exercise the clinician would ask the patient 'What do you need to do now to make yourself more anxious?' Or they could make a specific suggestion as the aim is to maximize symptoms in order to test out catastrophic misinterpretations. There are other methods that can be used to induce panic symptoms such as asking the patient to engage in physical exercise, which can induce palpations and chest pain. For further guidance in this area see Bennett-Levy et al. (2004) and Wells (1997).

It is also possible to ask the patient to deliberately bring to mind their panic-related NATs e.g. 'I will collapse, I'm losing control, and I'm going to die.' This would be helpful with patients who have difficulty inducing panic symptoms. It also helps to build the connection between thoughts, feelings and behaviour, which is the crux of the CBT treatment rationale.

Once the exercise is complete and the person is more composed then it is important to carry out a debriefing process. This would include asking in general how the person found the experience, but importantly the clinician should return to the hypothesis A versus hypothesis B metaphor to evaluate the outcome and collect the available evidence to support or refute each hypothesis. A further aspect of this process would be to re-rate how much they now believe (on a scale of 0–100) the catastrophic NAT that was tested in the intervention and the hope is that their strength of belief had reduced. The next step is to collaboratively devise behavioural experiments for homework to further test out the two hypotheses and modify the catastrophic NAT further. Again this could be graded, e.g. inducing mild symptoms while another person was in the house, inducing severe symptoms when another person was in the house, then out of the house, inducing mild symptoms in a situation where they had panicked before, then inducing severe symptoms in such a situation. This last type of experiment can be challenging, not only in that they may be difficult to do, but also in that it may be realistically embarrassing to make any attempt to induce symptoms in a crowded situations. The clinician may have to use his imagination to try to facilitate this situation. It may not be necessary to do this situational work if the degree of belief in the catastrophic misinterpretation reduces as a result of the in-session behavioural experiments.

What can go wrong with this intervention?

THE PATIENT IS UNABLE TO INDUCE SYMPTOMS

One explanation for this is that he is engaging in subtle safety behaviours that have not been picked up before; it is the job of the clinician to enquire into such behaviours and get the patient to eliminate them. Another explanation is that the environment of a clinic with a health professional at hand is too safe to induce panic symptoms. In this case the patient should induce panic symptoms with these factors being minimized, for example the clinician could go out of the room and not tell the patient when she is coming back. Another problem is that the person may be reassuring himself too successfully: 'He wouldn't ask me to do anything that was dangerous so nothing bad can possibly happen to me.' Here it may be helpful to get the patient to think the opposite of this, although plainly there is a tension between the formulation and rationale that states that the patient is catastrophizing and attempts to make the panic induction more successful by implying that they may be in danger.

If the patient does panic and yet his strength of belief in the feared outcome does not diminish, then this should be enquired into carefully. Again it is likely that the person has engaged in a mental or behavioural safety manoeuvre or avoidance.

Occasionally this procedure produces muscle spasm, in that the patient may have some initial difficulty in fully moving their arms or fingers. They should be informed that this sensation would pass.

The patient is then encouraged to tackle situational (agoraphobic) triggers. If the patient's NAT is 'I will have a panic attack here and collapse/die' it may be more appropriate for the person to do a panic induction exercise in that situation, to test out the validity of the prediction. The patient needs to tackle these situational triggers consistently and the authors recommend patients engage in such behavioural experiments to test their catastrophic NATs at least four times per week.

There would be a confidence that the patient could be discharged into follow-up if the patient's strength of belief that the symptoms were dangerous was very low, that they were not significantly avoiding, and that the naturally occurring panic was declining.

TROUBLESHOOTING

The evidence would support a view that if the CBT approach to panic is followed then it is fairly successful. However the typical problems that occur in the treatment of panic are as follows:

- Failure to do panic induction exercises because of anxieties in the patient or clinician. This has been dealt with earlier, but the clinician's NATs about 'causing harm', 'losing control of the situation' or 'being cruel' may need to be addressed.
- Failure to recognize or deal with comorbid disorders or ongoing stress in the person's life may make the panic problem harder to treat.

Social phobia

As described in Chapter 3, the key characteristic of social phobia is the fear of negative evaluation by others in a social situation (Wells, 1997). In the triggering situations patients' rules for living and core beliefs about performance, self and the implications of showing anxiety symptoms are activated: this leads to NATs such as 'my hands will shake' (and I'll appear weak) or 'my mind will go blank' (and I'll appear foolish) and the person feels anxious. A further aspect of the CBT social phobia model is what Wells (1997) refers to as 'self as a social object'. That is the socially anxious person self-consciously visualizes in his mind's eye himself performing badly and then engages in a variety of behaviours to try and minimise this. These vary according to the individual's specific fears but can in some instances become a self-fulfilling prophecy. These may include avoiding or leaving the situation, avoiding eye contact so as not to draw attention to themselves, gripping objects to prevent hands shaking, avoiding speaking or altering speech patterns to reduce the likelihood of speaking problems and so on.

These safety behaviours are unhelpful because they lead to a heightened self-focus, prevent the worst fears being disconfirmed, can make the symptoms worse, draw attention to the person and finally damage the actual social situation by making the person appear unfriendly and awkward.

Patient example

Paul is a 24-year-old man who was referred from the physicians because investigations of his twitching and shaking had been negative.

On assessment it was clear that he did suffer from social phobia and the shakiness symptoms only occurred in social situations. It was noted on assessment that he had a number of unhelpful rules for living. These were 'people must always think highly of me', 'I must not make a wrong decision' and 'if I look anxious or twitchy then people will think I'm weird'. In social situations such as interviews or meetings with friends, these rules for living would be activated, anxiety would occur which worsened his shakiness and he would engage in a variety of safety behaviours. These included making an excuse and leaving situations early; not saying very much; over-rehearsing comments to get them right; not saying anything too controversial and not initiating conversation.

He also shifted his mental attention to his physical symptoms of trembling, which impaired his ability to interact with others and made him more anxious. He had a powerful mental image of himself shaking uncontrollably and everyone staring and considering him to be weird. He therefore minimized the social situations he went into and, at the time of assessment, had not been in one for six weeks. If he had to go into situations he would ruminate before and after them, thus heightening his anxiety.

Treatment

As always in describing treatment there is an assumption that the clinician has developed and shared a formulation with the patient that has identified developmental and maintenance factors contributing to the problem. The patient should have a clear understanding of this formulation. Paul's goals for 6 months' time were: to be in education full time and to attend as the course required; to have one close female friend and see her once per week; to be in the pub with his friends two or three times a week and not attend to his tremor.

If the patient is avoiding, then behavioural experiments need to be arranged to encourage the individual to test out their negative predictions, which are driving the avoidance. Complete avoidance of social situations is unusual, and safety behaviours are the main target for treatment. With Paul a formulation was developed with which he was reasonably happy, based on the rules for living described earlier and the situational NATs, feelings, physical sensations and behaviours that he reported. Treatment then consisted of engaging in a number of behavioural experiments aimed at entering specific social situations in order to test out his negative predictions relevant to that situation. He agreed at the beginning to find out what educational resources were available in his area, by making various phone calls. He also agreed to go and see the tutor of the course he was interested in doing and ask him various questions. He also agreed to go out with two close friends to the pub in the evening. Over a number of sessions specific behavioural experiments using the hypothesis A versus hypothesis B format were constructed and carried out in these situations. This involved Paul identifying the two hypotheses to be tested if he dropped a specific safety behaviour, carrying out the experiment and then reviewing the outcome in relation to the two hypotheses. For example, one behavioural experiment was to switch his attention between his internal focus on his anxiety symptoms and outward focus on to the actual conversation that was going on around him and compare how these two forms of attentional focus affected his social performance. Paul was able to recognize that the internal focus served to heightened his anxiety and increase his safety behaviours while the external focus enabled him to participate in social interaction. A further experiment was to maintain eye contact in social situations and he would focus on asking and replying to questions.

Paul's treatment went fairly well. The main problem was an initial anxiety to engage in behavioural experiments per se. This was usually expressed to the clinician as what we eventually termed 'excuses' such as, 'I did not see the relevance of doing it' and 'I was too busy'. It was fairly easy to help him see that this was a type of subtle avoidance. The clinician moved the situation forward by carrying out some behavioural experiments with Paul in social situations. This involved the clinician going with Paul on a number of occasions and enabling him to engage in carrying out the agreed behavioural experiments. The advantages to carrying out a limited number of behavioral experiments with the patient are that it can provide the clinician with extra clinical information and it allows more direct engagement of the patient in testing out the predictions that need to be tested. It also enables the clinician to identify subtle avoidances the patient may not be aware of but which may be impeding progress. However, the clinician must guard against becoming a reassurance to the patient in that the clinician's presence leads the patient to conclude progress is due to the clinician's presence in the social situation.

In Paul's case, he walked round the hospital (where the CBT sessions took place) with the clinician and he went into various shops and departments and he initiated conversations. He also set up a teaching session and on several occasions he did a 10-minute talk to colleagues on his favourite topic of ice hockey. All these aimed to test out his predictions as expressed in his NATs and rules for living. By the end of treatment he was moving toward his goals, he had enrolled in a college course and was socializing with his friends three or four times per week.

Troubleshooting

Many of the problems here are common to other anxiety disorders and particularly include avoidance of carrying out behavioural experiments and subtle safety and reassurance seeking behaviours.

Distinctive problems in social phobia are:

1   The patient views the treatment session as another threatening social encounter where he has scope for making a fool of himself. The clinician needs to be alert to this and the NATs that are present in the session and sensitively turn these into an opportunity to make therapeutic gains, by helping the patient to test out these thoughts via an in-session behavioural experiment in order to begin to develop an alternative perspective.

2   The patient has been socially avoidant for so long that he has lost his social networks and there are no natural situations that the patient can face. One then has to be imaginative in thinking of alternatives. These could be hobby clubs, social clubs, self-help groups, people in shops, bus stops, queues, relatives and so on. As the patient may find these exercises less personally meaningful, he may be less motivated to engage in them. It is also important to consider the role avoidant personality traits may play if the patient has a longstanding absence of a social network. This is a common comorbid problem in social phobia and will add a degree of difficulty in using CBT interventions due to the lack of social arena and the patient's reluctance to engage with one.

Obsessive compulsive disorder

As described before, OCD is characterized by upsetting intrusive thoughts that the individual finds subjectively distressing in some way, giving rise to NATs about the meaning of these intrusive thoughts. This, in turn, gives rise to anxiety and leads to compulsive behaviours (washing and checking rituals, reassurance seeking behaviour and avoidance) in order to neutralize the intrusive thought and to reduce anxiety.

Salkovskis (1985) developed the influential model that we describe here and in an earlier part of the book. Research evidence (Rachman and de Silva, 1978; Salkovskis and Harrison, 1984) suggests that unpleasant intrusive thoughts are a normal human experience and the intrusions that occur in the general population do not differ from those reported by individuals who suffer with OCD. This leads to the suggestion that the important psychological factor that leads some people to go on to develop OCD is the meaning people attach to these intrusions with individuals who experience OCD believing that the intrusions are in some way personally relevant and threatening. It is this appraisal or meaning attached to these intrusions in the form of NATs that generates anxiety leading to washing and checking rituals and reassurance-seeking behaviour.

Salkovskis suggested that in OCD responsibility for harm to self or others is a key theme in rules for living. Thus a person with OCD experiences an intrusion of his partner's car crashing and feels anxious and guilty. He is then compelled to think a 'good' thought in order to neutralize the intrusion. This may involve deliberately invoking an image of his partner driving safely along the road, happy and content. The meaning he attaches to the intrusion may include NATs such as 'that is a bad thing to think' and 'I must want it to happen' and the related rule for living might be 'if something bad happens it is my fault'. Other theorists have suggested other appraisals that may maintain the OCD problem: overimportance of thoughts (related rule for living may be 'if I think a thought it must mean I want to carry it out'); excessive concern about controlling one's thoughts (possible related rule for living 'if I am not in control of my thoughts then I may do something dangerous'); overestimation of threat (possible rule for living related to this theme could be 'if there is any chance of risk it must be avoided'); intolerance of uncertainty (possible rule for living 'unless I have certainty I cannot act'); perfectionism (possible rule for living 'I must strive for perfection in everything otherwise I will be discontent'). A summary of the model is provided in Figure 8.2.

From the original assessment, one should have identified the environmental triggers, the obsessional intrusions and their appraisals (in the form of NATs), themes in the person's rules for living and core beliefs, emotional response (anxiety, guilt, low mood), and behavioural response (washing and checking rituals, cognitive neutralizing strategies, reassurance seeking and avoidance). Treatment will therefore consist of a variety of cognitive and behavioural interventions to modify the appraisals (NATs) that have been identified and eliminate washing and checking rituals and reassurance-seeking and avoidance behaviours. The following is an outline of the basic CBT treatment principles for tackling these types of appraisal. It is important to note these are used in conjunction with a CBT treatment rationale and a collaboratively developed CBT formulation of the patient's problems.

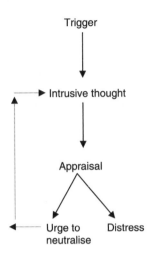

Trigger

Biased appraisals
Overimportance of thoughts
Overestimations of danger
Overestimations of the consequences of danger

Intrusive thought

Inflated responsibility
Overestimations of the consequences of responsibility
Need for certainty and control over thoughts

OCD maintained by failure to evaluate and consider
alternative appraisals and and beliefs in the light of
contrary experience

Appraisal

Urge to   Distress
neutralise

Figure 8.2   A cognitive behavioural model of OCD (reprinted with permission from Simos, 2002)

Responsibility appraisals

The standard technique here is to use a pie chart. So, say for example the patient had inflated concerns about dirt and contamination and following a meal she cooked one of the guests became ill, she thus believed the illness was her fault (100 per cent). The patient and clinician would draw out a pie chart and list all the factors contributing to the guest becoming ill, the patient placing herself at the bottom of the list. The patient is then asked to assign percentages of responsibility (out of 100) to each item on the list. The aim is to try and introduce flexibility into the patient's perceptions by taking into consideration other factors that may influence the situation rather than operating on the assumption sole responsibility lies with her. This also begins the process of modifying what may be the related rule for living 'if something goes wrong it is my fault':

1   *Overimportance of thoughts.* Patients may hold a rule for living such as 'if I think a thought it is significant and I must attend to its meaning because it is important', 'if I think a thought this increases the probability of my acting on the thought' or 'if I think something bad this is the same as doing something bad'. This may lead the patient to invest a great deal of mental attention in monitoring their thought processes, to be on the look out for unwanted, upsetting or potentially dangerous thoughts. Ways to work with these types of thought revolve around behavioural experiments aimed at deliberately and repeatedly thinking a specific thought and recording whether this leads to an increase in the occurrence of these thoughts. For example, the patient could be asked to deliberately and repeatedly think the thought 'I will cause an accident when I drive the car next', and record whether this occurs. A further method here is to carry out a survey where the patient and the clinician each ask five people to monitor the occurrence of intrusive thoughts over a period of a week and then examine the results, drawing together the patient's viewpoint regarding the results of the survey. A further experiment is to ask the patient to record every time they experienced an intrusive

thought and monitor how often the feared consequence in the intrusion actually occurred.

2   *Need to control thoughts.* Patients who adhere to rules around a need to control thoughts may put excessive efforts into controlling intrusive thoughts by pushing them out of their mind. This is called *thought suppression.* Research shows this is counterproductive and leads to a rebound effect in which the thought that is being suppressed re-intrudes into the mind with greater intensity thus setting up a vicious cycle of suppression, re-intrusion and increased distress (Purdon, 1999). In order to tackle this, the patient is asked to engage in a behavioural experiment in which he is asked to compare two strategies for dealing with intrusive thoughts. The first strategy is to suppress the intrusions and write down the effects in terms of frequency, severity and duration of intrusive thoughts. The second strategy is to just allow the thoughts to come into mind and write down the effects in terms of the frequency, intensity and severity of intrusive thoughts. The next step is to compare the two sets of results, the outcome being the more intrusive thoughts are suppressed the more frequently they occur with a greater degree of intensity and severity, while when intrusive thoughts are allowed to come into mind they eventually fade leading to a significant decrease in the frequency, intensity and severity of intrusive thoughts. This can also be used to challenge over-control of thoughts as described above and reduce thought suppression, which is a key maintenance factor in OCD.

3   *Overestimation of threat.* Some feared consequences of OCD are easier to disconfirm by the setting up of behavioural experiments than others. It may be possible to face fears and reduce safety behaviours if the person believes he will be immediately contaminated if he touches a door handle, or become ill if he eats chicken from a takeaway and plainly this will be a key element of treatment. The clinician should construct behavioural experiments that help the patient repeatedly face his fears in order to reduce his estimation of threat. For example, to touch a door knob, with both hands, rub his hands all over his hair and clothes and then resist washing his hands for the rest of the day while continuing with usual activities. This behavioural experiment would be repeated frequently (i.e. daily) until concerns regarding con-tamination had reduced significantly. However, some threats are in the distant future: 'I will get cancer from radioactivity poisoning' is not so amenable to this disconfirma-tory approach. This specific approach is most similar to the principle of exposure and response prevention (see Chapter 10 for a description of this intervention) in the behavioural tradition. It is important to ensure that the patient eliminates all washing and checking rituals (including cognitive rituals) and avoidance behaviour over the course of therapy.

4   *Intolerance of uncertainty.* If the patient has a rule that 'I must be 100 per cent certain about everything' or something similar then it may be helpful to challenge it. Plainly this rule is likely to lead to checking and reassurance seeking in a variety of domains in the patient's life not just related to his OCD. The patient can experiment in making changes to this behaviour. As already stated, this type of rule is also often an indication of the presence of comorbid generalized anxiety disorder that adds a level of complexity to the treatment.

5   *Perfectionism.* This is best understood as avoidance of criticism and failure. If the patient describes such themes as part of their rules for living or core beliefs then these can be a targeted as part of treatment. However, perfectionism can be formulated as a

personality factor in which case the intervention may be more complex to implement with less clear-cut outcomes.

What is described here is a basic cognitive behavioural model for working with OCD with more emphasis on tackling cognitive aspects of the presentation. The more traditional behavioural treatment for OCD, namely exposure and response prevention, is a more straightforward intervention to master for clinicians new to CBT and when it works it is very effective. However, in more complex presentations of OCD attention to cognitive maintenance factors is crucial. The cognitive behavioural model described here emerged directly from the research and clinical evidence that a proportion of patients presenting with OCD did not respond well to pure behavioural treatments. Research is ongoing to the further development of CBT treatments for OCD and one fruitful area currently under investigation is whether certain types of appraisals are more fundamental to the maintenance of the disorder (Whittal and O'Neill, 2002).

Treatment progress will be measured by a reduction in the frequency, intensity and severity of intrusive thoughts, change in the meanings attached to these intrusions, feelings of anxiety, guilt and low mood, and elimination of washing and checking rituals, covert mental rituals and reassurance-seeking behaviour.

Troubleshooting

The main problem in using CBT to treat OCD is the construction of behavioural experiments. These could focus on testing out predictions in relation to tackling avoidances, disengaging from rituals, not controlling thoughts, not attending to thoughts, anti-perfectionism and uncertainty tolerance. The research evidence from the behavioural literature (Marks, 1987) would suggest that behavioural change involving behavioural experiments aimed at facing feared avoidances and not engaging in cognitive or behavioural rituals is essential. A particular problem, as mentioned earlier, is that some behavioural experiments do not allow for the possibility of 'disconfirmation': for example the patient who says 'if I am exposed to hospitals I will get cancer when I'm older, because of the radiation there'. Obviously, the patient can expose himself or herself to this risk but he will not necessarily learn that he is unlikely to get cancer because the feared event is in the future. This would indicate standard cognitive interventions would need to be used to elicit his NATs regarding his overestimation of risk in relation to hospitals, radiation and cancer in the future. It would still be correct to help him address his avoidance of hospitals by engaging in behavioural experiments to go into hospitals.

Health anxiety (hypochondriasis)

Health anxiety can easily be conceptualized and treated as an anxiety disorder. Patients misinterpret bodily sensations as evidence that they have a severe, often fatal, physical disorder. This causes understandable anxiety and the physical component of anxiety (e.g. shortness of breath) is interpreted as further evidence of serious illness. The condition differs from panic in that, in panic, patients believe that a catastrophe is going to occur immediately, whereas in health anxiety the catastrophe is located somewhere in the future.

Again, Wells (1997) has developed a sophisticated formulation of this condition, based on the earlier work of Warwick and Salkovskis (1989). Early experiences in the patient's life that may predispose him or her to be anxious about their health include difficult experiences of illness in childhood (either to a loved one or self), mistakes by doctors, near misses of serious illnesses, seeing a relative suffer and/or die from an illness and a parent or relative who is overprotective or anxious about health and models this to the child. These experiences may lead to rules for living such as 'if you get cancer/heart disease you will always suffer and die', 'if you get cancer/heart disease you always die a slow and painful death', 'if you get a terminal illness it is a form of punishment', 'doctors get it wrong all the time'. It is important to note that there may be some truth in these statements, however they are usually held with a high degree of conviction and inflexibility. In addition, the themes of control and a need for certainty are often present here.

Critical incidents that may occur to trigger health anxiety could be actual illness, disturbing health information in the media and medical errors. However, it is not uncommon that concerns about health have always been present for the patient. The maintenance factors that then occur are NATs about normal bodily sensations such as 'I haven't had that pain in the side before – it could be cancer', 'I'm a bit breathless, perhaps that's the first sign of heart trouble'. Plainly these NATs are associated with anxiety (occasionally depression and anger), and then the physical symptoms of anxiety will occur, leading to further NATs and more bodily sensations to misinterpret in a typical vicious circle maintenance formulation. Information processing biases are also important including selectively attending to bodily sensations, and thinking processes/errors, like catastrophizing. Often patients will move between avoiding medical resources for fear of finding out the worst and constantly utilizing them to be reassured that they are well. The next maintenance factor is behavioural change, namely reassurance seeking from medical sources (e.g. GP) or friends with some medical knowledge, avoidance of 'triggers', for example medical resources, TV programmes, hospitals, possibly the patient's GP, ill people and so on. The person may also engage in physically poking and prodding his body, in an attempt to reassure himself that bodily parts feel the same as before in terms of size and shape and there is no abnormality present. This is problematic; as the person does not really know what he is looking for, the poking and prodding can cause redness and soreness and the mental effort required to do it keeps him focused on his fear.

The patient with health anxiety may be difficult to engage. They often present as accepting that they worry excessively about their health, but at another level often believe there may be something wrong with them that 'has been missed'. He may wish in the interview to speak at excessive length about his symptoms and may seek reassurance from clinicians. Sometimes he is awaiting the results of further tests and it may be worth waiting to get all the results back before commencing CBT. However, because of the patient's tendency to always 'demand' further investigations, it may be worth beginning to work with their health anxiety and addressing the issue of investigations as a problem to be worked on.

If the patient is reluctant to engage in CBT, certain strategies can be used to assist this (Wells, 1997). The treatment can be presented as a 'no-lose' strategy. It is presented that CBT may be helpful, but if he does not find it so then he is at liberty to return to the 'medical' strategy he was following before. Explain to the patient that a psychological approach does not suggest that he is imagining the symptoms but that what the patient and clinician are trying to do is examine together all the possible explanations for the symptoms described, one of which may be physical illness (based once more on the principle of hypotheses testing). Try to engage the patient in behavioural experiments at an early stage that help him see the potential benefits of a CBT intervention.

Patient example

Hazel was a 26-year-old woman, referred from a medical clinic. She described herself as suffering from severe anxiety particularly around illness. She responds to pain in her abdomen by thinking that she has got ovarian or bowel cancer. She also has frequent headaches and convinces herself that she has a brain tumour. She is sure that she will die from these and she becomes very anxious in response to symptoms. Her behavioural response is to seek reassurance from her GP and particularly her husband; to read health books and browse the internet for reassurance; to monitor her symptoms by checking her colour in the mirror; by taking her own pulse; and by poking and prodding and feeling any part of her body that is painful. She has physical symptoms of anxiety such as nausea, poor appetite, racing heart and dizziness. She has spent quite a lot of money on private healthcare and has successfully asked for and been given two scans without obvious clinical need. Assessment revealed that she had a number of rules for living such as 'if I am to cope I need people around me', 'if you take risks catastrophe occurs' and 'I must stay in control at all times otherwise I will be overwhelmed'. She had an experience of minor misdiagnosis and this had led to the belief 'doctors always get it wrong'.

Further back she had suffered the experience of nursing her mother through a painful death from cancer and this had left a mark. More recently she had suffered some minor ill health with stomach ulcers.

Treatment

The stages of treatment are the same as other disorders. Agreement on a formulation must be an early task, although, as stated earlier, this could be acceptance of the formulation as one possible explanation of the problems alongside the explanation that the patient does indeed have a serious illness. Questionnaires will be administered and a problem and goal statement will be developed.

In terms of sequencing treatments, the first step is to engage in behavioural experiments to test out the validity of reassurance-seeking and specific safety behaviours. The clinician should discuss with the patient a strategy to eliminate verbal reassurance seeking:

C   'You often go to your husband for reassurance because he's an ambulance man?'
P   'Yes, and he always gives me some. Bless him!'
C   'He's a great man, but going back to the formulation, why did we agree it was not helpful seeking reassurance?'
P   'I suppose I need to deal with my worries myself.'
C   'It's also very tempting to keep seeking reassurance because of the relief you get.'
P   'Yeah.'

C   'But it doesn't really reassure you does it?'

P   'What do you mean?'

C   'Well, I am quite prepared to give you as much reassurance as you need in order to overcome your problems. So, we have 40 minutes of our session left. How much reassurance would I need to give you to help you get thought the week?

P   'Well, it doesn't work like that. Any reassurance only lasts till the next twinge.'

C   'Okay, so we are in agreement that it works as a short-term strategy until as you say the next twinge. But if you were having twinges every hour you would need the reassurance every hour?'

P   'Mm . . . yes.'

C   'So no matter how much reassurance I gave you it would not help in the medium and long term?'

P   'No, not really.'

C   'So can we agree we need to understand two things: what the reassurance gives you in the short term and what your predictions are about what will happen to you if you do not get the reassurance you think you need at times when you are worried about your health?'

P   'Yes, I guess so. But how can we do that?'

C   'Well, let's spend some time thinking about that in more detail; behavioural experiments are often very useful; let me explain the purpose of these in terms of our treatment rationale.'

The clinician would engage in this Socratic dialogue and use behavioural experiments to test out the hypothesis that in the long-term reassurance seeking keeps the patient's attention focused on the issue of illness. It also is a transfer of responsibility on to the person that is reassuring. For a detailed description of using behavioural experiments to tackle reassurance seeking, see Garland (1996). The next behavioural strategy is normally the reduction of specific safety behaviours e.g. poking and prodding, constantly seeking information about the feared symptoms on the internet, checking one's appearance in the mirror and so on. These should be set up as behavioural experiments, with the question: 'What are your predictions about what will happen if you stop doing that?'

It is suggested that the next line of treatment is the modifying of negative automatic thoughts (NATs). These thoughts will typically be 'I've got cancer' 'I'm definitely going to get this illness' and 'I'm definitely going to die from it'. The CBT intervention here would be to use Socratic questioning to explore with the patient the meaning they attach to the symptoms they are experiencing and make a written summary of the outcome of the discussion. For example:

•   Have you had this symptom before and if so how did you make sense of it?
•   If you went to your GP how would she account for this symptom?
•   If a friend reported a similar concern, how would you talk it through with him?
•   What other explanations are there for the symptom?
•   How can we test out the validity of each explanation? (behavioural experiments)

As with other anxiety disorders, it is important to try and increase the patient's tolerance of discomfort by trying to modify the 'awfulness' of how they are feeling and to try and modify the patient's overestimation of the risk of getting it.

At times it may be worth working with the patient's ideas that they would never cope with a terminal illness by asking whether they have ever coped with difficult situations before, what support they would have with the illness, how they would support someone else in managing a terminal illness. It may be important to modify, as much as possible, the fear of dying and the idea that death from terminal illness invariably means acute suffering and pain. A fear of death may contain distortions (often based on experiences of witnessing others' terminal illness and informed by religious and spiritual beliefs) that can be modified using CBT interventions. These include the distortion that the person will be aware of his own physical suffering after death or that it will be impossible to control their pain when dying or the person's family will suffer and be completely unable to cope with the consequences of their death.

The clinician and patient can build on the process of modifying NATs as described earlier by the use of further behavioural experiments. For example, if a patient is very frightened of particular symptoms then one could induce those symptoms as one would in panic disorder. For example the patient who thought that dizziness meant he was very likely to have a stroke could make himself or herself progressively dizzier. If the patient is collecting information about how to manage particular symptoms, then they could be asked to seek out evidence (once only) from credible medical sources, for example about self-examination for disease and be asked to consider following these.

It is possible for the health anxious individual to actually become ill and often patients are concerned that CBT is encouraging them to let their guard down. One should explain that the treatment is about helping them to be appropriately concerned about symptoms and not be over- or under-preoccupied with them. This often leads to a discussion about the circumstances in which a person should go to the doctor. Again the patient can find out what other people do, or can if possible look at what the 'official' advice is. A constructive rule could be 'I will attend my doctor if I have significant or persistent symptoms' and obviously some leeway must be left for individual judgement.

The next, and perhaps more complex step of the CBT intervention is to get the patient to experiment with switching their attention between focussing on and off their symptoms. For example, for one day the person intentionally focuses on the symptoms and the next day he focuses away from them and their frequency and severity is noted for each part of the experiment. The intended outcome being that the more the individual focuses on his symptoms the more frequently they are noticed and more severe they are. Indeed many patients are able to recognize that if they focus on a symptom long enough it will occur. This is often very powerful in shifting the patient's belief away from the idea that the symptoms they worry about are a sign of physical illness toward the idea they are related to anxiety generated by a preoccupation with their health.

The next step of the CBT intervention would be to consider working with rules for living and core beliefs such as 'doctors get it wrong all of the time', 'I must be 100 per cent certain that I will not get a serious illness' and 'if you have a pain in your body it must mean something serious is wrong'.

At this point the patient's anxiety around his symptoms should reduce to a manageable level and he should be doing more and coping better. When the clinician is confident that this is happening and that the patient is able to continue to utilize the treatment by himself or herself, it is time to consider discharge into follow-up. The relapse prevention process should be followed and questionnaires administered to objectively measure improvement in the presenting problem.

Troubleshooting

The typical problems that occur in the treatment of health anxiety are:

1   The patient accepts that he worries excessively about his health and addresses this, but still has a 'what if . . .' attitude to his symptoms. This problem may reflect demands for certainty that are impossible to achieve and may be an indication of a comorbid GAD, which makes treatment more complex, lengthier and less clear cut in terms of outcome.
2   The patient may actually have a diagnosed physical illness that causes symptoms alongside a more general worry about his health. What it is worth trying to do (perhaps with the help of the patient's GP) is to try to distinguish between symptoms of the diagnosed illness and anxiety symptoms related to his health anxiety.

Generalized anxiety disorder

As described in Chapter 3, the CBT model of GAD is based on three themes within rules for living and core beliefs: uncertainty, unpredictability and uncontrollability (Barlow, 2004). The CBT model also pays attention to the content (NATs) and process of thinking (intrusions, threat cue detection and thought suppression). However the defining cognitive feature of a CBT formulation of GAD is worry (Borkovec and Inz, 1990, Wells, 1997). Wells has developed a specific CBT model for formulating worry based on positive and negative beliefs about worry formulated as rules for living, for example 'if I worry I am prepared when something goes wrong' (a positive belief about worry) and 'if I don't control my worry I will lose my mind' (negative belief about worry). Key maintenance factors in GAD are information processing biases (*how we think*) including thought monitoring, thought suppression and threat cue monitoring and behaviours including safety behaviours, reassurance seeking and avoidance. Treatment will therefore focus on formulating these processes in the maintenance of the disorder and behavioural experiments to test their validity and to tackle avoidance, reassurance seeking and safety behaviours (for a detailed account see Garland, 1996). Rules for living related to perceived lack of control and a striving for certainty are also modified using relevant behavioural experiments.

Other CBT interventions have been developed by Newman and Borkovec (2002):

*   early detection of internal and external cues for worry and anxiety (so the person can act quickly)
*   stimulus control methods such as scheduling a 30-minute 'worry time' and being given instructions not to worry at other times. The rationale is that because GAD patients worry in multiple situations there are a lot of potential triggers, so having a specific time and place is an attempt to make these situations less triggering. If the patient wants to worry at other times he must tell himself that he has a worry time set aside and can think the issue through then if this is difficult he should absorb himself in another activity. Often patients find it difficult to postpone their worry
*   relaxation methods: the rationale for this is to reduce physiological arousal. Methods that can be used are 'slowed, paced, diaphragmatic breathing' or progressive muscle relaxation in which patients progressively tense and relax muscle groups.

There is some debate in the literature and among CBT practioners about the efficacy of the strategies advocated by Newman and Borkovec (2002). For some patients interventions such as relaxation are used as safety behaviours and become counterproductive. Meanwhile the idea of paying attention to internal and external cues to worry in order to take action quickly may inadvertently feed rules for living and core beliefs that worry is dangerous and needs to be controlled. The authors would express a preference for using a formulation-driven intervention based on the Wells (1997) model.

Patient example

Alice is a 46-year-old woman who has a lifelong tendency to worry. Her mother suffered from panic attacks and her father was prone to depression. Her main problems were significant episodes of worry, the worst being around her own potential ill health and death, and the second being anything happening to her husband. We identified a core belief namely 'I am vulnerable' and 'disaster is just around the corner' and related rules for living 'I must do everything I can to prevent harm to others and myself' and 'people can't be trusted with their own safety'. These lead to behavioural patterns of risk avoidance, seeking excessive reassurance, warning others about perceived risks and taking responsibility for others' well-being. Treatment consisted of developing a detailed written formulation of the development and maintenance of her GAD, setting goals around tolerating normal risk, not worrying excessively about health, and pursuing avoided activities. Treatment had a cognitive and behavioural focus with the goal of using behavioural experiments to test out NATs, rules for living and core beliefs. These included testing out her predictions regarding resisting not monitoring and checking the body for symptoms, not seeking reassurance from the GP over minor symptoms and not over-questioning her husband about his activities as a form of reassurance seeking (to ensure he was not engaging in anything potentially dangerous). She also used behavioural experiments to engage in new activities that she perceived to be potentially dangerous and therefore avoided. This included hill walking, attending a reading group and cycling. She eventually returned to work part time as it was realized that having a lot of time on her hands allowed her more opportunity to worry. At the end of treatment there was a 50 per cent improvement in questionnaire scores.

Troubleshooting

More often than not patients who present with GAD recognize they have been worriers all their lives. In this respect, the disorder is often difficult to treat as many of the factors implicated in the maintenance of the disorder are well established by the time treatment is sought. In addition, avoidant coping is always present in a GAD presentation and this impacts significantly on meaningful engagement in treatment. As a result of this avoidance patients with GAD engage in a great deal of reassurance seeking and use of subtle safety behaviours and often the very CBT interventions aimed at helping the patient tackle their problems become safety behaviours or forms of reassurance and are rendered ineffective. Therefore, using CBT as an intervention in GAD requires high-level skills in making a CBT formulation of the problem and much persistence and effort is required by both patient and clinician to bring about small changes. Treatment contracts generally extend beyond 20 sessions and often CBT is used with a rationale of managing the problem more effectively rather than treating it per se. CBT interventions often require multiple strands, including behavioural experiments to face avoidances, modifying NATs, rules for living and core beliefs, including beliefs about worry. In addition behavioural experiments that tackle the information processing biases in GAD (e.g. threat cue monitoring, thought monitoring and thought suppression) are usually key. These require a significant level of CBT training in order to carry them out effectively and the novice is advised to consider his CBT training needs in this area and discuss the use of such interventions in CBT clinical supervision before attempting to utilize the interventions that are only briefly described here.

Further reading |

It has been referred to several times in the chapter, but Wells' (1997) book *Cognitive Therapy of Anxiety Disorders* is a classic in that it is scholarly, detailed and feels accurate in its treatment recommendations. It does demand some knowledge of cognitive behavioural theory and cognitive science. Some of the books in the Robinson 'Overcoming' series are very useful for clinicians because of their clarity of style. An example would be *Overcoming Panic* by Silove and Monicavasagar (2001) and *Overcoming OCD* by Veale and Wilson (2005). A scholarly review of the subject would be *Anxiety and its Disorders: The Nature and Treatment of Anxiety and Panic* by Barlow (2004). With regard to behavioural experiments, the *Oxford Guide to Behavioural Experiments* (Bennett-Levy et al., 2004) is a key text for the treatment of anxiety disorders.

Chapter summary |

Anxiety disorders are characterized by an increased sense of threat and a diminished sense of one's ability to cope and involve catastrophic thinking and various types of avoidance, safety and reassurance-seeking behaviour. In panic disorder, there is a catastrophic misinterpretation of normal bodily sensations; in social phobia, there is a fear of negative evaluation by others in a social situation; in OCD, there is an inflated sense of responsibility for harm to self and/or others and anxiety about the meaning of normal intrusive thoughts; in health anxiety (like panic), there is a misinterpretation of bodily sensations, but here the sensations are thought to mean that the person has a severe or fatal disorder; in generalized anxiety disorder, there is a great deal of worrying, thought to be influenced by unhelpful rules for living and metacognitive beliefs. Strategies are described to help treat these disorders.

Treating acute depression effectively

THE COGNITIVE BEHAVIOURAL MODEL OF DEPRESSION

The cognitive behavioural model of depression was first described by Beck and colleagues (Beck et al., 1979). The model identifies several cognitive themes as being central to the onset and maintenance of depression. These are as follows.

Formulation of the theme of loss

The theme of loss in depression does not originate in cognitive therapy. This concept was first articulated by Freud (1936), and subsequently other commentators have elaborated on this theme, notably Bowlby (1980). The specific contribution made by Beck is to differentiate between actual and perceived loss in relation to depression. Actual losses may be life events such as bereavement, redundancy, divorce or children leaving home. Beck develops this theme further by considering the perceived losses that may accompany these actual losses. These perceived losses might include loss of purpose, loss of status, loss of role, loss of security or loss of companionship and the like. The drawing of this distinction highlights a central feature of the cognitive model, namely it is not events in themselves that make us happy, sad, angry, guilty, but the view that we take of them. For example, within a Rogerian counselling model (Rogers, 1957) there is an assumption that experiencing a life event such as bereavement is distressing per se and attention is focused on enabling someone to express their distress openly. While at face value an experience such as bereavement is likely to be distressing to the individual experiencing it, within the cognitive model the clinician is seeking to identify the specific perceptions regarding the loss event.

Patient example

Alan, a 55-year-old man, became depressed after the death of his mother, following a protracted illness. He described experiencing overwhelming feelings of guilt whenever he thought about his mother. In discussing this with him it became apparent that when his mother died he felt a huge sense of relief. He had found caring for her over the previous 18 months very stressful and frequently experienced thoughts along the theme of wishing she would die so that he could get on with his life and escape his own emotional turmoil. To Alan, the fact he had such thoughts meant he was a selfish person who did not deserve any happiness. He viewed his depression as a suitable punishment for being such a bad son and having, as he viewed them, such despicable thoughts.

This can be contrasted with Joanne, a 28-year-old woman, who became depressed following the death of her father. She had not had contact with her father for many years due to his abusive behaviour toward her throughout her childhood. While discussing her father's death she stated that she was glad he had died and did not express any feelings of sadness regarding his passing. Indeed, she did not attend his funeral. However, Joanne was readily able to identify her sense of loss for her childhood, which was marked by physical violence and for the lack of a 'loving and caring father who did the things regular dads did'.

Negative cognitive triad

A second aspect of Beck's cognitive model of depression is what is termed the negative cognitive triad (Beck et al., 1979). This refers to three specific themes that describe the content of depression related NATS. These three themes are:

- negative view of self: 'I am useless.'

- negative view of the world: 'Everyone hates me.'
- negative view of the future: 'Everything is pointless.'

There are research data to support the occurrence of these themes in depression (see Blackburn and Twaddle, 1996, for a review of these data).

Patient example

Audrey, a 55-year-old woman, became depressed following a complaint being made against her at work, over which she was exonerated. Audrey frequently berated herself and reported typical NATs such as 'it's entirely my fault', 'I'm such a failure', 'people are so cruel', 'I don't know why I bother, nothing makes a difference'.

How to identify and work with these typical thoughts encountered in the depressed person is described later in the chapter.

Hopelessness

The theme of hopelessness is a crucial aspect of depression and is related to the third theme in the negative cognitive triad, a negative view of the future. Hopelessness is defined as: 'A perception that the future is bleak and will remain so for the foreseeable future.' There is a wealth of research data (Beck et al., 1975; Beck et al., 1985c; Dyer and Kreitman, 1984; MacLeod et al., 1992; Petrie et al., 1988; Wetzel, 1976) which demonstrates that a high level of hopelessness is predictive of suicidality rather than level of depression. Thus, in a nutshell, an individual who is displaying low levels of depression but high levels of hopelessness will be much more at risk of attempting suicide than someone with a high level of depression and low level of hopelessness. Equally, someone who is very depressed may not have the motivation to harm themselves. However, when depression starts to remit, if high levels of hopelessness are present then the risk of suicide may be significantly increased. Beck has devised specific, well-validated questionnaires to measure both depression and hopelessness. These are the Beck Depression Inventory (Beck et al., 1961) and the Beck Hopelessness Scale (Beck et al., 1974). Used in combination these can be an effective way of monitoring mood and level of hopelessness. However, these should not be a substitute for carrying out a thorough ongoing assessment using clinical skills.

Patient example

James is a 50-year-old man who has become depressed following the loss of his job at a company where he had worked for 25 years. James described a loss of role, purpose and status both in his own eyes and the eyes of the community. He reported feeling hopeless with a score of 18, indicative of a high level of suicidal risk on the Beck Hopelessness Scale. On the Beck Depression Inventory (BDI) he scored 24 indicative of a moderate level of depression but scoring 3 on question 2 (pessimism) and 2b on question 9 (self-punitive wishes), both of which questions refer to hopelessness-related constructs on the BDI. James reported thoughts such as 'my life is over', 'everything is pointless', 'nothing is ever going to change', 'I have no future'.

How hopelessness can be addressed clinically using CBT is discussed later in this chapter.

Helplessness

The theme of helplessness in depression has emerged from the work of Seligman (1975) and is defined as: 'A perception that there is no action an individual can take to influence a given set of circumstances.' This theme is prevalent in many depressive presentations. It is perhaps most common in patients who find themselves in adverse social circumstances over which they perceive they have little control or influence. It can be particularly paralysing to clinicians and is often used as a reason not to consider CBT as a treatment option with the caveat: 'If I lived in those circumstances then I would be depressed.' Thus the reason for depression is ascribed to social environment rather than to how the individual's perceptions regarding their place in that environment are shaping their behaviour.

Patient example

Angela is 35-year-old woman living on an inner city council estate. She has been depressed for the past 5 years. She has three children by three different partners all of whom have been physically violent. Having ended her most recent relationship 6 months previously her ex-partner continues to harass her in the street and try to break into her house. She is anxious and tearful and feels unable to exert any influence over the situation. It would be very easy to conclude that Angela's problems lay with her ex-partner until there is some examination of Angela's perceptions regarding her ex-partner, which explains her sense of helplessness with regard to his behaviour. Her automatic thoughts included 'I deserve this', 'at least I have his attention, I must be annoying the bastard, that's good', 'the police won't be interested in helping me, I have a criminal record'. From this perspective there may be an opportunity to use CBT to help Angela examine some of these perceptions and act differently, which may reduce her sense of hopelessness.

For an in-depth case example of dealing with helplessness-related depression see Moore and Garland (2003).

USING CBT TO WORK WITH DEPRESSION

The evidence base for CBT for the treatment of acute depression is well established (Beck et al., 1985b; Blackburn et al., 1981; Blackburn et al., 1986). For the interested reader an excellent chapter summarizing the evidence base for CBT for acute depression and the debate that surround its efficacy can be found in Williams (1997). There is increasing evidence to demonstrate the utility of CBT in the treatment and management of chronic depression (Paykel et al., 1999). The treatment protocol from which this evidence base is derived is described in Figure 9.1. The standard number of sessions for delivery of this treatment protocol, excluding assessment sessions is between 12–18 sessions for acute depression (Beck et al., 1979) and between 18–25 sessions for more chronic presentations (Moore and Garland, 2003).

- Assessment of presenting problems within a CBT framework including socialization to the CBT model (1–3 sessions)
- Problem and target setting (1 session plus 1 homework exercise)
- Behavioural intervention: activity scheduling and graded task assignment (3–6 sessions)
- Cognitive intervention: attentional focus strategies; counting thoughts and task interfering cognitions (TICS) and task orienting cognitions (TOCS) (Burns, 1990) (1–2 sessions)
- Cognitive behavioural intervention: identifying negative automatic thoughts; modifying automatic negative thoughts and behavioural experiments; tackling psychological/situational problems (4–6 sessions)
- Relapse prevention: identifying and modifying rules for living and behavioural experiments; managing setbacks; blueprints for change (2–4 sessions)

Figure 9.1   CBT treatment protocol for depression

The assessment process, socialization to the model and problem and goal setting using a CBT framework, is discussed in detail in earlier chapters. In addition, the assessment of depression using a CBT framework is covered in a number of texts and the interested reader is directed to the following: Chapter 1 in Hawton et al., (1989) and Chapter 1 in Moore and Garland (2003).

Protocol-driven intervention

The purpose of a protocol-driven intervention is to deliver each element in a stepwise way that builds on itself. In this respect, there are some advantages in trying to follow the protocol as intended, not least because this is the process from which the evidence base for CBT for acute and chronic depression is derived. Depending on service setting and time constraints, some elements of the treatment protocol may be emphasized over others. For example, in a primary care setting where there is a limit of 6–12 sessions, activity scheduling and graded task assignment used comprehensively may be the most effective intervention for managing mild to moderate acute depression.

What does the clinician need to do to maximize the benefits of a protocol-driven intervention?

HANDOUTS

Psycho-education is a fundamental aspect of CBT. Giving the patient written information to support each intervention is essential in order to maximize the chances of the patient using the strategies outside of the session.

When treating depression, a number of aspects of the illness need to be taken into consideration when deciding what written information to give. Commonly, patients who suffer with depression have impaired concentration and memory and motivational deficits, as well as reduced abstracting and recall abilities (for a comprehensive discussion of this aspect of cognitive psychology see Williams et al., 1997). It is important to take these into consideration when preparing written material. The following guidance may be of help:

- Keep handouts short (ideally no more than two pages).
- Keep language simple and straightforward (the average reading age of the nation is 9). Add to this the cognitive impairment that can result from depressive symptoms and it is easy to see that the clinician is going to have to work hard to enable the patient to use psycho-educational material.
- Ensure good-quality print both in terms of font size and clarity of print. Old worn photocopies with words missing are difficult for anyone to read – a depressed patient is likely to abandon it more quickly.
- Consider presentation and strive for the handout to be laid out in a readable style.
- Always read handouts yourself so you are familiar with the content and can discuss this in detail with the patient.
- Check for and eliminate mistakes.

There are a number of handouts in existing texts that are central to the treatment of depression using the protocol just described. These are as follows:

- socializing the depressed patient to the CBT model: Mooney and Padesky, 2000; Moore and Garland, 2003
- activity scheduling and graded task assignment: Fennell, 1989
- identifying and modifying negative automatic thoughts: Fennell, 1989, 1999; Greenberger and Padesky, 1995; Moore and Garland, 2003.

TAPE RECORDER

Within the original randomized controlled trials on which the protocol is based each therapy session was audiotaped and the patient was encouraged to listen to this in between sessions. The initial rationale for this was to combat the memory and concentration difficulties in depression. It is important for both clinician and patient to recognize and make an allowance for the deficits in memory and concentration that the depressed patient experiences that are real and exert a detrimental effect on the individual's ability to function. It is therefore crucial that the clinician working with the depressed patient does the following:

- makes an allowance for the impact of these symptoms and aims to minimize their impact on CBT interventions
- tailors the intervention according to how impaired the patient's memory and concentration are.

Audiotapes of the session can therefore be extremely useful as prompts to the patient for homework assignments and to review the content of the session.

TREATMENT FOLDER

CBT is a self-help model, and in this respect the clinician should maximize this aspect of treatment from the outset. The rationale for the treatment folder is to encourage the patient to keep in one place all the handouts, written notes and completed diary sheets that are produced during the course of treatment. The patient is asked to bring the folder to each CBT session and the clinician works actively with the patient to use the contents of the folder. This is a small area in which the patient can be encouraged to take active responsibility for change.

DIARY SHEETS

Every CBT intervention makes use of diary sheets, so the clinician has to have these at hand. There are a number of standard diary sheets in existence in a variety of texts. For the depression protocol the minimum required diary sheets are as follows:

- activity schedule
- diary for recording automatic negative thoughts
- diary for modifying automatic negative thoughts.

Several texts contain examples of these.

Service providers need to consider financing the provision of these essential tools. In addition, clinicians need to consider how these are accessed effectively in routine clinical work. For example, a clinician who carries out all their work from one office can allocate a proportion of a filing cabinet to handouts and diary sheets. However, for individuals who see patients in their own homes, more preparation and organization is required. Many clinicians view these tools as unnecessary luxuries. In fact, in order to use CBT effectively diary sheets and appropriate storage and free access are essential tools of the trade. No plumber would arrive at work saying 'my tools were too heavy so I left them at home' or 'I have no space to store them so I don't use them'. Diary sheets and handouts are to the clinician practising CBT what tools are to a plumber.

USING CBT IN THE TREATMENT OF ACUTE DEPRESSION

One of the most distressing aspects of depression is that it robs people of their ability to engage in activities that most people take for granted. Many individuals who experience depression describe its grinding inertia, which makes everyday activities difficult.

Patient example

Julia is a 45-year-old woman with a 12-month history of depression, the onset of which coincided with changes in her role as a bank clerk. At assessment Julia identified the following problem list:

- Low mood on a daily basis that is managed by retreating to bed.
- Poor concentration, tiredness, lethargy and sleep disturbance which lead to putting off activities of daily living.
- Withdrawal from hobbies and social activities.
- Inability to return to work due to fear of failure.
- Need to maintain high standards when engaging in most activities that leads to procrastination and avoidance.

When Julia first began treatment she had withdrawn from activities such as household chores. Getting washed and dressed each day took great effort and she had abandoned her interests and hobbies. She was plagued by thoughts of failure and was critical of her perceived inability to maintain her previously high standards.

As stated previously, there is a strong evidence base for the use of CBT in the treatment of acute depression. This evidence is based on using a standard treatment protocol as described in Beck et al. (1979) and consists of the following elements:

- activity scheduling and graded task assignment
- identifying automatic thoughts
- modifying automatic thoughts with behavioural experiments
- identifying rules for living
- modifying rules for living with behavioural experiments.

The aim in following a treatment protocol is to deliver specific interventions in pre-determined stages. The protocol has three broad aims. First, to provide relief from depressive symptoms; second, to problem solve situational problems that may be maintaining depression; finally, it is to modify psychological vulnerability to depression. This chapter will look at how the standard treatment protocol can be applied to the treatment of acute depression giving consideration to these elements.

Typically, once a thorough assessment of the patient's problems has been carried out the treatment protocol consists of 12–20 1-hour sessions delivered using the protocol format just described.

The frequency of delivery recommended in a standard treatment protocol is two sessions per week for the first 2–3 weeks. This is followed by 6–8 weeks of weekly sessions. As treatment progresses the time intervals between sessions is increased initially to fortnightly, then monthly. In some circumstances it may be appropriate to offer extended follow-up at 1 month, 3 months, 6 months and 12 months after treatment has been completed. This can be beneficial where depression has been severe and where there have been previous episodes of depression.

Research evidence indicates that the effectiveness of this protocol is maximized when it is used in conjunction with a therapeutic dose of antidepressants. For a full discussion of this aspect of treatment see Moore and Garland, 2003; Williams, 1997.

Activity scheduling and graded task assignment

Within the early stages of implementation of the treatment protocol for acute depression there is an active and deliberate targeting of depressive symptoms. Tackling these first can often lead to a rapid improvement in mood over 2–6 sessions. Generally the first intervention used to tackle depressive symptoms is the introduction of activity scheduling and graded task assignment (Beck et al., 1979; Fennell, 1989). Activity scheduling can be introduced after the very first assessment session. This is a useful homework task in order to gain a baseline measure of the depressed individual's current activity levels.

Figure 9.2 illustrates what an activity schedule looks like.

The treatment rationale for using activity scheduling

As stated previously an important aspect of CBT is to give the patient a meaningful treatment rationale based on the assessment of their current problems. When treating acute depression a useful starting point can be the impact of reduced activity levels on overall functioning. This can be illustrated using the vicious circle maintenance formulation described previously (see Greenberger and Padesky, 1995).

An example of such a formulation would be drawn out on paper with the patient and discussed as follows:

'Julia, in considering the vicious circle it seems that key symptoms in terms of how your depression affects you are tiredness, lethargy and poor concentration. As a result most activities seem a tremendous effort and your first thought is "I can't be bothered" often followed by "it's pointless, I won't enjoy it" and "I won't be able to finish so why bother starting". As a result you put off starting tasks and either take to your bed or sit and stare into space. It seems however that as time passes you notice that you are feeling much more depressed, your tiredness and lethargy is worse and your mind is full of thoughts such as "Look at me I'm so lazy", "I can't even do simple tasks", "I'm useless", "I just sit around all day doing nothing". You seem to be saying that this can go on intermittently over days, putting things off, feeling really low in mood and criticizing yourself for not doing what you feel you need to do. This seems like a vicious circle. What I would like to propose to you is that we try and find a way of helping you break out of the vicious circle; rather

Instructions for completing the activity schedule.

Please record each activity on an hour-by-hour basis. Then rate each activity for both mastery and pleasure on a scale of 0–10 where 0 is the low end of the scale and 10 is the high end of the scale. Mastery is defined as *How well I did the activity given how I was feeling.* Pleasure is defined as *How much I enjoyed the activity.*

	Monday	Tuesday	Wednesday	Thursday	Friday	Saturday	Sunday
6–7a.m.							
7–8a.m.							
8–9a.m.							
9–10a.m.							
10–11a.m.							
11–12a.m.							
12–1a.m.							
1–2p.m.							
2–3p.m.							
3–4p.m.							
4–5p.m.							

Figure 9.2 Activity schedule

5–6p.m.						
6–7p.m.						
7–8p.m.						
8–9p.m.						
9–10p.m.						
10–11p.m.						
11–12p.m						
12–1a.m.						
1–2a.m.						
2–3a.m.						
3–4a.m.						
4–5a.m.						
5–6a.m.						

than being so hard on yourself, let's see if we can help you make an allowance for your symptoms. With this in mind if it is okay with you I would like to introduce the first step of this process.'

How patients respond to this rationale

Generally speaking, this rationale is effective because most people who suffer with depression recognize the impact the illness has in undermining usual daily functioning, so that straightforward tasks become very difficult to engage in. Being given the opportunity to re-engage in everyday tasks is something most people with depression respond to positively. It is also helpful to work on a problem that reaps identifiable improvements in 2–5 sessions and tackling depressive symptoms offers this. This engenders hope in the patient and promotes active engagement in treatment. In this respect targeting depressive symptoms in the first instance will produce faster results than, for example, trying to modify someone's longstanding view of himself or herself as a 'failure'. Equally working with someone's rules for living and core beliefs requires a strong therapeutic relationship in which the patient can trust the clinician with emotionally sensitive material. Rules for living and core beliefs usually represent to a greater or lesser extent how someone defines themselves in terms of their worth and working too soon on these can significantly worsen depressive symptoms. Thus an important aspect of the symptom relief phase is to equip the patient with specific skills to manage mood so that when work on rules for living and core beliefs commences they can effectively manage any downturn in mood.

Exercise

Imagine for a moment that if over the next few weeks all you did was work and meet your family and household responsibilities. Now, your life may be very busy and it seems a lot of your time and energy goes into this type of activity. However, imagine in addition, on top of only doing what you felt you ought to do you also experienced great difficulty watching television, reading the newspaper or a book, preparing a meal, talking to family and friends, having sex, playing with your children or tending to your plants and garden. After a while you may start to feel pretty miserable. Hopefully, you are not suffering with depression. This is the exact position many people who suffer with depression find themselves in. Add to this the disabling effects of biological symptoms of the illness, possibly feelings of guilt and a mind plagued by a sense of inadequacy and failure because you can't even engage in the everyday tasks that most of us take for granted. Consider also which household tasks you particularly dislike, perhaps the ironing, the weekly supermarket shop, organizing the washing for the family, imagine the effort it can sometimes take you to get on with these, imagine how hard they become once somebody is experiencing depressive symptoms.

In carrying out this reflective exercise you may be able to catch a glimpse of how debilitating and distressing an illness like depression can be. Most depressed people will tell you that feeling robbed of the capacity to do everyday things is often the most devastating part of the illness. It is also the aspect of the illness that contributes significantly to relationship tensions which then compounds the depression further.

Next time you are working with a patient who is suffering with depression try to talk to them in detail about this aspect of their experience of the illness. Is this something the patient would like to work on?

Introducing activity scheduling as a homework assignment

Having introduced to the patient the hypothesis that there may be a relationship between their appraisals of their depressive symptoms, the constraints these place on their usual functioning and how they view themselves as a result, the next step is to begin the process of finding out what current activity levels are actually like. The following dialogue can be used as a guide to introducing the method:

'Julia, it seems important that we try and get some understanding of your current activity levels. This will help us to make sense of your problems in concrete terms, identify possible patterns in relation to your mood and activity levels and provide a baseline for what you are doing from which we can measure improvement as treatment progresses. What I have here [clinician shows activity schedule to patient] is a diary sheet, which is called an activity schedule. As you can see [talking through the diary sheet] there is every day of the week broken down into hourly slots over a 24-hour period. What I would like you to try and do is basically record what you are doing each hour of the day. Then for each activity I would like you to take two ratings as follows [pointing to the written instructions on the activity schedule]:

Mastery and pleasure on a scale of 0–10 where 0 is the low end of the scale and 10 is the high end of the scale.
Mastery is defined as *How well I did the activity given how I was feeling*
Pleasure is defined as *How much I enjoyed the activity*

So, for example, between 11–12 today which is Tuesday you are in your CBT session [looking at Tuesday between 11–12 on activity schedule] so we could write here CBT session and can I ask you just to rate your sense of mastery right now on a scale of 0–10 and, I know this may seem a bit odd, your sense of pleasure in the session [clinician makes a record on appropriate part of schedule].'

It would be important at this stage to check out with the patient their understanding of what you are asking them to do and to elicit any concerns they may have. It is also helpful to support this with a written handout that summarizes the instructions you are giving (see Fennell, 1989). In terms of rating mastery the statement 'given how I am feeling' is a crucial element of the instruction. As stated previously most depressed patients do not take into account the real deficits that depressive symptoms have on their ability to engage in and complete activities. Presenting the mastery instruction in this ways begins the process of asking the patient to make an allowance for the impact of their depressive symptoms on their day-to-day functioning and to begin to question how they view themselves (i.e. 'useless', 'lazy', 'failure') and the unrealistic expectations they often set themselves (i.e. 'I should be able to do everything to the same standard as before I became depressed') in relation to activities.

The discussion could then continue as follows:

'When you are recording your activities everything you do counts. So even if you are lying on the bed asleep, watching TV or staring into space all of these are important and it is helpful to record them because they may give us useful information about your mood at these times. In terms of filling the schedule in then it may sometimes be impractical to complete it every hour. However, also leaving it to the end of the day may decrease your chances of doing it. Therefore, can I suggest you try and fill it in every 2–3 hours? If possible try and keep it somewhere that reminds you to complete it, e.g. your coffee table.'

It is useful to check out with the patient how optimistic they are about completing the task and to problem solve obstacles. A final part of the instructions from the clinician might include: 'We are not looking for a perfectly filled in diary. We are trying to get some sense of your current activity levels. If you find that you sometimes forget to do it don't try and catch up. Just start at the time it is and continue from there. If it feels too much to do it every day do it every other day. Like everything we do in CBT the method requires practice and so there is no expectation you get it right first time.'

This type of baseline measurement of activity levels with mastery and pleasure ratings is useful to carry out throughout the assessment phase and helpfully prepares the ground for the next intervention graded task assignment which aims to re-establish the patient in a daily routine as well as re-engaging in activities they may be putting off or avoiding. This is now described.

Purpose of graded task assignment

The purpose of using graded task assignment when treating depression is as follows:

- to re-engage the patient in activities and begin to tackle procrastination and avoidance
- to improve concentration and combat tiredness and lethargy
- to re-establish daily routine.

Using the principles of collaboration and guided discovery (see Chapter 2) the clinician needs to work with the patient through the following steps.

Step 1: establishing an activities list

In order to begin the process of using graded task assignment the clinician needs to establish a list of the following activities:

- previously enjoyable activities
- activities the patient is putting off or avoiding as a result of becoming depressed.

Alongside this the clinician needs to make a clear assessment of what makes it difficult for the patient to engage in these at present. It is important to remember that the biological symptoms of depression, (tiredness, lethargy, poor concentration and memory, sleep disturbance, loss of libido, irritability and the like) severely impede the depressed individual's ability to engage in most activities. It is not only important to explicitly acknowledge this with the patient but also to educate them that this deficit is real. Written material is vital at this stage. Many people who suffer with depression will attribute their inactivity to laziness or stupidity. In addition, they will place an expectation on themselves to function at the same level as they did before they became depressed. Thus, they expect to complete tasks at the same speed, be able to do several tasks at once and for their energy and concentration levels to last across several hours. The biological symptoms of depression usually make this impossible. As a consequence the depressed individuals use this as evidence against themselves, often reporting thoughts such as 'look how pathetic I am, I can't even clean the house any more' or 'I'm just so useless, I can't even do simple things'.

When introducing the concept of graded task assignment the overall message the clinician is trying to promote is:

- one of compassion toward self, rather than self-criticism and self-loathing
- acceptance that these deficits are real and impede current functioning
- the need to make an allowance for symptoms in order to break out of the vicious cycle of inactivity.

In the face of limited capacity for activity the depressed individual often invests their limited resources into engaging in tasks they feel they ought to do. This usually includes work, family and parental responsibilities and household chores. As a result they abandon enjoyable activities as they feel unable to prioritise these, seeing self as undeserving or unimportant or prioritizing duty and responsibilities over everything else. Therefore, in constructing a list of activities the patient is avoiding or putting off it is useful to break these down into different categories. For example:

- 'Enjoyable activities I have stopped doing'. This may include hobbies and interests, social activities, shared family activities, self-nurturing activities (e.g. hairdresser's, manicure, soak in the bath, reading a magazine).
- 'Household tasks I'm putting off.'
- Work-related tasks.

Initially, it is important not to make these lists too comprehensive, as this can be overwhelming to the patient. Equally it may be helpful with some people to focus on one activity from each category as a starting point and to tackle each activity one at a time. As a general principle it is often helpful to start with re-engaging the depressed patient in a previously enjoyable activity. A central aim at the start of treatment is to try and tackle a problem that will see improvement in 2 or 3 weeks. This builds hopefulness in the patient and facilitates rapid engagement in the treatment process. Helping the depressed individual re-engage with a sense of pleasure, if successful can result in a relatively rapid improvement in mood.

Step 2: give a rationale for grading tasks

In order to use this intervention with a patient you will need the following materials:

- Written instructions for the patient giving the rationale for graded task assignment and how to use this (see Fennell, 1989; Greenberger and Padesky, 1995).

How to introduce the concept of graded task assignment is illustrated in the following clinical vignette.

Ways of grading a task:

- breaking it down into composite steps
- simplifying the task.

Patient example

To return to Julia, while generating a list of previously enjoyed activities, she identified embroidery as something from which she had previously derived a great deal of pleasure. However, over the last 12 months she had given up on this activity, reporting thoughts such as 'I can't be bothered', 'I can't concentrate', 'I always make a mistake'. In asking Julia what in her view made the task difficult she stated 'I think I've just become lazy'. The clinician enquired as to which symptoms of depression particularly hindered her ability to engage in embroidery. Julia identified poor concentration and tiredness as the most problematic and discussion established that the two symptoms tended to reinforce each other. Thus when Julia was tired her concentration was poor. A further piece of information that was necessary was to clarify with Julia how, prior to becoming depressed, she had worked on her embroidery. At this point, Julia replied: 'Oh I used to sit and do it for 2–3 hours at a time, I really miss it, but I just can't think straight now, so there is no point in trying.' The clinician also clarified with Julia that, at its best currently her concentration span was approximately 15 minutes. Further, her concentration was at its best between 11–12 noon and 3–4 p.m. At this time she rated her level of concentration at 3 on a scale of 0–10 where 0 'unable to concentrate' and 10 'able to concentrate as I could prior to becoming depressed.' Finally, the clinician enquired as to what Julia had being trying to embroider to which she replied a larger tapestry of

---

the Last Supper using fine embroidery silk. This began to enable the clinician to consider the overall formulation of Judith's difficulties, and the theme of high standards and doing things properly was flagged up.

Summary of steps:

- Identify previously enjoyed activity patient is currently not engaging in.
- Identify symptoms that interfere with task completion.

Using the vicious circle maintenance formulation to illustrate the cycle of inactivity the treating clinician put it to Julia that indeed her view that she had become lazy is one hypothesis (hypothesis A) that might explain her difficulty in doing her embroidery. The clinician then presented a second hypothesis (hypothesis B) that her significantly reduced concentration span and degree of tiredness may be impacting on her ability to carry out the task: this was, if the way in which she approached the embroidery was modified by breaking the task down into smaller steps in order to make an allowance for her symptoms, then would this enable her to resume her hobby once more? Julia was very sceptical and reported a raft of automatic thoughts about the idea.

Step 3: how to grade a task

In order to use this intervention with a patient you will need the following materials:

- a blank activity schedule
- written instructions for the patient giving the rationale for graded task assignment and how to use this (see Fennell, 1989; Greenberger and Padesky, 1995)
- list from step one
- 45–60 minutes to work with the patient.

The clinician worked with Julia to develop a concrete and specific written plan of how to re-engage with the activity of embroidery. The first step was to simplify the task and it was agreed that the Last Supper would be put to one side and Julia would attempt to embroider a small greeting card. Part of the rationale for choosing this activity was that it was clearly a skill Julia had. In addition she had all the materials at home in order to begin the task. These things are important to consider when choosing a task, as the ease of access to materials will impact significantly on the individual's ability to get started. Equally, this is not an appropriate time to start trying to learn a new skill. The aim is to re-engage the patient in activities they used to enjoy.

The next task was to identify with Julia all the steps involved in reaching the point where she could begin her embroidery. Then two columns were created on a sheet of paper one which stated 'how long this step would have taken me prior to becoming depressed' and one which stated 'given my current difficulties with concentration and tiredness how much time will I allow myself to complete this step' (see Table 9.1).

Table 9.1 Activity scheduling steps

Each step of the activity	How long each step would have taken me prior to becoming depressed	How long I am going to allow myself to complete each step given the symptoms of depression*
Draw pattern for embroidery	20 minutes	40 minutes
Choose embroidery silks	15 minutes	30 minutes
Sort embroidery silks onto a card	10 minutes	20 minutes
Cut out material on which to embroider	10 minutes	20 minutes
Start embroidering	Complete in one 2-hour sitting	10 minutes then a break of 20 minutes, which will be drinking a cup of coffee

* Symptoms include tiredness, reduced concentration and memory. Patient will calculate at least double amount of time, perhaps more.

What is the rationale for allocating time to this stepped approach?

As observed in Table 9.1 the column indicating the time allowance to be made for symptoms is roughly doubled. This may seem overly generous initially. However, this can play an important role in motivating the patient to move from step to step, particularly if they complete the step well within the allotted time.

Using the activity schedule to develop a concrete plan

Once you have agreed on an activity and identified the steps involved, the next phase is to plan how these steps are going to be implemented on a blank activity schedule. It is at this point that the information regarding concentration span and the time of day at which tiredness and poor concentration are least problematic is used. In the example of Julia, she identified her concentration span to be of 15 minutes' duration and at its best between 11–12 noon and 3–4 pm. These were chosen as the times when the patient would plan to implement a specific step. At this point it is important to be concrete and specific in terms of planning. At this initial stage of treatment Julia was meeting with her clinician twice per week. So together they planned which steps from Table 9.1 they would attempt to implement during the 3 days between sessions. It may be tempting to fill the patient's day, but the idea is to maximize the patient's chances of completing each step. It is also important not to buy into demands the patient may make of themselves, that if they start something then they must finish it (possibly a theme in their rules for living such as 'if I start something I should finish it'), or more typically, they know they won't be able to finish it (due to poor concentration, lack of energy etc.) so they don't start it. Thus an active and deliberate part of the rationale for graded task assignment is to consider the impact of depressive symptoms and rules for living and not necessarily aim to complete the whole task before the next treatment session. You might therefore decide to plan one or two steps on one day and nothing on the next. This then affords the opportunity to help the patient compare their mood on days when they are engaged in some structured activity and days when they are not engaged in such a way. An example of Julia's first graded task assignment follows. In addition to the steps being planned at the previously identified time the following instructions were added:

- To only engage in 10 minutes of activity.
- The 10 minutes was to be timed using an alarm to prompt Julia to stop.
- On stopping, Julia was to 'have a break' for at least 20 minutes which was defined as having a cup of coffee.

'What about me, the clinician?'

One of the common mistakes novice clinicians make in trying to use CBT interventions when working with depression is not making an allowance for the genuine deficits the depressed individual experiences. Thinking is slowed, concentration is reduced and abstracting ability impaired. These are some suggestions:

- Slow the pace at which you give information.
- Ask for frequent feedback (every 5–10 minutes) from the patient, to check you are moving in the right direction together.
- Encourage the patient to ask questions and give them time to ask them.
- Make short, frequent written summaries of important learning points.
- Use diary sheets to illustrate examples which are personally relevant to the patient.
- Support your verbal rational with a good-quality handout, the use of which you model in the session.
- Audiotape the session and encourage the patient to listen to it in between CBT sessions.

Sometimes delivering an intervention in a methodical way can seem time consuming. Under pressure to get through a busy clinic it can be tempting to skim over details and press on quickly with the patient. Taking time to teach the patient CBT skills in a stepwise way is, in the authors' view, time well spent. If you consider your own attempts to learn to use CBT skills ask yourself the following questions:

- Did CBT make sense the first time I heard about it?
- Could I naturally use the interventions without practice?
- Did I read about a CBT intervention that all made sense, and the first person I used it with everything went smoothly?

Or:

- Did I have to practise repeatedly in order to develop CBT skills?
- Are there still some things I need to practise?

- Did I make mistakes and need to reflect on these in order to learn?
- Have my skills developed over time and with the assistance of colleagues and supervisors?

Patients are no different – they are learning a new and unfamiliar skill. They do have a much harder task – they are trying to learn a new skill while grappling with a major mental health problem – one which can significantly interfere with their ability to use the very skills they need to tackle their depression. Thus, they need to be guided by a compassionate and patient clinician who is able to personalize the CBT treatment rationale to meet their needs and promotes hopefulness in the patient. A key aspect of being a productive practitioner of CBT is being clear in your own mind what the rationale is for using a particular intervention at a given point, understanding blocks to progress and having sufficient tenacity to persist with a particular intervention.

Reviewing the graded task assignment the following session

Reviewing how a homework task has gone is of paramount importance in CBT and routinely at least 10 minutes of the session should be devoted to this. In the early stages of treatment, 20–30 minutes of the session may be given over to the review of homework or more, if there has been significant learning or, in contrast, obstacles to completing the homework. In this respect there is no such thing as homework failure. This is a concept that both clinician and patient need to embrace. Just as much can be learned about a patient and their problems from non-completion of a task or from it not going according to plan, as can be learned from its success. The motto here is that everything is 'grist for the mill'. If as a clinician you can accept this, then you will have less frustration in your therapeutic work. If you have a tendency to see task completion as an end in itself then you will run into problems. Thus when a patient completes their homework you say 'well done' and move on without opportunity to learn, both you and the patient have missed a rich opportunity to pinpoint what has made the difference and incorporate this into future therapeutic work. Equally, if the patient does not complete the task and you ignore this without addressing the reasons, you may continue to encounter an unidentified obstacle to progress, which will extend treatment and potentially lead the clinician and patient to feel despondent. The clinician may experience NATs such as 'I'm useless, the patient isn't making progress, it's my fault' or feelings of irritation with NATs such as 'this patient is not trying, they don't want to get better, they are wasting my time'.

Exercise

Develop a concrete plan during the session to re-engage the patient with a previously enjoyed activity, using the principles of graded task assignment. Use the whole hour to work on this goal. Agree that the homework assignment will be to implement the plan. Use the following questions to guide your self-reflection on your practice:

- What were your feelings and NATs during the session while trying to prac-
tise this skill?
- How did these influence your behaviour in the session?
- How did the work in the session proceed?
- What aspects of the task went well?
- What aspects were more difficult?
- What did you learn in this session that you can apply in the next session or
when working with other patients?
- What were your feelings and NATs when you reflected on the session?
- What specific question regarding mastering this skill can you formulate to
take to clinical supervision?

How do I react when things go according to plan?

How do I react when things don't go according to plan?

From this, what can I learn about myself as a clinician/person?

What are the pitfalls of using activity scheduling and graded task assignment?

This intervention can look deceptively simple. Equally, novice practitioners can assume that it is so simple it cannot possibly be effective in tackling the grinding inertia that characterizes depression. Enabling the patient to gain real and lasting benefits from using this intervention in a productive way requires skill, time and tenacity. There are a number of ways in which graded task assignment can go wrong. Being able to anticipate some of these, particularly when you are using it in the early stages of treatment can impact significantly on the patient's overall investment in it as a treatment strategy. Given the strong evidence base for its use it would seem useful to try and maximize the chances of its success from the outset. The following guidelines are aimed at trying to minimize common pitfalls that can arise when using activity scheduling and graded task assignment.

Activities dependent on the weather

In the UK, the defining feature of the climate is changeability. Therefore, if any task you plan with the patient involves being outdoors, always develop a contingency plan should the weather prevent the implementation of the original plan. Typically, activities that fall foul of the weather are gardening, DIY, walking and the like. Remember the aim in the early stages of treatment is to choose a task that is going to bring the patient pleasure and present them with a 'no-lose' scenario. One of the authors is reminded of an example early in her career when activity scheduling and graded task assignment came unstuck. A plan had been made to use graded task assignment with the goal of enabling the patient to put a new roof on his shed. He was pleased with the plan at the end of the session and expressed some hope he would be able to do it. It was February and an hour after the session ended it began to snow. It continued to snow for three days. The patient arrived at the next session having completed very little work on his shed. He reported feeling very low, along with strong feelings of guilt. He was very tearful and expressed NATs that he had 'let the therapist down' and he was 'a waste of space'. He was unable to make an allowance for mitigating circumstances. The next three sessions were taken up not only trying to lessen the impact of this train of thought but also trying to engage him in continuing to use graded task assignment. While his response to the situation provided valuable information (which included excessive responsibility taking and a sense of self as a failure leading to avoidance behaviour) that developed the formulation of his problems, some timely advanced planning may have averted activating these rules for living and core beliefs so early in treatment.

Activities dependent on others

Like the weather, significant others in the depressed person's life can, for fair or foul reasons, be unreliable. Therefore, if you are planning activities that are dependent on others always build a contingency plan into the schedule. This can be achieved by asking questions such as:

'If X cancels what alternatives are there?'
'If Y is busy who else could you ask?'

Many depressed individuals are interpersonally sensitive and perceive themselves to varying degrees as a nuisance or undeserving of help and attention from others. These perceptions can interfere significantly with activity scheduling and graded task assignment, which involve interactions with others. In the early stages of treatment the aim is not to tackle such perceptions directly using cognitive interventions, but it is important to try and anticipate their likely impact should they be activated in a specific situation. Therefore, a general principle when planning activities, which involve interacting with others, is to try and choose people with whom the patient has a good relationship, who are tolerant and understanding of their illness and who in general are reliable in keeping to agreed plans. Also check out the nature of the relationship with the individuals with whom the activity is to be shared, and try and make some assessment of the degree of mutual support and reciprocity that exists in their interactions. Many depressed people spend much of their time meeting the needs of others to the detriment of their own well being. Thus on the surface they may seem to have lots of contact with others but closer observation can often reveal that the patient's role in a particular relationship is to take care of others while their needs are neglected or ignored. Once depression has set in many depressed people recognize this type of pattern and experience interacting with others as a source of anxiety and exhaustion, but feel unable to set limits with others who make excessive demand on their time and resources. Activity scheduling and graded task assignment provide an opportunity to identify more productive relationships and encourage the patient to engage in behavioural experiments to foster these relationships.

The patient who has no enjoyable activities in his life

Depressed people often lack enjoyable activities. People who fall into this category either tend to spend their time and energy taking care of others and their home, or are overcommitted to work. For such individuals their sense of enjoyment is closely bound up to being approved of by others or goal attainment and being productive. Thus they derive little pleasure from activities that to them can seem frivolous and a waste of time such as lying in a bath, reading a magazine, relaxing in the garden, having a facial and the like. They often have no hobbies or if they do have hobbies they are pursed in an unrelenting way to a very high standard, to such an extent that rather than being enjoyable the hobby becomes a source of stress and disappointment when desired standards are not achieved. Equally, these individuals are often overactive rather than inactive.

When depression hits and these individuals are prevented from caring for others or robbed of their ability to work, they often seem without direction and purpose and often describe activities as having no meaning or pleasure. Such individuals can present a challenge when using activity scheduling and graded task assignment as it is often difficult to re-engage them with activities. Introducing the idea of 'enjoyment for enjoyment's sake' is often a new idea for these individuals and is not going to be accepted very readily. The clinician can be rendered helpless by the absence of previously enjoyed activity not related to productivity and it is easy to fall into the trap of suggesting activities the patient might like to engage in. This is to be resisted. It is important to remember the intervention needs to be tailored to the needs of the individual and careful discussion is needed in order to work collaboratively to find activities to focus on. These need to take into consideration how the person views the world and what type of activities they value. Negativity is a defining feature of depressive thinking. Even when introducing previously enjoyable activities this can be met with a barrage of NATs giving reasons why it will be 'pointless'. However, when it comes to trying to engage someone who has never really had hobbies or interests outside of work, introducing new activities can seem so alien that they will be rejected out of hand. This is likely to result in frustration for both patient and clinician. Activities the authors have found useful as a starting point are as follows:

- a graded programme of exercise
- crosswords
- using computer skills
- gardening

- golf
- activities with grandchildren
- graded DIY.

The patient who is always active

When the depressed patients seemingly have too much to do this is often central to making psychological sense of their difficulties and is a useful guide to formulating rules for living and core beliefs. Constant activity can be a manifestation of the following:

- *Difficulty saying no to others.* Requests for help may be indicative of rules for living around the theme of approval and subjugation. For example, 'if someone asks for help I should always give it'. An example of a related core belief may be: 'Others' needs are more important than my own.'
- *Taking excessive responsibility for other people's needs or problems.* A relevant rule for living here may be 'if someone has a problem it is up to me to sort it out' with the core belief 'I am responsible for other people's well-being'.
- *Excessively high standards.* Patients with rules for living around the theme of doing things properly often find themselves overactive because tasks take longer to complete as they are carried out to such a high standard. An associated core belief may be a sense of self as a failure.
- *Avoidance.* For many depressed patients constant activity is a means of distracting themselves from their mood and NATs. This tactic is often associated with rules for living around the theme of control; where thoughts and feelings are experienced as out of control and potentially overwhelming the overactivity is used as a means of managing this.

When faced with the patient who is overactive all of these factors need to be considered in the context of their impact on activity scheduling and graded task assignment.

Tackling household chores

For many depressed people household chores frequently become neglected. Once out of hand these tasks can quickly be experienced as impossible to tackle as they appear overwhelming and time consuming. Graded task assignment is ideal for tackling these problems. Rules for living around the theme of high standards and perfectionism often manifest themselves in this arena. The reality of depressive symptoms, in particular tiredness, lack of energy and poor concentration, may well mean that the patient is unable to tackle activities with the same gusto as previously. Thus tasks may take longer and be much harder to engage with. Equally, if you hated ironing before you became depressed, it is going to seem like an overwhelming chore once depressive symptoms take hold. The sense of dissatisfaction with not being able to maintain their usual standards may lead the patient to give up completely (e.g. rule for living: 'If I can't do something properly, there is no point in doing it at all').

Depending on how long a task has been neglected, using graded task assignment may actually be insufficient. Often getting on top of household tasks requires a combination of graded task assignment and problem solving.

There needs to be negotiation regarding what it is realistic to achieve in between sessions and the clinician should be conservative in estimations. For example, James had been depressed for 3 years. He wanted to go back to using his study. However, it was full of boxes and other clutter that had accumulated in there over a 2-year period. This included a year's worth of unopened mail. It would have taken James months to sort this out alone. He knew this, which is why he avoided tackling it. Thus we focused on tackling just one study related job at a time and agreed to spend no more than 4 hours a week on it at first. The instruction was just to focus on this task and not attend to everything else that needed doing. In addition, we identified a friend who would work on the task with him. The friend proved vital in maintaining motivation and in helping James when his NATs got the better of him and he wanted to give up.

Simplifying tasks

A very effective way of introducing graded task assignment is to simplify tasks. This is something that often does not occur to the patient and can very quickly enable the patient to re-engage in activities. Good examples of simplifying tasks include reading, crosswords, watching television, cooking and the like. Thus with reading there are a variety of ways this can be simplified. Some patients can be encouraged to re-read their favourite children's stories as a way of getting back into reading. Julia, described earlier in this chapter, worked as a primary school teacher and enjoyed children's stories. She began by reading one of her favourites and found the easy sentence structure, short chapters and large print useful simply as a means to re-engaging in the act of reading and gradually stretching her concentration. Other methods for simplifying reading might be starting with a newspaper or magazine, perhaps one that has glossy pictures or short stories. Poetry is also a useful beginning to returning to reading provided it is reasonably short and not too complex or serious. Similarly with television, watching a cartoon or a short programme of 30 minutes and then turning it off may be a way of starting to interact actively with television programmes, as opposed to doing what a lot of depressed people do which is have the television on continuously but register very little of what they are watching. Re-engaging with regular food preparation and eating is also a useful activity to grade as well as contributing by giving the patient the benefits of improved diet, which will impact significantly on energy and concentration levels. This may start off with very simple meals such as a bowl of cereal or a sandwich and progress to snacks such as beans on toast. Such activity lends itself well to planning and to helping the person establish a normal daily routine.

Working with NATs and rules for living in acute depression

In Chapter 6, we discuss the core features of NATs and their role in the maintenance of mental health problems. This chapter also outlines the basic principles involved in identifying and modifying automatic thoughts and the role of behavioural experiments in testing out the validity of such perceptions. All the information and clinical skills outlined in this chapter are relevant to beginning the process of identifying and modifying depressive NATs. Therefore in this section of the chapter the focus will be on the special features of thinking in depression that need to be taken into consideration when working with the depressed patient. These are as follows:

- memory biases in depression and their implications for working with the depressed patient
- working with hopeless and suicidal thinking.

Identifying and modifying automatic thoughts

As outlined in Chapter 3, thinking can be considered to have two aspects, content (*what we think*) and process (*how we think*).

WHAT WE THINK: CONTENT OF THINKING IN DEPRESSION

Research shows that when people are depressed their thinking is more negative in terms of content (for a review of this aspect of cognitive psychology, see Chapter 6 in Williams et al., 1997). When working with depression the content aspects of cognition that require attention are those identified in the model described at the beginning of this chapter. That is to say, when assessing and working with a depressed patient the following themes should be targeted in terms of content:

- actual and perceived loss
- negative cognitive triad
- hopelessness
- helplessness.

   Thoughts that fall into these content-based themes can be tackled using the strategies described in Chapter 6.

HOW WE THINK: PROCESS OF THINKING IN DEPRESSION

In considering how information is processed when an individual is depressed, there is a range of research evidence on which to draw. These can be summarized as follows. Depressed individuals in comparison to control subjects demonstrate:

- Difficulty in remembering and recalling information.
- More readily access negative memories, in comparison to neutral or positive memories.
- More over-general memories (they can't recall specifics) and problem-solving deficits.
- A tendency toward a 'black and white' (miss out the shades of grey) position in terms of how information is processed.
- A tendency to ruminate (go over and over in the mind particular themes).

   While this seemingly complex cognitive science may seem to have little relevance to treating depression, there are a number of practical consequences that result from these mood-related memory biases, which have to be taken into consideration when using CBT to treat acute depression.

DIFFICULTY REMEMBERING AND RECALLING INFORMATION

Basically this means that when the depressed individual is presented with new information the brain has difficulty taking it on board and storing it in memory. Further, once stored the individual has difficulty accessing it and retrieving it from memory in order to use it. This memory bias has huge implications for how the clinician presents information to the patient. Information needs to be simple, succinct and concrete and there needs to be opportunity for repetition. The following can aid this process:

- straightforward and simple language
- shorter (maximum 30 minutes) CBT sessions given more frequently (twice weekly) from the first 3 weeks of treatment
- illustrations of points using examples from the patient's own recent experience, described using the patient's own language
- the use of short handouts (maximum two pages), using simple, straightforward language and which the clinician has talked through in detail with the patient
- written summaries of learning from each session
- written summary of agreed homework assignments
- use of audiotape of session for patient to review at home.

MORE READILY RECALL NEGATIVE MEMORIES

An aspect of depression that clinicians often find frustrating is the patient's unending capacity to always focus on the negative. How many times have you sat with a depressed patient as they cite a catalogue of negative events? You spend a good deal of time trying to shift their perspective and at the end of the session several positive events emerge seemingly out of the blue. It is not uncommon for clinicians to attribute this frequently observed phenomenon to personality traits and inherent pessimism and become frustrated with the patient and give up trying to help. This perspective can discourage both patient and clinician. A more helpful perspective for the clinician to take is that of 'this is how the depressed mind works and part of my role in treatment is to help the patient to become aware of this and actively help the patient to counter this'.

Several aspects of CBT are specifically geared toward helping patient and clinician strive toward a balanced perspective. These include:

- Use of an activity schedule to record activities and using this as a basis for reviewing the events of the week in the early part of treatment.
- Actively recording activities that go well and summarizing their impact.
- Educating the patient that this tendency to recall the negative more readily is a symptom of depression the result of which is that it may seem everything is bleak and pessimistic because when mood is depressed then memory gives preferential attention to negative memories over positive memories.
- Teaching the patient to recognize this process when it is present.

RECALL OF MORE OVER-GENERAL MEMORIES AND PROBLEM-SOLVING DEFICITS

Using problem solving with a depressed patient can be painstaking. As you work through each step of problem solving asking, 'what is the problem?', 'What are your options in solving it' etc. the patient frequently says, 'I don't know' or stares at you blankly, unsure how to answer. This is often a good point for the clinician to be mindful of his or own feelings and NATs, which frequently revolve around feelings of frustration and demoralization, with NATs such as 'he is doing this on purpose' or 'I'm useless at this'. However there is a good reason why the patient finds problem solving difficult, which is that depressed people report more over-general as opposed to categorical memories and being able to problem solve effectively is based on being able to access categorical memories. So what is the difference between categorical and over-general memories? A categorical memory is one that exists in time, place and person and extends over time, e.g. 'on holiday for a week last year in Vienna in Austria with my sister and friend Jane'. In contrast an over-general memory consists of a shorthand summary, for example 'on holiday'. When a depressed individual is given a cue word such as 'happy' and asked to recall a relevant memory they are much more likely to retrieve an over-general memory than a categorical one. It is easy to see from this example that if the ability to solve problems is based on being able to retrieve categorical memories then this explains why problem solving is difficult for them. More importantly, the patient's lack of response to the clinician's attempts to use problem solving may not entirely be accounted for by a lack of intelligence or a pessimistic personality or plain stubbornness, but by over-general memory which is a symptom of depression.

A further factor that needs to be taken into consideration in terms of problem-solving deficits in depression is that in comparison to non-depressed controls, depressed individuals tend to underestimate the effectiveness of their problem-solving skills. Thus there is a good chance, even if a potential solution to a problem is generated during a session the patient may not carry it out because they may experience NATs such as 'it won't work' 'I'm not capable of doing it' and the like. So it is important to give consideration to over-general memory and poor problem solving as a symptom of depression and how this impacts on treatment. The following guidance may be of benefit:

- Educate the patient that this over-general recall is a symptom of depression in order to minimize the impact of self-deprecating thoughts.
- Do not abandon problem solving if it is a useful tool but use it in a way that takes into consideration the presence of over-general recall. In the initial stages of using problem solving the clinician my need to be more proactive and take a lead on behalf of the patient.
- Proactively identify negative automatic thoughts that have potential to interfere with using problem solving and teach the patient to tackle these.

TENDENCY TOWARD AN ALL OR NOTHING POSITION WHEN PROCESSING INFORMATION

The tendency to think in black and white terms is described in Beck's original cognitive behavioural model for acute depression (Beck et al., 1979). Recent research has shown the tendency toward processing information in a black and white or all or nothing way as being predictive of both poor outcome and relapse in depression (Teasdale et al., 2002). In this respect, this processing bias needs actively addressing as part of treatment. Research examining how cognitive therapy achieves its effects supports the idea that rather than modifying content per se it also impacts on how information is processed, breaking down global, black and white information processing biases and helping the patient to see thoughts as thoughts rather than facts. In this respect, several standard CBT interventions may be helpful in promoting more flexible, less black and white information processing because the patient is asked to consider problems in concrete and specific terms. Certain rules for living are also important to consider in relation to black and white processing. For example, the behavioural consequences of the following such rules are likely to be pro-crastination and inactivity driven by the individual taking an all or nothing approach to a task: 'if I can't do something properly there is no point in doing it at all' or 'if I can't complete a task there is no point in starting it'. In this respect, behavioural experiments directly targeting this black and white perspective would be important in minimizing the impact of the rule on day-to-day functioning and thus begin the process of modifying it. One very useful intervention within the depression treatment protocol is graded task assignment, which involves taking a stepwise approach to task completion which actively counters the all or nothing perspective that typifies depressive thinking processes.

RUMINATION

Rumination is a common thinking process in depression. Rumination has been shown to be associated with the both the severity and persistence of low mood (Nolen-Hoeksema et al., 1993; Nolen-Hoeksema et al., 1994). Rumination is typically self-critical and self-blaming in focus and most commonly in depression focuses on previous upsetting memories and events. One of the overall aims when using CBT to treat depression is to disrupt ruminative processing cycles. This work currently represents the cutting edge of treatment interventions in depression with much of the work being focused on mindfulness (Segal et al., 2002) and attentional training (Wells, 2000). There is increasing evidence for the role of these interventions in the treatment of chronic depression, which is beyond the scope of this current text. Mindfulness-based interventions have been specifically devised as relapse prevention strategies for individuals who have recovered from an acute depressive episode, but who are experiencing residual depressive symptoms. However, mindfulness training is not currently part of the treatment protocol for acute depression. Attention is being turned toward how the findings from the mindfulness research can be integrated into Beck's original treatment protocol for acute depression. This represents an exciting development in the field of depression, which hopefully will continue to develop into more robust CBT protocols for the treatment of acute depression.

Tackling hopelessness and suicidality in depression

There is an assumption in acute depression that hopelessness and suicidality are a transient phenomenon and that the intensive use of CBT interventions can lead to a rapid reduction in level of hopelessness and suicidality. The following section takes an overview of some of the standard CBT interventions that can be used to target hopelessness and suicidality in an individual who presents with acute depression. It is important to distinguish between patients with acute depression who are hopeless and suicidal and those who may engage in repeated acts of self-harm in the context of more complex, comorbid presentations. For this last group of patients, while some of the interventions described now may be of benefit, such individuals are likely to require a different approach to the management of their difficulties. There are CBT treatment packages specifically designed with this patient group in mind. Interested readers are directed to the following texts: Beck et al., 2004; Linehan et al., 1991; Young, 1994.

As stated previously, level of hopelessness rather than severity of depression is predictive of suicidal intent in depression (Beck et al., 1985c). Therefore identifying and modifying hopelessness is a key CBT skill. As outlined in the introduction to this chapter the theme of hopelessness is one of the aspects of the negative cognitive triad (Beck et al., 1979), namely, negative view of future. Thus, the content of hopelessness-based negative automatic thoughts is a perception that the future is bleak and will remain so for the foreseeable future. The memory and processing biases described earlier also play a role in maintaining the hopeless perspective in particular rumination and the global, all or nothing perspective. With regard to the research evidence, poor problem solving has been shown to be positively correlated in individuals who engage in repeated acts of parasuicide. Equipping these patients with problem-solving skills significantly reduced their level of hopelessness and depression and reduced the number of repeated suicide attempts (Salkovskis et al., 1990).

Key CBT interventions for targeting hopelessness and suicidality are:

- assessment and measuring suicidal intent
- problem solving
- activity scheduling and graded task assignment that is used with a slightly different rationale to that described in that activity is scheduled for every hour of the day in order to provide structure and focus
- identifying and modifying hopeless and suicidal NATs
- identifying the key emotions in suicidality of anger and guilt and blame-related NATs (self-blame 'it's my fault, 'I'm a burden to my family' and blame of others 'that bastard left me, I'll show him')
- identifying and modifying assumptions regarding methods of suicide (e.g. 'an overdose will be painless I will just go to sleep')
- advantages and disadvantages of suicide
- examining the perceived consequences of suicide.

There are a number of texts that outline these interventions in detail including Beck et al., 1979; Hawton et al., 1989.

Further reading |

Cognitive Therapy of Depression by Beck et al. (1979) is the original work on this subject and is still worth reading. A recent description of the standard CBT protocol is *Cognitive Behavioural Treatment of Depression* by Klosko and Sanderson (1999). *Cognitive Therapy for Chronic and Persistent Depression* by Moore and Garland (2003) addresses the complexities of chronic depression. Two excellent self-help books that patients and clinicians can both use are *Overcoming Depression* by Gilbert (2000b) and (a different book!) *Overcoming Depression: A Five Areas Approach* by Williams (2001).

Chapter summary |

The CBT model for acute depression is formulated around the theme of perceived loss and the negative cognitive triad in which there is a negative view of self, world and future. The CBT protocol for acute depression begins with activity scheduling and graded task assignment with the goals of tackling procrastination, avoidance, tiredness and lethargy. The overall aim is to re-establish a daily routine and re-engage the depressed patient in activities they are putting off or avoiding. It is important to be aware of the potential difficulties in using this intervention. The next stage of treatment is to modify negative thinking, primarily by the use of standard CBT interventions, which include identifying and modifying NATs and rules for living using verbal methods such as thought diaries and experiential methods such as behavioural experiments. Both the content and the process of thinking should be considered as part of the formulation and treatment of acute depression. The application of standard CBT interventions when working with hopelessness and suicide is also briefly described.

Other CBT models and approaches

INTRODUCTION

In this book, the CBT model associated with Beck has been described. It is important to be aware that there are alternative models of CBT, and the most important of these are (arguably) behavioural therapy, rational emotive behavioural therapy and, more recently, acceptance and commitment therapy and dialectic behavioural therapy. In this chapter, these approaches, particularly behavioural therapy, for which there is a very strong evidence base, will be described. In doing this, it will be considered how these approaches compare to the Beck model.

BEHAVIOURAL THERAPY

History of behavioural interventions within CBT

Without going in to the history of psychotherapy it is important to say that current CBT is heavily dependent on ideas from behavioural therapy. Behavioural therapy developed in the 1960s and was based on emerging ideas in learning theory. There are important ideas in learning theory including classical conditioning, operant conditioning, habituation, preparedness and modelling, which it is useful to try and understand.

The first concept is *classical conditioning* associated with Pavlov (1927). He showed that if a stimulus produces a response, it can be paired with another stimulus and the second stimulus will produce the same response. In the classic experiment, the stimulus of food produced salivation in the dogs and, when the food was paired with a bell, the bell alone produced salivation. This is important in that it led to researchers considering that phobias were a part product of an experience in which the person responds to the phobic object with fear and that this fear in the future will not just be provoked by the phobic object but by anything associated with it.

The next idea is *operant conditioning*. The essence of this is that a response is altered as a result of its consequences. Essentially, the consequence of reward will increase the behaviour and that of punishment reduce it. If an animal (and most of the laws of learning theory were worked out with animals) is rewarded with food every time it does a task, it is likely to repeat the task. This may happen with a human, but because of their cognitive abilities they are more likely to question the necessity of continuing the behaviour or the desirability of the reward. It is held in behaviour therapy that because escaping from a phobic situation is rewarding in terms of the massive reduction in anxiety, then the escape is held to be highly rewarding and therefore will be repeated next time the person faces the situation. One can also use this idea in clinical practice by rewarding the patients with praise or asking them to arrange a reward for themselves, if they complete a therapy task.

Another key concept is *habituation*: this means simply that repeated exposure to a stimulus will reduce the response. If a car alarm goes off our response is to attend to it and listen carefully to decide if it is our car. However, we habituate to it as the exposure continues and eventually our response is much reduced in that we hardly hear it. This was a crucial concept in the development of treatments for anxiety disorders like panic, agoraphobia and OCD. It was discovered that repeated exposure to the feared stimulus, the phobic object, would lead to a habituation of the anxiety response. It is an interesting question as to how this process of habituation interacts with cognitive processes in humans.

Another important idea is *preparedness* and this means that, because of our evolutionary history we are 'prepared' to be more fearful of some things rather than others. These things are spiders and snakes, being alone or with strangers, being out in the open or enclosed, heights and the sight of blood (Richards and McDonald, 1990). If one considers how people lived thousands of years ago, one can see why a wariness of these situations could enhance survival.

The next key idea is *modelling*, again from observations of how animals learn. This means that the individual models his response on that of another. The therapist can model the desired behaviour in a way that shows a good coping response.

There is extensive discussion of these topics in the book *Phobias* (Davey, 1999). Behavioural treatment of anxiety disorders makes use of these concepts. For example, a therapist may *model* an *exposure* to a spider which the patient has been *prepared* to be phobic of, but which they have actually become phobic of because of *conditioning* process. *Exposure* is encouraged until *habituation* occurs. It should be remembered that there is a good evidence base for this approach: 70–85 per cent of specific phobics are effectively treated by exposure, there is 'substantial effect sizes for agoraphobic symptoms and somewhat smaller but still large effect sizes for panic', in OCD, exposure and response prevention brings about a '30–50 per cent improvement in 75 per cent of patients' (Roth and Fonagy, 1996).

Problematic behaviours

It is proposed at this point to look at a number of problematic behavioural patterns that occur in anxiety and depressive disorders and describe an approach to them that is based more on the behavioural therapy approach. The behavioural approach is to encourage behavioural change and to argue that this is enough in itself to bring about change in problems like anxiety, depression, poor sleep and so on. A format will be followed of describing the unhelpful pattern in detail, discussing why the abnormal behaviour occurs within the context of behaviour theories and consider how the patient can be helped to change the behaviour.

In general when we are helping patients change behaviours it is suggested that this process is gone through: an understanding is developed of why this behaviour was prob-lematic and this can be drawn from the formulation and from the theory. The patient would be helped to consider that their behaviours are unhelpful because they are leading to a disturbed emotion, they are stopping them eliciting the desired response from the physical or interpersonal environment and finally they are blocking them acting in a way that is consistent with their values, standards and goals. Obviously it is important for the patient to relate to this formulation. Again linking to the assessment and formulation we would prioritize which behaviours should be changed. This should be drawn out from the patient and a hierarchy can be made.

Behavioural change statement

A typical statement that can then be made to the patient would be: 'When we are working on behavioural change it is important that you are clear in your mind why we are agreeing that you make this change. In this case, we agreed that when you panic you immediately rush out of the crowd and go home and you identified in our discussion, that it stopped you facing and getting used to your fear. It also stopped you achieving your personal goal of going shopping with your husband' (behavioural emphasis).

'When we talk about behavioural change I realize that it can be difficult to do it all at once. We often use the term "difficult but do-able" in trying to decide what change you should make. Also when we write down the behavioural change it is useful to put it in the first person, to specify when, where, and how, you will make the change, and particularly to discuss the potential problems that you may have in making the change. I realize that it is easier writing something down here than it is to do it in practice.'

SPECIFIC PROBLEMATIC BEHAVIOURS

Avoidance

Avoidance is something that is typically seen in patients with anxiety disorders. People will avoid things they have associated with anxiety, so patients with specific phobias will avoid the phobic object (the spider, the needle), and possibly things associated with it (dusty dark garages, hospitals). Patients with panic disorder who repeatedly panic in certain places such as the supermarket or in a crowd will avoid those places. Some patients with panic do not make an association with a pattern of triggers; this is likely to be because they purely panic in response to internal irregular events like an anxious thought, a missed heartbeat or a small change in their breathing pattern. The patients who avoid external situations are likely to associate their panic with specific situations that trigger these internal bodily sensations, (this would be the cognitive rationale). The more they avoid, the more it becomes a habitual behaviour to deal with their fears, it is reinforced and therefore likely to be repeated, and avoidance stops the process of habituation.

In terms of dealing with avoidance, the evidence would suggest (Richards and McDonald, 1990) that when facing up to a situation (in behavioural theory called 'exposure'), the following rules apply.

Exposure should be *graded*. The patient should have a hierarchy or should follow the idea of 'difficult but do-able'. It is possible to get the patient to face his fear completely at once (flooding) and if he can do this then the outcome can be just as good. Most patients won't want to do this.

Ways that exposure can be graded are as follows. In social phobia, consider whom the person feels most comfortable with e.g. males/females, older people/younger people, friends/strangers. Consider what would be easiest for the person to do e.g. smile, ask a question, pay a compliment, reveal something about themselves etc. Consider the environment where the patient would be most comfortable e.g. at home, in the pub, with a few or many people. In specific phobias of insects, bees/wasps, thunder/lightning, flying, vomiting, needles (these are ones that are typically seen in the clinic) one could move along a hierarchy that might involve for some people; listening to the therapist saying the phobic word, saying it themselves, listening to its sound at different volumes (if applicable), looking at pictures of it from different distances, watching a video of it from different distances with the sound off or on, experiencing a mild form of the phobic object when accompanied/ unaccompanied, experiencing a more severe form of the phobic object right up to repeated exposure to the ultimate fear (e.g. 'having a spider in my hair'). In symptom induction exercises in panic disorder, for example, with a patient who is fearful of being breathless and stopping breathing, one could get him to imagine being breathless, to say phrases like 'stop breathing', to visualize being very breathless, to actually do a hyperventilation exercise or to take vigorous exercise to be breathless. Obviously here one would draw out from the patient where they would place each of these on the hierarchy. In patients with agoraphobia who are situational avoidant, one could start off with them going outside their house accompanied, then unaccompanied, then going further afield, going into a slightly crowded situation, more crowded situations, busy situations. Again one would create a hierarchy with such a patient.

Regular. By this it is meant that the patient practises the exposure regularly and this is likely to mean once a day. The patient should persist with the exposure until they are regularly able to face the phobic object with little anxiety. It is probably better for the patient to work every day to expose themselves to one thing rather than irregularly facing up to a number of things, mainly because their success will boost their confidence.

Prolonged. This is particularly important because many patients will tell you that they have faced up to their fears, but on questioning they did not stay there long enough for their anxiety to diminish.

If one is measuring the patient's anxiety in the situation then it is probably wise to wait until it reduces to 2–4 on a scale of 0–8, and that the patient then remains in that situation for a while longer, in order to get the full benefit of habituation.

Focused. Here we mean that the patient should actually be fully attending to the situation that he is facing. He may be averting his eyes, daydreaming, visualizing that he is elsewhere. One should explain to the patient that these behaviours are unhelpful in that they block habituation and one can try to grade them out.

When a patient has been avoidant, especially for a long time, he will be particularly fearful about facing situations, worrying that the anxiety will be overwhelming or be convinced that his worst fear will come true. Other patients, for whom the problem does not have a big impact on their lives, are reluctant to face it because the reward of overcoming it is not worth the potential distress. Possible strategies to use here are:

- motivational ones, such as looking at the advantages and disadvantages of overcoming the problem
- helping the patient see that the exposure gets easier the more they do it
- helping them realize that they are significantly exaggerating the dangerousness of the situation (although no one can guarantee that it will not happen)
- helping them see that they may be significantly exaggerating how bad their feared outcome would be if it actually happened
- discussing with them whether they are downplaying their ability to cope with potentially difficult situations.

Escape

Escape, in this context, means rushing out of a triggering situation in response to intense anxiety: the person will usually rush to somewhere that seems safe and where the phobic stimulus does not seem present. In terms of learning theory, the person is rewarded by the reduction in anxiety that occurs and is therefore much more likely to repeat the behaviour in the future.

A common problem patients make is to go into a situation briefly, but to leave again before any learning occurs. Again, when addressing escape behaviours it is important to urge the patient to stay in the situation until new learning happens and the patient's anxiety significantly diminishes. Often the phrase 'stand your ground' is an important one for the patient. A problem with helping the patient to do this is that one can write down a specific behavioural change such as 'when I am in a crowd in the supermarket I will stay there, even if I feel panicky'. However, the patient may forget this at the time, so it is important that he is aware in what situation he needs to be able to make this behavioural change, he is prepared to do it and it is at the forefront of his mind. If the patient is unable to stop escaping from situations then the best thing to do would be to grade the behavioural change downwards. However, it is not a good idea to do this so that he spends less time in the situation; for example suggesting that he only spends 2 minutes in the situation, rather than 10 minutes. Again, the danger is that it is not long enough for habituation to occur. It would be better to grade it towards a generally less anxiety inducing situation, for example: 'I will go into the supermarket in the early morning when there is no one around and I will stay there even if I feel panicky.' Exposure as an approach is particularly well suited to the treatment of phobias (see Chapter 3).

Safety behaviours/rituals

Safety behaviours are defined (Salkovskis, 1991) as behaviours that the person suffering from an anxiety disorder will engage in to protect them against danger. Cognitive theory would suggest that these behaviours are unhelpful because they maintain preoccupation with threat and prevent disconfirmation of negative thoughts. A behavioural rationale would say that they block the full arousal and habituation process. For example, a patient with social phobia always gripped his drink glass very tightly. His cognitions are: 'If I don't hold this glass tightly then my hands will start shaking and I'll spill my drink. People will think I'm clumsy.' He was preventing himself learning that he was unlikely to spill his drink or, even if he did, then this was not a terrible situation and people would not necessarily think of him as clumsy. The behaviour also kept him preoccupied with threat simply because of the mental and physical effort required gripping the glass so. There are lists of safety behaviours in Chapter 4. It is important to have a full list of safety behaviours from the assessment process: failure to make progress in the treatment of anxiety disorders can often be because the therapist and patient are not aware of all the safety behaviours. When tackling this one should go about it in a graded way, starting at the easiest behaviour to eliminate and again tackling this behaviour could also be done in a graded way, for example: 'I will grip the glass slightly less tightly.'

In considering rituals, and these occur primarily in OCD, then the mechanism is likely to be the same as safety behaviours. In cognitive theory they prevent disconfirmation of, and keep the focus on, the threat, in behavioural theory they prevent habituation. Rituals usually take the form of checking or cleaning, are viewed as senseless by the patient ('ego-dystonic'), and are usually resisted to some degree. Typical checking rituals would be checking the door is locked many times before leaving, checking the oven/taps/heating are off many times before leaving or going to bed, driving back over one's route to ensure that one has not caused an accident, over-checking the correct dose of a medicine or the correct address on an envelope and so on. Typical cleaning rituals would be washing one's hands or body abnormally (duration, amount of soap, degree or force of scrubbing, doing it in a fixed pattern etc.). In some patients with OCD there can be very many rituals and they can be engaged in for very long periods.

Some of the rituals in OCD can be hard to make sense of, for example counting in a strange way such as saying all the even numbers from one to 10 before doing an action. This type of ritual is best viewed as a being like a superstitious thought ('don't walk under ladders') that many of us may have and we realize they do not have any common sense meaning. Sometimes, if it is difficult to make sense of why the patient is engaging in a particular ritual, it is because they have been doing it for so long that they have forgotten what danger they are trying to ward off. Another explanation is that the danger the person is warding off is so disturbing that they are unable to contemplate it.

The principle of working with rituals is the same as for any other safety behaviour. They are identified and behaviourally the person is helped to eliminate them in a gradual way, and sometimes a course of treatment for OCD can feel like systematically working to eliminate a large amount of rituals. This can be technically difficult if the person's feared consequence is in the distant future ('I'll get cancer') or unable to be tested ('I'll go to hell'). Further advice on the treatment of OCD can be found in Chapter 8.

The main problems in dealing with safety behaviours are, first, identifying them all, second, the patient's reluctance to give them up because of a fear of increased anxiety and, third, although the patient gives them up there is no significant improvement. Regarding the first point this is best addressed by completing a thorough assessment. If one suspects there are more safety behaviours one can say 'are there any safety behaviours/rituals that we haven't talked about?', 'do you do anything else in that situation to keep yourself safe/reduce your anxiety that we don't know about?', 'are there any other actions you do similar to the counting and checking?' One could ask the patient to do an exercise at home keeping a record of any extra behaviours that have not been addressed. One could ask the person's next of kin if they have noticed any rituals/safety behaviours that have not been identified. If one was stuck one could spend a half-day going with the patient into challenging situations, and observing what he does. If the patient is reluctant to give up the safety behaviour because of their concerns about increased anxiety then one should explore this. Often the person feels they will be 'out of control' and by that they usually mean that they will appear anxious in front of others and this will be embarrassing and humiliating. Also the patient may need reminding that the anxiety will come to an end and that the more frequently the person makes the behavioural change then the easier it will get.

If the patient seems to have dropped all safety behaviours and still is not much better then it is important to probe for subtle avoidances or substitute safety behaviours or types of mental reassurance.

Reassurance

Reassurance in itself is not a problem and it is something that we all engage in. It can be a problem in the anxiety disorders particularly obsessive compulsive disorder, panic disorder, phobias, hypochondriasis and generalized anxiety disorder. What is meant by reassurance is when a patient seeks information from other people that his particular feared outcome will not occur. The patient may say 'will I be all right?' or 'is it safe?' The answer is usually given by the reassuring person in a definitive way such as 'of course a panic attack won't kill you', 'spiders are completely safe – you'll be all right' or 'there's no possibility that you can be contaminated by that'. Sometimes reassurance can be sought in a very subtle way such as just looking at another person who gives the patient a nod to reassure them or just even a smile or a touch.

This is problematic in that it does not allow for the little bit of uncertainty and reinforces an attitude that one can be 100 per cent certain. It is also problematic because it allows the patient to deflect the problem and, to an extent, a negative outcome on to the reassuring person. This acts as a transfer of responsibility. Also the person gets a great reduction in anxiety, which in learning theory terms can be a negative reinforcer and therefore likely to be repeated and become a dysfunctional strategy. Again in learning theory terms it blocks habituation.

It is probably acceptable for a person or therapist to reassure the patient once in a reasonable way that expresses the reality of the situation. The success of this would be to judge whether the patient accepts the reassurance and is satisfied. Repeated requests for reassurance have to be viewed as a clinical problem and addressed. Usually, one would want the person to reduce this behaviour to test out what happens. One would ask the patient to become aware when they are seeking reassurance and stop this and continue to stop it. If they were unable to stop seeking reassurance and this is quite common because there is a strong compulsion to do so, then it is important to speak to the people who reassure him and give them a statement to say when this occurs. This would typically be 'the therapy does not allow me to reassure you' or 'it's not helpful for me to reassure you' and this should be said in a calm and caring way. It can sometimes be the case that the reassuring people are exasperated by the demands of the patient and get angry. One needs to help them not to deal with reassurance seeking in an angry manner. If the sufferer persists then the other person should walk away from the situation. One can also deal with this issue at the same time as discussing how the patient's relative could be a co-therapist. This is important in that although the patient has their reassurance stopped, the relative is helping them in a constructive way.

The main difficulty when trying to implement this behavioural change, which is usually done at an early stage of treatment, is that the patient may not be aware that he is seeking reassurance because it is such a habitual practice. Again it is important that all instances of reassurance seeking are identified at the original assessment. If it is felt that some have been missed, then additional questions may be 'are there any other ways that you seek reassurance that we haven't talked about?', 'what do other people do for you when you're feeling anxious?' and 'what do you say to people when you're panicky/anxious?' Again the reassuring person can be asked for further examples, and the therapist can be alert to examples in the session.

If the patient becomes much more aware of this behaviour, but has difficulty stopping it, one could try and grade it and phase it out, although this could be difficult. For example, the patient could agree to only seek reassurance once a day or only seek it once but not repeatedly. It may be helpful to do a role play with the patient and relative around stopping this behaviour.

Unassertiveness/people pleasing

It would be the authors' opinion that the issue of assertiveness is not adequately emphasized in the CBT literature. Many of our patients are unassertive and being so can cause them great problems. Assertiveness is generally associated with anxiety, but may be associated with depression if the person constantly berates herself for not expressing her wishes. Assertiveness would be understood from a cognitive perspective as rising from unhelpful thoughts and beliefs and, in behavioural terms, as a failure to learn. A definition of assertiveness would be a willingness to stand up for oneself in situations of actual or potential conflict (Neenan and Dryden, 2002). To understand this problem from a CBT point of view, it is important to understand typical triggering situations, typically dysfunctional beliefs and rules and how they then lead to unhealthy beliefs and behaviours. Typical triggering situations are often conflicts and disagreements; these may be at work or in the home and may be worse with people who are viewed to be stronger, more threatening, more successful or in a position of authority. These people may be spouses and partners, bosses or colleagues at work and people managing shops and services.

Potentially unhelpful beliefs that unassertive people may have are (Hauck, 1981):

- *Fear of violence.* 'If I stand up for myself, I could be attacked.'
- *Fear of failure.* 'If I get what I want here and it goes wrong it would be awful.'
- *Fear of hurting others.* 'If I tell her what I think she'll be devastated and not get over it.'

- *Fear of rejection.* 'If I stand up for myself then the person would reject or dislike me. I couldn't cope with that.'

Gilbert (2000a) identifies:

- *Fear of counterattack.* 'If I criticize him, he'll retaliate, I'll be tongue-tied and I'll blush. I'll be worst off.'
- *Fear of loss of control.* 'If I'm assertive I could get carried away and become abusive or aggressive.'
- *Fear of losing a sense of yourself as a 'nice person'.* 'Demanding your rights isn't a nice thing to do.'

When assessing the individual, if one gets the sense that they may be unassertive then it is a good idea to ask them directly if they are – they will usually know! One can then probe for these beliefs. Of course, one does not automatically assume that these beliefs are dysfunctional. Particular care should be taken with beliefs about physical violence. It is quite possible that being more assertive in an abusive marriage could lead the woman to suffer (more) violence. The advantages and disadvantages of being more assertive in this instance would have to be carefully considered.

People pleasing is related to unassertiveness. Typical beliefs here would be 'other people come first' and 'my needs are unimportant'.

The typical emotional states that come from lack of assertiveness are anxiety, if the person has to be assertive, depression and frustration if they are unable to be assertive, and, at a physical level, tiredness from doing too many tasks. There is, unfortunately, a tendency for others close to the unassertive or people-pleasing individual to give them, deliberately or not, extra tasks, jobs or responsibilities. This may because they believe they can get away with it without the person complaining or they do not realize the person objects because they do not say.

The behavioural aspect of unassertiveness will include the following:

- not stating one's opinion
- keeping quiet
- meekly agreeing
- avoiding the person or situation
- procrastinating over being assertive
- complaining to oneself or to other people, the latter in the hope that the message will get through
- sulking: this is an attempt to give the person a message, by withdrawing and looking hurt, that they are unhappy with the outcome of the interaction
- being passive.

With people pleasing one can add:

- doing lots of things for others
- volunteering to help, to give lifts, to do household tasks
- agreeing to every request
- taking inadequate rest and time for oneself.

Again, these behaviours are not absolutely wrong, but are likely to lead to problems if taken to excess. They may be associated with strong religious beliefs that emphasize self-sacrifice.

It is important to differentiate at a behavioural level between behaviours that are passive as just described, assertive and aggressive. Often the unassertive person flits between passivity and aggression. This can happen because he gets so frustrated with his own unassertiveness, he becomes angry, usually with himself. Angry behaviour may include shouting, not listening, demanding his 'rights' and so on. If the person wishes to become assertive then the first stage will be developing a mini-formulation using the information collected. One must then evaluate the person's readiness and willingness to work on the problem. One should also correct misconceptions about assertiveness. These would include:

- Being assertive means you always get what you want. The key element in assertiveness is asking for what you want, but accepting that the other person does not have to give you it. The person should be willing to debate what the solution to the disagreement may be, but accept that people may have competing interests. Robb (1992) describes an 'assertive-backlash' in that if the person is too assertive then they may find themselves fired, divorced or friendless. This is probably not going to happen to most patients, as their problem will be not being assertive enough.
- That if you are assertive then you need to be assertive all of the time. An important part of the skill is to decide when to use it. Alternative strategies may be to judge the importance of the conflict, to ask for time to think, to get further information and so on.

If the person has a realistic perspective on assertiveness and wishes to work with the problem then one would use standard CBT strategies. One would use methods such as diary keeping to test out negative thoughts and assumptions as already described.

The key element of this will be repeated behavioural change. Behavioural experiments and changes will have to occur frequently and over a long period. A typical strategy would be developing a list of triggering situations. One should work with the person to start challenging and changing beliefs. One can then set about gradually altering whatever unhelpful avoidance, people pleasing and unassertive behaviours the person has and sub-stituting more helpful ones.

The specific steps in doing this would be (Dryden, 1992):

- Get the person's attention.
- Describe objectively what aspect of the other person's behaviour is a problem. It is better to stick to specific issues and not generalize or put the other person down because of his problematic actions.
- Express your feelings in a constructive way using the first person. A typical statement could be 'I am annoyed and upset that you did not pick me up from the station.'
- Invite a response from the other person and consider it fairly. Either accept their explanation or dispute it further.
- State your preferences clearly and specifically, 'Would you please pick me up from the station next Friday at 8 o'clock?' You may state why you feel your request is a fair one.

- Communicate any information about future episodes ('if you forget to pick me up again, I will have to take the car myself') and invite a response.

Specific constructive behavioural changes may be stopping automatically agreeing, stopping sulking, stopping avoiding the person, reducing procrastination and so. With assertiveness work a particularly good strategy is role play and this can be made good fun. The therapist can play a particularly difficult person and the patient should practise being assertive with them. Afterwards the exercise should be discussed.

Problems with being more assertive and less people pleasing:

- The patient is just reluctant to be more assertive. This is likely to be because of the unhelpful beliefs outlined above and these can be very ingrained. It may require quite a lot of work to try to break them down. Often the patient is tempted to procrastinate on this. As usual there will be a way of grading it. One could get the person to develop a hierarchy of difficult situations or people. For example someone may not be able to be assertive with his boss but it may be possible with a colleague or a friend. The person may not be able to be assertive with his boss over pay but may manage it over a holiday issue.
- The other person's response may not be desirable. They may become annoyed, obstinate or even angry. Sometimes this will happen if they are used to the newly assertive person usually being quite timid. There is no magic solution to this apart from getting the person to think clearly and act constructively in the situation. Acting out the other person's response would be helpful. If the other person is persistently obstinate or angry in the face of assertiveness, then the patient has to consider whether this is an individual with whom they are only able to use assertiveness warily. It may be necessary for them to reconsider their relationship with the person, possibly breaking it off. In real world situations this may be very difficult or impossible. Sometimes it may be possible to get peer or even legal support in helping the person be more assertive.

In general, given that most people are reasonable, we would predict that the person standing up for themselves will get a considered response.

Poor problem solving

In the literature on problem solving a distinction is made between emotional change and coping which we have focused on in this book and problem-focused coping (Lazarus, 1999). By problem-focused coping we mean addressing difficult situations in order to change them. It may be particularly helpful to use problem solving in the following situations:

- The person is in a dilemma or is facing a difficult life choice.
- The person has a number of 'real life' problems or crises, which could include dealing with a physical illness, a financial crisis, having to move home or dealing with a deteriorating personal relationship.

Whether one should adopt a more standard CBT approach or use problem solving may depend on whether the person was thinking about the situation in a dysfunctional way. If they were generally not then a problem-solving approach may be helpful, indeed the crisis may be leading to so many disturbances that standard CBT is difficult to use.

There is evidence that this can be used effectively as a sole therapy with depression, and indeed helping cancer patients cope (D'Zurilla and Nezu, 2000). If it is used then there is a well-established protocol (Neenan and Dryden, 2002):

1   *Problem identification*. It is important here to define the problem in precise language e.g. 'I am likely to be made redundant in March which will lead to a 75 per cent reduction of my income.'

2   *Goal selection*. Again the person should express this clearly and in a way that is measurable.

3   *Generation of alternatives*. This step is to generate as many possible solutions as possible, even if they are highly unlikely (often called 'brainstorming'). Sometimes the therapist needs to prompt the person to get them started.

4   *Consideration of consequences*. The next stage is to consider the advantages and disadvantages of each alternative. If one wanted to elaborate then one could consider this in the short and long term and even the consequences for significant others.

5   *Decision making*. Here the person is asked to consider the alternatives that most likely will help them reach their goals. There may be one or more. This is probably the most difficult stage, as one can be faced with several possibilities that look equally attractive or more often unattractive. It may help to give a numerical value to each alternative on a scale of 1–10. This could measure 'usefulness' or 'desirableness'. It is probably necessary at this stage to have quite a prolonged discussion with the patient and he is likely to require time to think about it and discuss it with friends/family. It is important that one does not impose one's preferred solution onto the patient, although that can be tempting.

6   *Implementation*. If the person has made up his mind then the next stage is to put it into practice. Depending on the task, this may be difficult. As before, role play, grading and discussion of the consequences are the things to do.

7   *Evaluation*. Did implementing the solution achieve the goal or move towards the goal? If it did not it may be the person has implemented the solution inadequately or without persistence or he is lacking in the necessary skills to do so. It may also be that there are real life obstacles to achieving it. Depending on the cause of the failure one might work with further coaching in the skill required to help achieve the solution or the person may have to return to considering rejected alternatives. Some problems may just not have a solution. One can just try and help the person cope with a very distressing circumstance (Sharoff, 2002).

Exercise

Help a patient to do a problem-solving exercise particularly if the patient is in a dilemma. Evaluate the effectiveness of the intervention.

Poor sleep

We will look here at the issue of poor sleep in association with anxiety and depression. Insomnia affects one third of adults occasionally and 8–12 per cent on a chronic basis (Ford and Kamerow, 1989). People will typically complain of difficulty getting to sleep, waking frequently through the night, early morning waking and that their sleep is not refreshing. Depressed patients will commonly complain of insomnia, with difficulty falling asleep, frequent or prolonged waking through the night and early morning wakening.

Occasionally depressed people will complain of sleeping too much (Benca et al., 2000). Patients with anxiety disorders frequently have problems. Sleep studies into various categories of anxiety disorder suggest sleep disruption including difficulty getting to sleep, increased time awake, early morning wakening, decreased sleep efficiency and reduced total sleep (Benca et al., 2000).

It is still somewhat unclear exactly how much sleep people need. The average amount taken is 8 hours and this reduces with age. If total sleep deprivation occurs then hallucinations are possible, although there are no long-term consequences (Benca et al., 2000). Another important issue is that most psychoactive substances will affect sleep either because of the direct effect of the drug or because of withdrawal effects (Benca et al., 2000). Also poor sleep hygiene can be the cause of sleep problems. By that we mean daytime napping, coffee and alcohol before bedtime, excessive noise, light, distractions and so on.

How can sleep problems be helped? Hypnotic drugs are frequently used but longer acting ones can cause morning lethargy and sleepiness and shorter acting ones can cause rebound insomnia and daytime anxiety as part of a withdrawal syndrome. Psychological therapy is effective and a recent review indicated that 70–80 per cent of patients benefited (Espie, 2002).

CBT for sleep problems consists of some of the following elements;

- *Sleep education and hygiene.* Information about normal sleep is given and the removal of bad sleep hygiene practices is planned.
- *Stimulus control.* This idea is based on classical conditioning. It aims to ensure that the bed is purely associated with sleep and that other domestic areas are not associated with sleep. It is suggested that patients should get up if they are in bed awake for more than 20 minutes, should not do things like watch TV in bed, should not nap in the chair and so on.
- *Sleep restriction.* The purpose of this is to ensure optimal sleep that is defined as the ratio of time asleep to time in bed. A diary is kept to calculate how much a person actually sleeps and the person aims to get that core sleep by manipulating bed and rising time.
- *Cognitive control.* The person is asked to set aside 15 minutes to end the day and think through any unfinished business and plan for tomorrow. It is aimed at reducing worry.
- *Thought suppression.* The person is urged to sub-vocally articulate the word 'the' every 3 seconds. This is an attempt to block anxious thoughts.
- *Imagery and relaxation.*
- *Cognitive restructuring.* As described in earlier chapters, but focused on negative thoughts about sleep such as 'if I lose sleep I'll be completely unable to function'.
- *Paradoxical intention.* The person is asked to remain quietly wakeful. This is an attempt to block the patient trying too hard to get too sleep.

It has not been established which of these techniques has the most potency: a typical brief programme to help the person with sleep problems will be described here:

1   Assess the duration and quality of sleep by means of a diary. Evaluate any interference with sleep arising from medication and substances such as alcohol, caffeine, benzo-diazepines and SSRI antidepressants. Assess poor sleep hygiene. Evaluate dys-functional beliefs about sleep. Assess pain and emotional states that may interfere with sleep.

2   Address poor sleep hygiene. Is the patient's bedroom warm, comfortable, quiet and sleep friendly? Does the person they sleep with interfere with their sleep (different bedtimes, snoring)? Does the issue of sex help or hinder their sleep? They may need advice that they should wind down for sleep and that heavy meals, vigorous exercise and stimulating mental activity should be avoided.

3   Advise them that caffeine will keep them awake, alcohol will be likely get them asleep but may lead to waking in the middle of the night and that benzodiazepines may cause a rebound effect. Think about them altering the timing of these substances, stopping them or changing them. This may need to be discussed with their GP.

4   Frequently anxiety (often in the form of worry) and other emotions interfere with sleep. Hopefully, this will be reduced if the person is correctly using their CBT strategies. Some people may have some significant problems and dilemmas that are difficult to switch off from. Sometimes the best that can be done is to ask the person to give themselves a 15-minute worry period and then to switch off from their worries, possibly by using the sub-vocalizing technique just described. In conjunction with this the people could teach themselves a meditation or relaxation technique and there are many available. Alternatively, the person could be asked to do an activity that they would normally find relaxing and absorbing (the absorbing may be important to reduce cognitive 'noise').

5   If the person has unhelpful beliefs about sleep then they should be encouraged to challenge them. These may include 'if I don't get x hours of sleep I'll not be able to function' and 'I'm sleeping very badly' (when the evidence contradicts this). Excessive attempts to make themselves get to sleep should be challenged in the paradoxical way described earlier.

6   If none of this works then a behavioural programme can be tried: the rationale for the programme is explained in terms of creating an association between bed and being asleep and vice versa; the patient is asked to go to bed and get up at the same time each day to create an association with time; if the person wakes through the night and they cannot get to sleep again within 20 minutes (the time is negotiable), then they should get up and not return to bed again until they are sleepy. This should be repeated every time they are awake for 20 minutes. An upper limit of times may be put on it, from kindness; the effects should be evaluated through diary keeping.

Poor self-care, eating and exercise regimes

It may seem that these areas do not have direct bearing on the person's mental health and this may be so but they do have a clear bearing on their well-being and are areas that are often problematic for patients and advice is often sought from the clinician.

Poor self-care will occur in depression and sometimes when anxiety disorders are severe. In depression it is often a product of poor self-worth combined with tiredness. Like many other withdrawn type behaviours it can perpetuate the depression through negative thinking like 'I look a mess', 'I haven't put my makeup on for ages, I'm letting myself go', 'what will people think of me looking like this?' Poor self-care behaviours may include not washing, dressing, getting up, grooming, doing makeup etc. One can empathize how difficult it is to do this when one is depressed, but encourage the person to take small steps towards doing the things they would routinely do before, while getting them to gently challenge their thoughts like 'it's too much effort'.

Again with eating there are a number of unhelpful responses. In depression and with severe anxiety the appetite is likely to be reduced. Also patients may be more inclined to eat snack food because of unwillingness to cook. This may not be a problem in the short term, if the person is going to recover fairly quickly, but a chronically impoverished diet may have an adverse effect on their health (Ogden, 2003). Comfort eating can also be a problem and can lead to weight gain that reinforces low self-esteem.

Exercise is also being increasingly seen as essential to well-being (Vita and Owen, 1995). It may be worth planning a graded programme of regular exercise with the individual.

RECENT DEVELOPMENTS IN BEHAVIOURAL THERAPY

There has been revived interest in behavioural concepts in recent years. For example, Jacobson et al. (2001) have built on behavioural theory and broadened it. Their approach in depression is to de-emphasize the idea of depression being caused by internal events like cognitions, but to see depression as a series of actions and behaviours. They would see depression as arising out of the context of the person's life, in the sense that thoughts and beliefs are learned from the environment and they then shape the environment. In that sense the person and their external environment are not separate. Individuals are seen to be moving towards personally desirable goals and seeking or receiving reinforcement. Crucially, depression will occur when this does not happen. Treatment, therefore, will address the depressed person's actions and its context and will be particularly interested in the function or outcome of an action. It will try to help the patient act in such a way that naturally occurring reinforcers are regularly available.

In practical terms treatment will consist of a detailed assessment that will put emphasis on the minutiae of what the patient does when depressed (e.g. staying in bed till noon, not phoning his brother, not opening certain letters, eating poorly). It will try to understand the purpose of these actions, but try to help the patient see that they are reducing natural reinforcers and stopping themselves reaching their longer term goals. As stated earlier a study has found this approach as effective as cognitive therapy. In summary, in the *Depression in Context* approach, the therapist is saying, 'you've had a really tough time, let's see if we can make it better' as opposed to 'for various reasons you're thinking in a distorted way, let's see if we can change that'.

Other recent developments in behavioural therapy are acceptance and commitment therapy (ACT), dialectic behavioural therapy and mindfulness, although mindfulness can be used in a number of psychological therapies.

Acceptance and commitment therapy

This strand is associated with Steve Hayes and his colleagues (Hayes et al., 2004b). The current position in cognitive therapy is criticized by these authors: first, it is argued that the addition of cognitive therapy does not add any value to the behavioural element (Dobson and Khatri, 2000). The next problem with cognitive therapy is that the model is 'showing signs of wear', with no improvement in effect sizes over recent years, in, for example, anxiety disorders (Ost, 2002). Finally, the rise of constructivism (in which the person constructs their own reality) has challenged the 'mechanistic' assumptions in behaviour therapy.

The emphasis in ACT is on context and function; the truth of a statement is dependent on how successfully it works. In contrast with cognitive therapy where thoughts and beliefs are viewed as incorrect (and unhelpful), the emphasis here would be on trying to understand these in the context of the person's life and evaluating how much they allow the person to be moving towards his goals and acting in accordance with his values. For example, there would not be emphasis on challenging a thought such as 'if I make a mistake in this talk people will think I'm stupid', but work would be done on helping the person consider whether such a thought was helpful to them and how they could be helped to move towards their goal of completing the task of giving the talk.

Their theory of psychology is based on the ubiquity of pain, meaning that humans can be conditioned to experience pain in a variety of situations associated with the original painful stimuli. The next problem is that humans are over-focused on verbal rules and evaluations (called 'cognitive fusion'), and this evaluation is unhelpfully linked with the experience of doing the task. This leads to problematic experiential avoidance, e.g. not doing further talks. The therapy therefore encourages the person to move forward towards goals and in accordance with values while accepting distressing thoughts and feelings in a mindful way (Hayes et al., 2004a). The patient would be helped to focus on doing the talk, as they value the importance of doing this, while being accepting of their anxious thoughts and feelings.

Dialectic behavioural therapy

This therapy has been developed as a specific treatment for borderline personality disorder (BPD). The theoretical model of BPD (Linehan 1993) suggests that the individual experiences an 'invalidating environment' during their childhood years. They are subject to environmental influences, sexual abuse is common, which leaves them in a position where they are encouraged to be self-controlling, are not helped to deal with stress and are unable to label and understand their feelings. It is speculated that they deal with this by switching between suppressing their feelings and strongly expressing them. It is suggested that this early environment leads on to the clinical picture of BPD that is seen later with the typical features of emotional instability, fear of abandonment and tendency to self-harm. The therapy is called dialectic behavioural therapy because the patient switches between extreme positions (dialectics) such as passivity in solving their own problems and an active stance in recruiting others to help them and solve their problems.

The treatment programme takes place in four formats: individual therapy; group skills; telephone contact; therapist consultation. The group skills, which are usually taught in a one-year programme, consist of mindfulness, interpersonal effectiveness, emotional modulation and distress tolerance. The course of the individual therapy is to negotiate attendance within a specific timeframe; deal with suicidality; address behaviour that inter-feres with therapy, skills training, PTSD work, self-esteem work; work on issues of the patient's choosing. A balance is struck between change where it is possible and acceptance where it is not.

Mindfulness

This approach is a type of meditation, which has been shown to be effective in preventing relapse in depression and is now being used with other problems (Segal et al., 2004). With depression it is used as a strategy to quickly break into the pattern of depressive rumin-ation, leading to depressed mood that can lead to relapse. Again, it is not the content of thoughts that are challenged, instead patients are encouraged through mindfulness to step back from their thoughts and observe them from a calm place. This calm place may be an awareness meditation of a particular object and patients are encouraged to use this medita-tion if they are becoming locked into depressive rumination.

RATIONAL EMOTIVE BEHAVIOUR THERAPY

This therapy was developed by Albert Ellis (1962), and has a reasonable claim to be the first cognitive therapy. It emphasizes that we are largely but not exclusively responsible for the way we see ourselves. It argues that healthy emotions come from rational thinking and unhealthy emotions come from irrational thinking. Healthy thinking is considered to be logical and promoting the person's well-being and movement towards their goals. It states that the four problematic types of unhealthy belief are rigid demands, 'awfulizing', low frustration tolerance and self-/other downing. These are contrasted with the healthy alter-natives of preferences, 'anti-awfulizing', high frustration tolerance and self/other accept-ance. The therapy consists of assessing the unhealthy beliefs and unhealthy emotions that arise from them and teaching the person to use vigorous cognitive, behavioural and emo-tional strategies to challenge these beliefs (Dryden, 1995).

The main differences between this and Beckian CBT are that the style is more direct and challenging and the work is done quickly at the level of beliefs. Negative automatic thoughts are viewed as inferences that arise from unhealthy beliefs and are given less attention.

There is less emphasis on case formulation and diagnosis and it is argued that the idea of the four key irrational beliefs can be applied to any neurotic disorder. The evidence base is much weaker than for standard CBT.

From an REBT perspective it is possible to break down the purpose of all behaviours into a few categories (Dryden, 1999):

1   To learn something or change one's thinking (for example, to complete a course of study or engage with a new experience).

2   To alter an emotional state (for example, to see a friend or to listen to music).
3   To elicit a response from the physical environment (for example, to buy a book or move furniture in a room).
4   To elicit a response from the interpersonal environment (for example, to ask for a date or criticize a person).
5   To act in a way that is consistent with one's personal values, standards and goals (for example, to help out in a church or to seek out a new job).

Figure 10.1 summarizes the differences between CBT, REBT, ACT and behaviour therapy.

Working on	CBT	REBT	ACT	Behaviour therapy
Cognitive content	+ + +	+ + +	0	0
Cognitive process	+ +	+	+ + +	0
Values	+	+	+ + +	+
Goals	+	+	+ + +	+ + +
Behavioural change to evaluate thoughts	+ + +	+	0	0
Behavioural change to reach goals	+	0	+ + +	+ + +
Mindfulness	+ +	0	+ + +	0
Conditioning	+	+	+ + +	+++

Figure 10.1   Main focus of different types of CBT

Further reading |

Mindfulness and Acceptance by Hayes et al. (2004a) explores the new behavioural therapies. *Brief Rational Emotive Behaviour Therapy* by Dryden (1995) is a good introduction to this subject.

Chapter summary |

Learning theory and its concepts of conditioning, habituation, preparedness and modelling has had a big influence on behavioural and cognitive behavioural therapies. The chapter describes how problematic behaviours can be understood and addressed from a behavioural therapy perspective: the problematic behaviours discussed are avoidance, escape, reassurance seeking, unassertiveness, poor problem solving, sleep problems and poor self-nurturance.

There are recent developments in CBT that are often more influenced by learning theory than by Beckian approaches. These would include behavioural activation, ACT, dialectic behavioural therapy and mindfulness.

Rational emotive behavioural therapy was developed in the 1960s and emphasizes rational thinking.

Integrating CBT skills into generic mental health roles

INTRODUCTION

In recent years governments have focused on clinical practice being evidence based and increasingly mental health workers are being encouraged to examine their clinical practice with a more critical eye. Many have welcomed this evidence-based approach as a means to improving the standard of healthcare accessed by patients (Chambless and Ollendick, 2001). Indeed, Salkovskis (2002) observes of the movement toward evidence-based practice that: 'It is encouraging that those who worked solely on the basis of clinical judgment and personal prejudices are now being encouraged to take a more systematic approach, and to base the choice of treatment on what is defined as "gold standard" outcome evidence.' However, Salkovskis also strikes a note of caution advising that relying solely on the outcome results of randomized controlled trials is too narrow a base on which to found practice. Rather he advocates the notion of 'empirically grounded clinical interventions' based on the scientist–practitioner model (Barlow et al., 1984; Salkovskis, 2002).

One consistent recommendation (e.g. Department of Health, 2001) is the need to increase patient access to cognitive behavioural interventions. Traditionally, such treatments are delivered in a highly specialized service setting where access is restricted due to limited number of clinicians who have undertaken the specialist training required to work in such a service setting. For many years, it has been recognized that the demand for cognitive behavioural interventions far outstrips supply. Lovell and Richards (2000) point out that, given the number of patients who could potentially benefit from cognitive behavioural interventions, there is currently a massive shortfall in the number of clinicians trained to deliver these interventions. Lovell and Richards also observe that the traditional method for delivering such interventions (an outpatient clinic offering weekly 1-hour appointments) and the access points for treatment (specialist services accessed via GP and/ or community mental health team referral) severely limits patients' opportunities to access this potentially beneficial treatment.*

While this is a very valid argument constructed by Lovell and Richards there is also a strong literature, some of which has empirical data supporting its efficacy, advocating the health benefits of integration of cognitive behavioural interventions into generic mental health settings. This includes inpatient services (Scott, 1988; Wright et al., 1993) and primary care settings (Scott et al., 1994). In addition, the authors are aware of the application of CBT principles in mental health settings such as community mental health teams and day hospital services. However, despite such an evidence base established over the last 30 years, as yet such integration has never taken place on a scale sufficient to actually increase patient accessibility to cognitive behavioural interventions outside of specialist services. The reasons for this are complex and on the whole beyond the scope of this discussion but will be briefly considered now.

CHALLENGES OF INTEGRATING CBT INTERVENTIONS INTO GENERIC MENTAL HEALTH ROLES

As the previous discussion testifies models of mental healthcare, which aim to integrate cognitive behavioural principles into generic health settings, have been described in the literature for the past 30 years. However, as the reader will recognize this literature is yet to be translated into clinical reality in the UK. From a practical perspective given current Department of Health guidance on the use of evidence-based psychological interventions and the need to increase accessibility to these by upskilling the current workforce to deliver on this agenda offers a pragmatic solution. There are a number of challenges that arise in integrating cognitive behavioural interventions into generic clinical roles some of which will be briefly outlined later. The aim here is to stimulate thoughtful reflection and provide a focus around which the reader can formulate their own ideas regarding the brave new world of modernized healthcare.

---

* At the time of writing there has, however, been a welcome announcement of UK Government investment in CBT services.

Professional training vs. CBT model

A primary challenge is the degree to which the philosophical underpinnings of the cognitive behavioural model match or clash with that of the clinicians' generic professional training. How this is considered and reconciled will have significant implications for the CBT interventions that emerge within services.

Exercise

Consider the following basic principles of the CBT model and then reflect on the degree to which these sit comfortably with you in terms of your current clinical practice.

Consider your own thoughts and feelings in reaction to the statements. If there are any that elicit a strong reaction, try and identify the reasons. Also consider what changes you may need to make to your own philosophical position in order to use a CBT model effectively. If you feel unable to contemplate such changes what are the implications of this for your practice?

- A problem-solving-based, active and directive intervention geared toward reaching specific and concrete goals.
- A collaborative venture where patient and clinician meet as equal partners to work to on explicitly identified problems within a limited timeframe.
- A self-help model where the clinician is seeking to equip the patient with skills that they can use to tackle their problems using their own initiative.
- Primacy given to the influence of psychological and environmental factors over biological and genetic factors in the onset and maintenance of problems.

While there is insufficient scope here to discuss this in any great depth it is a matter worth much consideration. It is a challenge for anyone to be asked to re-orient their practice and take on board theory and practice that in many ways are very different from their core professional training. If this is not difficult enough, when whole teams are asked to consider new ways of working within a restructuring of services, this can add a further layer of complexity in integrating new theoretical principles and clinical interventions into existing models of clinical practice.

Access to adequate CBT training and clinical supervision

Within the CBT literature, high quality training and ongoing clinical supervision are seen as standard necessities in the process of developing clinical competence to practise CBT (Padesky, 1996). Therefore would-be practioners of CBT need to access CBT training and clinical supervision that is fit for purpose. That is, the training and supervision is sufficiently rigorous as to equip a clinician with sufficient CBT knowledge and clinical skills that they can deliver high-quality and effective CBT interventions that continue to develop the integrity of the current evidence base. This requires an organizational infrastructure that recognizes the following:

- The establishment of competencies for the practice of CBT interventions within the organization.
- Recognition that not all health service staff have the necessary generic interpersonal and clinical skills to be competent practioners of CBT. Therefore, if patients are to access effective and high-quality CBT treatment, systems need to be developed that proactively identify and train staff that are fit for this purpose.
- A clear programme of continuing professional development in the area of CBT knowledge and skills that recognizes high levels of clinical competence is best assured by investing in staff training on a medium to long term basis. This should not only include developing roles where staff are trained to deliver high-quality CBT interventions but also proactively equip them with skills to train and supervise others to develop CBT skills. This will require the creation of more specialist CBT roles.

USING CBT INTERVENTIONS IN AN INPATIENT SETTING

With pressure to limit the financial burden exerted on healthcare systems by inpatient admissions there is an increasing pressure to reduce the amount of time patients remain on a hospital ward. This has occurred in the context of a reduction in the number of inpatient services. Taken from this perspective some would argue such changes are a serious challenge to the idea of using psychosocial interventions in an inpatient setting. Alongside this change the past decade has seen the rise of the user movement in mental health, which has expressed a great deal of dissatisfaction with standards of care in inpatient services and a call for increased access to psychological help while an inpatient. The following case example outlines the pragmatic use of CBT principles in the care of one patient who had experienced a series of hospital admissions. The overall outcome for the patient, both short term and at 4 years follow-up was good with a complete remission of symptoms. AG's experience of working in an inpatient setting provided food for thought regarding some of the institutional changes that need to occur if access to CBT interventions is to become a routine aspect of an admission to hospital. These are discussed at the end of the case example. There is a strong body of literature supporting the use of CBT interventions in an inpatient setting. The interested reader is encouraged to consult Wright (1996) and Wright et al. (1993).

Patient example

Arthur was a 62-year-old retired headmaster who has been an inpatient on an acute psychiatry unit for the last 5 weeks. This is his third admission to the ward in 12 months and since the onset of his illness he has only spent a total of 6 weeks out of hospital. The onset of his difficulties occurred 3 months after retirement from his career in education. Arthur was very committed to his profession and worked long hours, including weekends. His social life revolved around work-based activities. He had a number of retired colleagues with whom he had some contact and two very close friends who visited him weekly both at home and on the ward.

Arthur was married to Mary and the couple had been together 38 years. They have a son, age 32, who was married and lived locally. The ward staff had observed some degree of tension in their relationship and noted that Mary was at times critical of Arthur, sometimes putting him down in front of others.

Each admission to hospital had been characterized by the same presentation, which had been diagnosed by the consultant psychiatrist as psychotic depression. At the time of his first admission Arthur was not eating or drinking, had disengaged from all self-care activities, withdrawing into himself and expressing paranoid ideas against his wife as well as threatening to kill her. Arthur was deemed a risk to himself and to his wife and had been admitted to the ward on a detention order. This is in order to assess his current mental state and offer appropriate treatment. On each admission Arthur was treated with electro-convulsive therapy (ECT) in combination with antidepressant medication in the form of Venlafaxine 225mg. During his third admission Arthur's wife and his close friend James expressed concern at what they perceived to be Arthur's overall lack of progress in making a full recovery from his illness. They went on to request the possibility of other treatments and James enquired about the possibility of cognitive behavioural psychotherapy. The consultant psychiatrist explained that routinely this was only available on an outpatient basis as part of the trust's tertiary psychotherapy service and at present there was a 12-month waiting list for treatment. Arthur's wife and James expressed their dissatisfaction, which prompted the ward manager to contact the recently appointed nurse consultant in psychological therapies. As a result of this discussion the nurse consultant agreed to visit the ward and meet with the staff and Arthur.

On meeting with the nursing staff they expressed concern that Arthur was not progressing as they hoped and were having difficulty finding a way forward. They reported having established a good rapport with Arthur and expressed concern he may be becoming dependent on the ward as a refuge from what they assessed as difficulties adjusting to retirement and managing tensions in his relationship with his wife. They also identified their own difficulties with dealing with Arthur's wife whom they perceived as critical of them.

At the first meeting with Arthur, which lasted 45 minutes, he presented as low in mood and anxious. He was very inactive on the ward spending the majority of his day lying on his bed. Verbally he reported NATs as follows: 'look at the state I'm in', 'I'm a complete mess', 'I can't even do simple tasks'. At this point Arthur would hang his head and say, 'I'm so useless'. Having spent 20 minutes listening to Arthur's story it was decided to share with Arthur a basic cognitive behavioural treatment rationale using a vicious circle maintenance formulation (Greenberger and Padesky, 1995) in order to assess whether he felt the treatment rationale held validity for him and whether he could work using this model.

Having carried out a brief assessment of Arthur's most pressing problems at the current time, the following problem list was drawn up with him:

- Inactivity and lack of structure to the day.
- Worry on a daily basis regarding his lack of progress in overcoming his illness and returning home.
- Lack of appetite leading to weight loss.

This problem list was not based on a comprehensive assessment of Arthur's problems as outlined in Chapter 5. Given the care setting in which cognitive behavioural strategies were being implemented the intervention was used to target immediate problems that were impeding Arthur from making a sustained recovery to the extent he could be discharged from the inpatient services and remain at home. The overall plan was to target more medium and long term problems using cognitive behavioural interventions on an outpatient basis.

The following goals were established as targets over the next 2 to 4 weeks:

1   To eat a small amount of food at each mealtime.
2   To go for a 15-minute walk each day and buy a newspaper.
3   To try and complete three crossword clues from the crossword in the paper (an activity Arthur had engaged in every day prior to becoming ill).

The cognitive behavioural intervention chosen by the nurse consultant to try and tackle the problems initially identified during the brief assessment was activity scheduling and graded task assignment (Beck et al., 1979; Fennell, 1989). The rationale for this intervention and guidance on its planning and implementation can be found in Chapter 9. This method was introduced to Arthur, his wife, his key worker and two of the student nurses on the ward.

It is to be noted that at this stage the goals set were deliberately more behavioural and that tackling his worry was in the initial stages put to one side. The rationale for this is to test out the role the worry plays in the maintenance of Arthur's problems. Therefore the experiment is to investigate the impact of re-establishing a regular routine of daily activities with Arthur. It may be that if he can re-engage with activities of daily living this will enable Arthur to experience the first steps of recovery and if he can maintain these gains over time then his worries about never functioning as he used to should recede. At this point his levels of worry can be re-assessed and a decision taken about what further cognitive work may be needed to directly tackle his worry.

While Arthur's care plan identified the same problems and reflected an overall goal of re-engaging with activities of daily living there were no specific goals within the care plan that targeted the problems identified. Thus, using this more focused and structured cognitive behavioural intervention, would enable both Arthur and the ward staff to be more proactive in working on quickly resolving the identified problems. There are several advantages to this approach when working with a patient with depression:

- Breaking tasks down into small steps makes them more achievable, which will increase the likelihood of overall task completion.
- Having the experience of completing an activity will increase motivation to

repeat the activity thus enabling the depressed individual to have a successful experience.

- Targeting specific activities allows the identification of obstacles to progress. These obstacles can then be targeted and resolved.
- Targeting one problem at a time enables the individual to develop a template of how the problem was tackled. This includes what tactics were effective in resolving the problem, what were the obstacles encountered during this process and how were these managed effectively. This process allows for the clear identification of a stepwise process to problem resolution, which can then be generalized to other situations. Thus the overall goal is not sorting the problem out for the individual but equipping the person with a set of skills so they can sort out their own problems.

The first task was for Arthur to buy a paper and attempt three clues from the crossword over the next 2 days. On introduction of this task, Arthur reported feeling very anxious with a stream of NATs as follows: 'I won't be able to do it', 'I won't be able to write' 'I'll make a mistake'. Rather than tackle these thoughts directly once the nurse consultant had identified how much Arthur believed each thought (see Chapter 6) she asked him to try the task as an experiment and this was written on a piece of paper (see p. 212).

The plan was also written on a blank activity schedule (see Chapter 9) and both Arthur and his key worker had a copy of this. The nurse consultant then agreed to visit the ward in 2 days' time to review how helpful Arthur and the ward staff had found using the intervention. As is often the case when activity scheduling and graded task assignment are introduced Arthur had grasped the principle and generalized it to some degree of his own accord. Thus when the nurse consultant returned to the ward 2 days later Arthur had not only completed three-quarters of one crossword but had enlisted the help of two other residents of the ward. When the nurse consultant and his key worker met with Arthur he appeared brighter in mood. He had been spending no time lying on his bed and had become more engaged in talking to both staff and residents on the ward. The nurse consultant began by returning to the behavioural experiments sheet. Arthur had not made any written summaries under the final two questions and so 10 minutes was spent helping Arthur to summarize his learning. Rather than the clinician completing these written summaries Arthur was encouraged to do this for himself. In asking Arthur what he had found helpful about the introduction of cognitive behavioural strategies he identified the following:

- The treatment rationale had given him hope that something could be done to tackle his depression.
- Once he started on the crossword he realized that his predictions that he wouldn't be able to write were not founded. This had motivated him to continue and made him question how accurate his predictions were.
- He felt a sense of pleasure and satisfaction from having completed the first three clues in 20 minutes. He had not experienced a sense of pleasure and achievement for 12 months.
- As a result Arthur was planning the following day to walk to the local library and borrow a book. He was somewhat apprehensive about this and a further behavioural experiment sheet was devised identifying his predictions regarding this activity.

Behavioural experiment sheet

Activity

To buy a paper each day and try and complete three crossword clues.

How do I feel at the prospect of doing this?

Anxious (75 per cent).

My predictions as to what will happen

'I won't be able to do it' (50 per cent), 'I won't be able to write' (80 per cent), 'I'll make a mistake' (90 per cent).

Having completed the task what have I learned from this?

Once I got going it was not as hard as I anticipated. I also gained some enjoyment from it and doing the crossword got me talking to other people on the ward.

How can I apply what I have learned to future situations?

Look out for my anxious thoughts and how they stop me trying things out. Going to the library across the road from the hospital and borrow a book to read.

Over the next 6 weeks Arthur generalized the application of activity scheduling and graded task assignment and continued to improve to the extent that he was discharged from hospital. The nurse consultant continued to visit Arthur and the staff twice a week for 45 minutes on each occasion. Once discharged from the service he was seen on a weekly basis for outpatient cognitive behavioural psychotherapy. This aspect of treatment focused more on his psychological vulnerability to depression which involved introducing cognitive interventions to tackle his more entrenched worry and modify conditional beliefs (see Chapter 7).

Impact of intervention on ward staff

The intervention had something of a mixed impact on the ward staff. Arthur's key worker and the student nurses directly involved in Arthur's care felt a sense of professional reward at his rapid improvement and discharge from hospital. They also reported having developed some basic cognitive behavioural skills and expressed an interest in accessing further training. However, within the broader nursing team there was some sense of feeling threatened by the introduction of a psychological approach to the ward environment. Some staff viewed such interventions as beyond the scope of their role and there was, as a result, difficulty in developing and maintaining continuity for the intervention across shifts. The ward manager expressed concern that the success of the intervention raised the expectation that the intervention be made available to other patients and the ward staff felt ill equipped to utilize it. Rather than this being identified, as a training and supervision need it was presented as a reason why the work should not be built on despite this being offered.

From the nurse consultant perspective it took time and effort to keep the key worker and student nurses involved in delivering the intervention. There was a tendency at times for the ward staff to view the nurse consultant as the 'expert' and to try and withdraw from the intervention. The nurse consultant saw her role not only as one of helping the patient but, importantly, empowering the nursing staff to help the patient. This complex task requires careful consideration and management.

The medical staff also made an interesting response to the intervention in that a direct request was made that no further cognitive behavioural work be carried out on an inpatient basis. This was in the context of the initial request for input coming from the medical team and there being a very favourable clinical outcome from the patient's perspective. Attempts to engage the team in discussion did not progress. It is, however, possible to hypothesise that the intervention may have been experienced as disempowering given the repeated, only partially successful medical interventions that were made prior to the request for a cognitive behavioural intervention. This discontinuity between team members and professions involved in delivering inpatient treatment clearly has implications for establishing cognitive behavioural interventions within an inpatient setting. A number of factors may be worth considering before attempting to integrate cognitive behavioural interventions into inpatient care:

- Work to develop a team perspective on using cognitive behavioural interventions that is advocated by the ward manager, the service manager and medical consultants.
- Once this is established, develop introductory level CBT training supported by CBT-focused clinical supervision facilitated by clinicians appropriately trained in CBT.

- The specialist clinician needs to devote time to getting to know the ward staff and to develop a good working relationship in order to maximize the potential benefits of changing practice. This needs to be based on valuing and shaping current clinical practice.
- Actively encourage the whole team to participate in developing the cognitive behavioural interventions model for the ward, including, nursing, medical and support staff.
- Provide staff with incentives to change their practice.
- Develop a model that is based on developing skills within the team rather than being dependent on the charisma of one specialist practioner.

USING COGNITIVE-BEHAVIOURAL INTERVENTIONS IN A PRIMARY CARE SETTING

Cognitive behavioural interventions have been identified as a central treatment strategy for the management of mild to moderate mental health problems in primary care (NICE, 2004a, b). Clinical presentations that typically fall into this descriptive category include panic disorder with or without agoraphobia, mild generalized anxiety, mild–moderate acute depression, bereavement and adjustment reactions, stress-related anxiety problems, mild to moderate social anxiety, obsessive compulsive disorder and social phobia. Within a primary care setting the aim is to offer a brief and targeted intervention, usually between 6–12 sessions, although the recently published NICE guidelines for depression and anxiety (NICE, 2004a, b) recommend cognitive behavioural interventions of between 6–18 weekly sessions. In addition, they advise an appropriately trained and supervised clinician should deliver these. These recently generated recommendations are conceived within the idea of a stepped care model (Haaga, 2000) in which treatment starts with the least intrusive and most cost-effective intervention with more intensive and costly interventions only being utilized when the person seeking treatment is not sufficiently helped by the initial intervention. Thus within this model in a primary care setting assisted self-help either computerized or manualized would be the first psychological intervention to be implemented within a stepped care intervention (NICE, 2002).

Anyone who has worked in primary care will understand the complexities that arise in trying to deliver CBT within a short-term (6–12 sessions) remit. One of the major difficulties in seeking to utilize CBT interventions in a primary care setting is how the term mild–moderate is defined. This can be based on symptom measurement, for example on the Beck Depression Inventory (1961) a score of between 10 to 18 would be defined as mild depression and 19 to 29 as moderate–severe depression. However, often individuals who present with scores within this range will respond successfully to antidepressant medication and therefore the primary carehealth worker is less likely to encounter depression that is mild–moderate in terms of a symptom measurement definition. A further factor that is relevant in the definition of mild to moderate problem is chronicity. There is a wealth of research evidence that demonstrates chronicity is an important prognostic factor in both depression and anxiety disorders. For the interested reader a useful summary regarding chronicity in the area of anxiety disorders can be found in Chapters 1 and 3 in Barlow (2004) and for depression the introductory chapter in Moore and Garland (2003). Clinical experience suggests the longer a problem has persisted the more difficult the problem is to treat. However, many factors can account for poor response to treatment including:

- prescription of antidepressant medication at sub-therapeutic doses
- difficulty accessing appropriate evidence-based psychological interventions such as CBT for treatment of the presenting problem
- appropriate evidence-based psychological interventions not being implemented as per protocol as they are delivered by untrained or poorly trained clinicians who receive inadequate or no appropriate model-specific clinical supervision
- the individual seeking help has more chronic and long-term difficulties which either require interventions delivered by clinicians with more specialist skills or who will require the long-term input of services to enable them to use CBT interventions to manage their illness more effectively. For example chronic depression, chronic generalized anxiety disorder, comorbid presentations and the like.

Case example

The following case example illustrates the use of assisted self-help for the treatment of mild anxiety-based problems in a primary care setting.

Mark is a primary care mental health worker from a social work background. He has undertaken an intermediate level of CBT training and is skilled in making a CBT assessment and treating individuals with mild–moderate mental health problems.

The remit of the service in which Mark works is 6–12 sessions of treatment. As a result, Mark has to make clinical decisions about which presentations to treat and how to best maximize the time available. Thus as the first intervention in a stepped care model with some patients Mark uses an assisted self-help package as a first treatment step when working with mild–moderate anxiety disorders and depression. An example of Mark's work with Andrew follows. Andrew became anxious and mildly depressed as a result of changes at work. Mark enables Andrew to tackle his problems by working with him to utilize a CBT self-help handbook (Williams, 2003).

In total, Mark completed six sessions of assisted self-help with Andrew. The first two sessions were delivered at weekly intervals, the second two at fortnightly intervals and the final two at monthly intervals. Mark's role was to introduce Andrew to the cognitive behavioural model using self-help material. The material Mark chose could be used as a CD-ROM or as a workbook. Andrew preferred to use the workbook approach. The workbook is interactive in style and encourages the completion of written exercises and practical homework tasks in order to tackle problems. The main aim in assisted self-help is to teach the patient how to access and implement the chosen self-help package. Thus, Mark sees his role not as solving Andrew's problems for him but assisting Andrew in using the self-help material for himself. Following a comprehensive assessment of Andrew's current difficulties over two 1-hour sessions Mark decided to offer six sessions of CBT-based assisted self-help. During the course of the intervention Mark worked through the following steps.

Session 1: helping Andrew understand his difficulties within a CBT framework

At the outset of the intervention Mark introduced the first two workbooks from *Overcoming Anxiety: A Five Areas Approach*. This consisted of explaining the layout of the workbooks and completing the first practical exercise with Andrew in order to model to him how to use the workbook. Mark worked within a collaborative framework and used Socratic questioning to check out how Andrew was responding to the self-help material. Frequent summaries were used to ensure Andrew understood how to gain maximum benefit from the workbooks and Mark actively invited Andrew to express any concerns he had regarding the intervention. At the end of the first, hour-long session homework was agreed in terms of implementing the practical exercises in the workbooks, which included making sense of your difficulties within a CBT framework and setting realistic goals for change. In order to maximize the chances of Andrew completing the homework Mark asked the following questions:

What is a realistic amount of time you can set aside for completing this homework?
When are you going to do this and where?
What factors are going to interfere with you carrying out the homework and how are you going to minimize the impact of these?
If, for whatever reason, you do not manage to complete the homework what are going to be the consequences of this for you?

In answering these questions Andrew and Mark negotiated that Andrew would spend 45 minutes four times per week working on the assignments and that this would be either between 7.30–8.30 in the morning or between 8–9 in the evening. The following factors were identified as potential obstacles: distraction from his friends; putting the task off; tiredness after work.

In order to combat these obstacles, Andrew decided to put a note on his fridge door reminding him to complete the homework, as well as to plan a reward for himself once the work was completed. The rewards included:

- Watch a DVD.
- Call a friend on the telephone.
- Visit his neighbour for a drink.
- Catch a taxi to work.

Session 2: reviewing the first week

There was only one week between the first two sessions. This timeframe is intentional in order to review progress and troubleshoot any difficulties early on in order to maintain focus and momentum in persisting with using the CBT self-help intervention. Andrew had successfully completed the agreed homework although he had not participated in as many self-help sessions as planned. Overall, Andrew had found the self-help useful and felt he had gained a new understanding of his difficulties and was beginning to find ways of tackling them. Given his progress Mark decided to give Andrew access to the complete

Overcoming Anxiety package and allow him to choose which workbooks best fitted his purpose. The session was used to review Andrew's goals and check these were realistic within the given timeframe and to develop a homework plan and strategy for troubleshooting obstacles. From this point onwards Mark allowed Andrew to take the lead in decision making as the aim with assisted self-help is for the patient to use the materials under their own steam.

Sessions 3 and 4: monitoring progress

These two sessions were both two weeks apart. Andrew was using assisted self-help to good effect and had achieved several of his goals. He reported an improvement in his mood and reduction in his level of anxiety. Given that Andrew was working well under his own initiative each of these sessions was of 30 minutes' duration. Mark's role was to briefly check Andrew was still on track in terms of utilizing CBT principles. However, the overall aim at this stage is to allow Andrew to use the self-help model at his own pace and in a way that best suits his needs. It is important to note that a crucial role of the clinician at this stage of the intervention is to ensure that the patient is implementing CBT strategies in a judicious way that is true to the principles of the model. Thus, if the patient reports a reduction in anxiety it is important to check that this is a result of positive action such as tackling avoidance or problem solving and not a result of instituting safety behaviours such as using alcohol to manage anxiety symptoms or only going out in the company of a trusted other. As outlined in Chapter 8, safety behaviours are an important maintenance factor in anxiety-based problems and it is vital that these are not actively or unwittingly developed by the patient as a means to solving an immediate problem. In the long term safety behaviours maintain problems. The clinician needs to be skilled in spotting safety behaviours and helping the patient to understand how they keep a problem going. It is also worth noting that the line between a coping strategy and safety behaviour is very thin and sometimes the very strategies you are aiming to help the patient use can actually become safety behaviour. A classic example of this is the patient who uses the workbook as a reassurance and reads it every time they become anxious and carries it everywhere with them, reciting passages in a ritualistic fashion. If this happens it is usually a sign the patient has a more complex and longstanding anxiety problem, which may require more intensive and specialized treatment.

Sessions 5 and 6: planning for the future

By this stage of the intervention Andrew and Mark were meeting once per month. Most of the problems Andrew had described at assessment had resolved themselves and he was feeling much better. These sessions lasted for 30 minutes and the main focus was planning for the future and relapse prevention. Andrew had successfully utilized six of the workbooks in the handbook and reported an 80 per cent improvement in his difficulties since the start of treatment.

USING CBT INTERVENTIONS IN A COMMUNITY MENTAL HEALTH TEAM

There are many ways in which integrating CBT principles into generic roles can be utilized within a community mental health team setting. The example chosen here is one of using CBT interventions to promote medication concordance in an individual with a severe and enduring mental health problem. The aim of the example is to illustrate how CBT interventions can be utilized within a monitoring framework to enhance treatment concordance. In addition a more proactive stance can be taken in terms of helping the patient to examine the impact their illness has on their functioning and develop methods for managing the real consequences a severe and enduring illness can exert on day-to-day functioning.

Case example

Audrey is a 50-year-old woman who is married with two grown-up children. She has had mental health problems since age 13 and has had contact with services since this time. Audrey has a diagnosis of bipolar affective disorder. She has had five serious episodes of illness, three with episodes of mania and two with profound depression. She has been reasonably stable for the past 7 years and currently has monthly contact with a community psychiatric nurse (CPN), Helen. Audrey is stabilized on lithium bicarbonate 800mg and Citalopram 40mg. Audrey struggles with the impact her illness has on her daily functioning and the fact that taking medication has a number of unwanted side-effects, which she feels inhibit her ability to function effectively. In the past she has stopped taking her medication altogether which has eventually resulted in a relapse of her illness. On two occasions a relapse of her illness has led her to engage in risky behaviour and has led to serious difficulties in her close relationships.

At a regular monthly session with Helen, Audrey confided that she had ceased taking her prescribed medication 3 weeks ago. Helen, who had undertaken specific training in CBT-based medication concordance, engaged Audrey in a process of examining her decision making with the overall goal of re-establishing Audrey on a medication regime, which was acceptable to her but that also managed her illness effectively. Helen worked through the following steps with Audrey.

Step 1: finding a position from which to discuss the subject

The initial stance Helen took was to be empathic with Audrey and to make a statement, which indicated to the patient that she must have had very good reasons for making the decision she has made and asking permission to talk it through with her. Helen also felt it important to convey to Audrey her concern that having ceased her prescribed medication there may be a risk of her becoming ill again and it was important that they examined this risk together. Audrey agreed that this was reasonable and this enabled a discussion to take place.

Step 2: identifying current circumstances that had led Audrey to cease taking her medication

Using Socratic questioning and guided discovery Helen reconstructed the circumstances that had led Audrey to make a decision to stop taking her medication. Through the discussion Audrey identified that she had been considering this action for several months. Several factors had influenced the decision:

- Worry that the lithium was causing kidney damage. This had been triggered by information she had read on an internet website.
- Feeling tired and lethargic and not having any energy, which was making activities of daily living difficult.
- An argument with her husband over Audrey's lack of interest in sex. This had been the actual trigger that had led her to stop taking the medication.

Step 3: to try and build awareness of the outcome of previous occasions when Audrey had stopped taking medication

Once more using Socratic questioning and guided discovery and taking an impartial stance Helen worked with Audrey to help her examine what had happened on previous occasions when she had stopped taking medication. Three instances were identified. Two had resulted in a severe relapse of her illness, which required hospital admission, and one had been managed by increased input from her previous CPN. At this point Audrey began to cry and shout at Helen, telling her that she did not understand. Helen worked with Audrey to identify her thoughts and feelings regarding taking the prescribed medication and how this was influencing her current behaviour. This was drawn out as a vicious circle maintenance formulation (Greenberger and Padesky, 1995), as illustrated in Figure 11.1. Helen was careful to be empathic with Audrey's perspective and not dismiss it without giving it credence and consideration before trying to help her examine the situation from other perspectives. It is particularly important to be empathic to the reality of the situation while remaining optimistic. The reality is that Audrey has a major mental health problem that at times exerts a significant negative effect on her day-to-day functioning. This can be managed well with prescribed medication, which, if she does not take it, can lead to a serious relapse in her illness that presents risks to her and her family and friends. However, taking medication, while having some benefits, also has a cost to it in terms of the impact of side-effects, which can make concordance with treatment at times hard to bear. Helen summarized the discussion so far by reiterating Audrey's position and making a written summary for Audrey to take away. This included a list of current reasons for ceasing taking medication and a summary of her current thoughts and feelings regarding this in the form of a vicious circle. Helen then moved on to try and help Audrey examine the situation from a variety of perspectives the first of which was the short- and long-term advantages and disadvantages of taking medication.

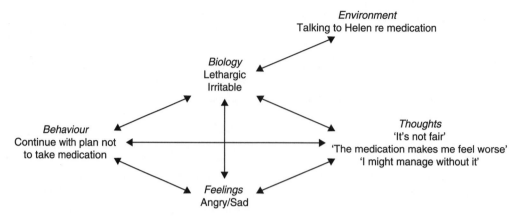

Figure 11.1   Vicious circle maintenance formulation for Audrey

Step 4: advantages and disadvantages of taking medication

Helen used Socratic questioning to identify the advantages and disadvantages of taking medication. Helen focused Audrey on concrete examples from her experience as a basis for generating this list. This is the most effective way of generating a personally relevant set of reasons rather than relying on an abstract set of reasoned principles as to why taking medication is a good thing. This activity was further refined by using Socratic questions such as:

- What does taking medication allow you to do which you may otherwise find difficult?
- In what way does taking medication impede your ability to function?
- In what way does medication enable you to function?
- What might be the short-term advantages of ceasing medication?
- What might be the long-term consequences of not taking medication?
- What will the advantages/disadvantages of not taking medication be to your relationships?

As is often the case the result of the exercise illustrated that there was no straightforward solution for Audrey and Helen and that managing the illness was part of a continual process of trying to reconcile often conflicting positions.

At this point Helen asked Audrey to go away and think about what they had discussed and arranged for them to meet in 4 days' time to discuss the situation again.

Helen was deliberate in not giving any instruction to Audrey to begin taking the medication again and observed that this was her decision. However, she did work through with Audrey a list of telltale signs that her illness was relapsing and encouraged Audrey to contact herself or the support services should she require help.

Step 5: making psychological sense of not wanting to take medication

At the next meeting 4 days later Helen began by collaboratively setting an agenda for the session. This included: a review of the previous session; Audrey's current position re taking medication; making sense of Audrey's decision from Audrey's perspective.

Audrey stated she had been feeling somewhat low in mood since the last meeting. This had been a result of recognizing that not taking her medication was probably a bad decision but that she was struggling with the fact she had to take it and didn't want to. This conflict had rendered her helpless. At this point Helen used Socratic questioning and guided discovery to try and build a formulation of the rules for living and core beliefs that may be driving Audrey's decision not to take medication. The issue of control was uncovered and Audrey was able to identify that when she took the medication she felt it was controlling her and the illness rather than she being in control of the illness and herself. From previous discussions with Audrey, Helen was able to observe that when Audrey is unwell she experiences the illness as controlling her and that this is equally painful. Audrey was able to concur with this view and the rule 'I should be in control at all times' was formulated. This need for control was then presented to Audrey as a dilemma with competing demands, which needed to be reconciled in a way that the advantages outweighed the disadvantages, but with the recognition there was no perfect solution. At this point Audrey became exasperated and stated that it seemed so unfair and expressed a desire for a perfect solution. Helen and Audrey both already knew that fairness and striving for perfection caused difficulties in other areas of Audrey's life and these perceptions were reiterated, as two rules: 'if I'm perfect then everyone is happy' and 'the world should be fair'. Helen also explored with Audrey what she found difficult about relying on medication and together they discovered that being self-reliant was very important to Audrey. This is encapsulated in the following 'rule': 'If you rely on anyone/anything it is a sign of weakness'.

These rules for living were summarized in written form and related back to her decision to stop taking medication with reference to the list generated at the previous meeting.

At this point Audrey reported feeling some improvement in her mood and began to reconsider her decision regarding taking medication. Helen put it to Audrey that the dilemma generated different NATs depending on the position from which it was viewed and it might be helpful to try and examine these NATs further. Helen proposed an experiment in which Audrey resumed taking her medication and together they would examine the impact of this on her functioning. Helen used the example of a NAT from Audrey's vicious circle that 'medication makes me feel worse' and that this is how she had felt at that time but on the basis of the work of this session then that may not always be how she views the situation. Audrey concurred with this and agreed to resume taking the medication with a view to proactively examining its effects and working together to find an optimal way for managing the illness. The homework between this session and the next was to monitor NATs regarding taking medication.

Step 6: modifying automatic thoughts and rules for living via behavioural experiments

Over the next 3 months Helen and Audrey met on a 2-weekly basis to identify and modify NATs regarding taking medication and living with the long-term consequences of having a major mental health problem. This also led on to work on modifying the rules for living that impacted on taking medication and adjusting to living with the illness (see Chapter 8). A self-help component was integrated into this phase of the intervention based on selected work from Scott (2001).

Outcome

Audrey found the whole intervention extremely helpful. In particular, she felt it had enabled her to engage in a meaningful dialogue regarding her illness which she felt had not occurred since its original diagnosis 35 years previously. She also found taking medication easier and was able to openly discuss her concerns about taking it with Helen whenever she needed to.

It is difficult in a short chapter to do justice to the breadth and scope of CBT applications that exist and the range of ways the interventions can be adapted to meet the needs of specific service settings. It is hoped that this chapter can act as a taster and inspire the reader to seek out further information and more comprehensive accounts of how CBT interventions can be utilized in generic mental health settings.

Chapter summary |

In this chapter, the application of CBT principles in generic mental health settings was examined. Specifically, these are an inpatient setting, a primary care setting and community mental health team. A number of examples, such as medication non-compliance, illustrate the ways in which CBT principles can be integrated into generic mental health settings. The ones chosen demonstrate some key skills, which if present in the general workforce would go some way to increasing service user access to CBT skills

Developing further CBT skills

DEVELOPING CBT SKILLS IN THE CURRENT MENTAL HEALTHCARE ENVIRONMENT

As described throughout this book, CBT has a strong evidence base supporting its use in the treatment and management of a range of mental health problems. The cognitive behavioural model has a strong research tradition and enshrined within its foundations is the idea that the treatments we use with patients should be tested and validated as part of an ongoing process of investigation (Salkovskis, 2002). In the current mental healthcare climate, which places increasing emphasis on using interventions that are evidence based, CBT has been endorsed as a treatment modality that patients should be able to readily access and that healthcare clinicians should be trained to deliver.

There is, of course, much debate regarding the validity of wholesale endorsement of the concept of evidence based practice and for many clinicians hackles rise at its mention. Standardly, the cognitive behavioural model emphasizes its strong tradition of randomized controlled trials as representing the gold standard and it is this type of evidence that informs the National Institute of Clinical Excellence (NICE) guidance that has so much currency at present in the National Health Service (NHS). In considering how the term 'evidence' is used in NICE guidance it does not purely mean data gathered from randomized controlled trials, but can also mean in descending order of importance:

- Well designed non-randomized trials.

- Evidence from well designed, non-experimental studies from more than one research group or centre.
- Expert authority opinion or reports of expert committees.
- CBT is undoubtedly strong in producing evidence from randomized controlled trials, and indeed all levels of this hierarchy. However, what irks many clinicians is the notion that greater weight is given to evidence gathered from randomized controlled trials than from data gathered using other research methodologies. Some would argue that while randomized controlled trials are very effective in establishing the efficacy of drug treatments, establishing the efficacy of psychological interventions using the same methodology is fundamentally flawed. In the spirit of the scientist–practioner model (Barlow et al., 1984) that resides at the heart of CBT the authors would encourage the reader to investigate their own views regarding their own position in this debate.

    However we would encourage a spirit of enquiry in this endeavour and direct the reader toward an excellent text by Mace et al. (2000) which debates the concept of evidence in psychological therapies from a philosophical and research perspective.

There are, of course, theoretical and practical problems associated with adopting this evidence-based approach and the CBT model does not ignore these. For a debate regarding the theoretical problems and discussion of the potential for their resolution the reader is directed toward Salkovskis (2002). In terms of practical problems from the clinician's perspective, these include:

- access to the evidence base
- skills in being able to appraise the evidence base critically
- time to access and use the evidence base
- developing the theoretical knowledge and clinical skills to implement this evidence-based intervention
- accessing appropriate clinical supervision to support the development of theoretical knowledge and clinical skills
- finding available evidence to inform the therapeutic interventions in the clinical area the clinician is interested in.

It is important for the clinician to address these problems with evidence-based practice and if they are considering a psychological approach for their patient, then to consider the evidence from CBT. This does not mean that CBT is automatically the psychological treatment of choice, as the evidence may not necessarily support its use. As stated earlier, when considering whether to provide a psychological intervention, the evidence is something that must be considered alongside the assessment and formulation of the patient's problem, their goals and the resources available.

Patients as consumers

Recently there has been an emphasis on the patient as consumer; this has occurred in the context of the decline of the asylum, the emphasis on self-help and scepticism about professional expertise, the growth of patients' rights groups and a general increase in consumerism in society. This has led to patients wishing to have greater choice in the treatment that they are offered. One aspect of this has been an increase in the demand for psychological treatment and counselling. Experience would suggest that CBT benefits from this as patients are aware of its effectiveness and frequently ask for it. This has led in recent years to a huge imbalance between supply and demand, with patients unable to access treatments of potential benefit. It is therefore possible to see the logic in more mental health professionals being trained to deliver CBT interventions. However, a responsible approach needs to be taken in terms of how this is achieved and what the implications might be for both patients and health services and their staff. It is important to say that just because a patient requests CBT it does not mean he or she will necessarily benefit. CBT interventions in theory can appear deceptively straightforward. However, in the hands of the untrained and unsupervised clinician they are at best rendered ineffective due to ill-informed implementation, or at worst can cause harm to the patient and their mental well-being. Therefore clinicians keen to develop and use CBT skills need to undertake an appropriate programme of CBT training and CBT-focused clinical supervision.

Learning from clinical supervisors and colleagues

Currently, in the NHS, CBT is practised by a range of mental health professionals across the disciplines including mental health nurses, clinical psychologists, psychiatrists, occupational therapists, social workers and forensic and educational psychologists. Most clinicians are exposed to some CBT principles as part of their core professional training but the nature and extent of this is highly variable according to the professional training and the educational institution where this training is based.

For any clinician who wishes to develop CBT knowledge and skills then it is important that you approach healthcare professionals who are appropriately trained in the use of CBT interventions and are in a position to support and encourage you in developing these skills. The most obvious starting point is to seek out individuals or teams within the organization in which you work and investigate what might be available in terms of CBT clinical supervision and training. It is probably wise to approach a clinician who works in the same clinical specialty, for example, if you work in adult mental health it is best to seek out a clinician who has undertaken CBT training to work with this client population rather than approaching someone who, for example, is working with children. This said, typically CBT-trained clinicians are much more likely to be found in adult mental health, forensic psychiatry, primary care, drug and alcohol services and physical health settings such as liaison psychiatry than, say, child and adolescent and older adult services. The majority of CBT training courses target clinicians who work on an outpatient basis with adults between the ages of 18–65. Therefore, if you work in a field other than adult mental health it may be necessary to seek support within other clinical areas while recognizing that the application of CBT in specialties such as older adults and child and adolescent services requires adaptation according to the needs of the population.

Once you have located a clinician who can potentially offer CBT clinical supervision and training it is worth trying to gain some information from them regarding their specific CBT training, whether CBT is their primary mode of working with patients (or they take a more eclectic approach) and whether their CBT practice is accredited with a recognized CBT accreditation body. This needs to be done respectfully but it is a legitimate request to make.

While factors such as where CBT training was completed and whether the individual is an accredited CBT clinician do not make any statement regarding the clinician's level of competence in carrying out CBT interventions, it may offer guidance regarding their specific CBT model (behavioural, Beckian cognitive therapy, REBT), and their approach to continuing professional development (CPD). For example, the British Association of Behavioural and Cognitive Psychotherapies (BABCP) requires an accredited member to participate in 30 hours of CBT-focused CPD every year across a range of activities including attendance at skills development-based CBT workshops; CBT seminars, reading; and the like. In addition, in the ever evolving field of CBT interventions, whether the clinician is accredited, may give some give some guidance as to how up to date their CBT knowledge and practice is.

It is important to be realistic here and observe that CBT provision varies widely across the country and depending on the local provision there may be severe limitations in terms of what action can be taken to begin to develop CBT knowledge and skills within some areas. In these circumstances, you may need to be more creative in your endeavours or look outside of the organization to develop these skills. The organizational obstacles to developing robust CBT skills is a crucial aspect to consider and for an informative and thought-provoking discussion of these issues the reader is encouraged to consult Chapter 16 in Grant et al. (2004).

There are a variety of ways in which the novice to CBT can begin to develop their knowledge and skills and starting with a formal CBT training course is usually not the first port of call. Reading introductory CBT texts is a good starting point and many of these can be found in our bibliography. Most organizations have library facilities and visiting these and finding your way around them will familiarize you with what is available in your area. Library staff can be helpful in enabling you to access appropriate CBT literature and if certain texts are not available will have mechanisms for helping you access these. Most libraries have an annual budget to purchase educational materials and will have a system for staff making suggestions regarding which materials could usefully be purchased. In addition, there is a great deal of information available on the internet through both educational establishments and the world wide web. Some caution needs to be exercised in using the last mentioned as some sites apply the acronym CBT in a very liberal sense which can be misleading to the novice practioner. Some clinicians may have anxieties about using library facilities and the internet. As the authors have encouraged elsewhere in this book, if you find yourself putting off using these resources try and identify your negative predictions and then set yourself a realistic behavioural experiment to try and test out these predictions; you may surprise yourself in terms of what you learn.

Another way of beginning to develop an understanding of CBT is to sit in on the assessment and treatment sessions of clinicians trained in the use of CBT interventions. This will give you first-hand experience of the CBT model in action and help you to consider whether you would like to develop your own CBT knowledge and skills further. This may be offered as a one-off experience but it likely to be more beneficial as part of a time-limited clinical experience carried out as part of your own CPD. Once more, applying CBT principles can be helpful in this sphere, for example setting yourself realistic goals in terms of developing your CBT knowledge and skills in a stepwise way.

A further step on the road to developing your CBT knowledge and skills is to attend introductory workshops and short courses. Many NHS organizations offer such events and these can be very helpful as a starting point. It would be our view that CBT training that is supported by CBT-focused clinical supervision is going to be of most value in terms of enabling you develop sufficient skill that you can put it in to practice.

In addition one-day workshops and short training courses can be accessed externally through nationally recognized training institutions and some privately run initiatives. Once more it is always worth carrying out a thorough investigation of the training that is on offer, the credentials of the training body delivering the programme and whether these fit with your own personal learning goals. For the novice to CBT this can be a daunting prospect. Seeking the advice of colleagues who are in a position to guide you through this process and make informed recommendations could be helpful. The BABCP website is a useful resource and more detail is provided later regarding what this organization has to offer.

Once some basic skills have been acquired these can be built on by undertaking a period of inhouse CBT training (usually 6–12 months minimum) under the supervision of a CBT clincian working with fairly straightforward presentations such as panic disorder, social phobia and mild to moderate acute depression. It is strongly advocated that the clinician attempts to gain this experience before applying to undertake a formal CBT postgraduate diploma course. All CBT trainings are part time (one day per week) and as such the learning curve is very steep even with previous experience. As a total novice to the approach starting at this point may prove overwhelming and seriously undermine your confidence in developing your CBT skills.

CBT-focused clinical supervision

In considering clinical supervision here the authors are referring to a process that enables the clinician to develop their CBT theoretical knowledge and practical skills and this is its exclusive focus. This can be contrasted with managerial supervsion, which generally deals with an individual's day-to-day functioning in their job role and professional supervision, which may relate to peer support and career development issues. While clearly these three forms of supervision have areas of overlap we would encourage a drawing of boundaries between them with discrete time being set aside for each type and in ideal circumstances facilitated by different individuals. For the purpose of developing CBT knowledge and skills the establishment of CBT-focused clinical supervision is vital and it is especially important that such supervision occurs that it is a good learning experience. The authors would recommend the following factors as important considerations when identifying a CBT clinical supervisor:

- The clinical supervisor should use CBT as their main treatment modality.
- The clinical supervisor has undertaken a recognized specialist postgraduate CBT training or is recognized by their peers within the organization (rather than by themselves) as having credibility as a CBT practioner with extensive knowledge and experience of using CBT interventions and is open to the process of accreditation of CBT practice.
- The CBT supervisory model (especially for novices to CBT) focuses primary on the acquisition of CBT knowledge and practical skills and the implementation of CBT interventions rather than the therapeutic relationship and issues of transference and countertransference or other psychotherapy models.
- The CBT supervisory model incorporates the philosophy of CBT and uses its

principles to guide the supervisory process. This includes: a collaboratively agreed agenda to guide each supervision session; the identification of supervisory needs and the setting of goals to measure their attainment; a problem or question is focused on in the supervision session; an action plan to answer the question or tackle the problem is developed and implemented; learning from the supervision session is reviewed and documented; homework is carried out by the supervisee in between supervision sessions to develop CBT knowledge and skills and this is reviewed at the beginning of subsequent supervision sessions.

- The use of audio and/or videotapes as part of clinical supervision. While this is standard as part of any postgraduate training in CBT it can also be very useful as part of CBT clinical supervision per se. It helps to develop robust clinical skills through a process of critical evaluation by the supervisee and supervisor and is good preparation for those considering postgraduate training, as it is one less obstacle to overcome when the training commences if you are already acclimatized to using this method, which at times is anxiety provoking for even experienced CBT clinicians. However, if the recording of treatment sessions is to be used as part of standard CBT clinical supervision it should be introduced in a graded way when the supervisor and supervisee have developed a good working relationship and the supervisee feels sufficiently safe to expose their clinical work to scrutiny. This said, many clinicians are highly avoidant of engaging in this process and if you find yourself falling into this category this is worthy of addressing as part of reflective practice and as part of your CBT clinical supervision.

Within the CBT model the supervisee and supervisor are viewed as having a shared responsibility for the content and process of supervision. The following points aim to act as a basic guide for supervisees when engaging in CBT clinical supervision:

1   The need to prepare for the session by bringing relevant case material and clear supervision questions. The purpose of identifying a supervision question is to ensure that the time available is used wisely and that the most pressing needs of the supervisee (and patient) are addressed. In addition, the use of a question focuses the discussion and activity of the supervision session in a way that is productive. For example, you may be struggling with a particular patient and not know how to proceed. You could bring to supervision a statement like: 'I am stuck with this patient and I don't know how to proceed.' Alternatively, you could spend time considering what it is you are stuck with and pose this as a question. For example: 'How can I help the patient to increase his activity levels?' Or 'How do I help the patient tackle her thought that her daughter's bad behaviour at school is her fault?' In this example, the supervisee may be recognizing a skills deficit and is seeking to address this in the question posed.

2   The need to present cases in a particular way that maximizes the learning process. It is a frequent observation that supervisees present case material in a rather disorganized way, jumping from the history to the treatment to the presenting problem and so on. This is not a criticism of them as individuals, but of possible inadequacies in their basic professional training. We would recommend that students present the case in the same order as they complete the assessment interview (as described earlier). The order would therefore be: the supervision question, presenting problem, vicious circle formulation, treatment goals, relevant life history, diagnosis, formulation and treatment

plan. It is probably something to be negotiated between the supervisor and supervisee whether the whole assessment has to be reported in detail (which is easier but more time consuming), or whether a stripped-down version should be given focusing on the main issues.

The internet, books and journals

The internet, books and journals are all excellent CBT resources. In this section a variety of sources are recommended and commented on. Looking first at the internet, nearly all sites have information about the specific organization, training and educational resources and sometimes a discussion forum.

www.aabt.org This is the website for the Association for the Advancement of Behavior Therapy, a leading American organization. It contains information about the organization's excellent journals, publications and videos.

www.academyofct.org Established by Aaron T. Beck and his daughter Judith Beck, the Academy of Cognitive Therapy is an American organization that provides details of its educational and training resources on its website. It also provides excellent articles in its newsletter. Trained CBT clinicians can apply to become members of the academy and the website provides information on how to go about this.

www.babcp.org This is the website for the British Association of Behavioural and Cognitive Psychotherapies. This is the main British CBT website. Anyone with an interest in CBT can become a member of BABCP (a small fee is charged) and no formal CBT qualification is required. It functions primarily as an interest group to promote the safe and effective practice of CBT. Membership provides the subscriber with an excellent free quarterly journal containing clinically relevant articles pertinent to the theory and practice of CBT, as well as a discount to the organization's annual conference. The site provides information for both professionals and patients. There is information about CBT training in the UK, details of the organization's annual conference and how to apply, and an excellent online discussion forum and a 'find a therapist' section, among other features. This organization has a voluntary accreditation process for clinicians who practise CBT and a separate accreditation process for those who work as CBT clinical supervisors and trainers. Information regarding accreditation criteria and application forms can be downloaded from this site.

www.beckinstitute.org This is the website for the institute where Aaron T. Beck works in Philadelphia, USA. Alongside other items, this site has details about the widely used 'Beck scales', a full list of Beck's books and publications, and a link to the Beck home page.

www.behavior.net This is an excellent site called Behavior Online, with interesting interviews with leading therapists, expert panels and Dr Katz cartoons. It is particularly useful because of its longstanding discussion forums, which are broken down into subject areas e.g. 'depression' or 'anxiety disorders', and which are a mine of useful information and comment.

www.iacp.asu.edu This is the website for the International Association for Cognitive Psychotherapy. It is primarily a gateway to membership of the organization, for which a small fee is charged. Membership provides you with an excellent free quarterly journal and information regarding the World Congress of Cognitive Therapy, which is held every four years at an international venue.

www.padesky.com   Christine Padesky is a leading CBT clinician and trainer. This is an enjoyable site that provides information about training provided by Christine Padesky and her colleagues around the world, as well as how to purchase her clinically informative audio and videotapes of how to implement key CBT interventions.

www.rebt.org   This is the leading resource for rational emotive behavioral therapy, being the site of the Albert Ellis Institute. It is possible to access articles on REBT and even to download books.

There are, of course, other sites; this list is by no means exhaustive. New sites are emerging all the time and many of those just cited have links to other CBT websites.

In terms of CBT books, we are in a period where there are a large number of superb CBT books in publication. However, as stated previously, the term CBT is a broad umbrella under which a range of behavioural and cognitive theories and models can be placed. Here is a list of the books the authors think would be particularly helpful in terms of learning about CBT.

Beck, 1995. This basic introduction to a Beckian model of CBT is very clearly written and helps the reader deal with both the basic principles of CBT and the more advanced concepts such as formulation and working with rules for living and core beliefs.

Blackburn and Twaddle, 1996. This book is particularly helpful in that it takes the learner through formulation and very detailed descriptions of several cases.

Hawton et al., 1989. This book has chapters on the principles of CBT, assessment and each of the commonly occurring mental health problems disorders. It is very clearly written by eminent clinicians who are expert practioners and researchers in the field. The main drawback is that it was published in 1989 and some of the interventions described have been further developed.

Leahy, 2003. This excellent book describes in detail tools and interventions that clinicians can use with their patients. The book uses a set format to cover a range of CBT interventions.

Leahy and Hollon, 2000. This book takes the reader through protocol driven treatment plans for depression and the various anxiety disorders. There is excellent photocopyable material in the text, and a CD-ROM of additional questionnaires and handouts.

Wells, 1997. This book, although it has some more complex theorizing about anxiety, also provides detailed formulations and treatment strategies for each anxiety disorder.

Journals are the best ways to keep up with recent developments. Some important CBT-related journals are:

Behaviour Research and Therapy
Behavioural and Cognitive Psychotherapy
Behavior Therapy
Cognitive Therapy and Research
Journal of Cognitive Psychotherapy
Journal of Consulting and Clinical Psychology

Formal training in CBT

Formal training in CBT is usually undertaken at a postgraduate, diploma or degree (masters) level. This is the type of qualification required to work in a CBT psychotherapy role. Such courses are usually accredited by academic institutions and generally speaking are completed on a day release basis in a year. Most of the available courses offer a training, which combines CBT clinical skill acquisition with the teaching of CBT theory. The BABCP website offers a comprehensive listing of CBT courses available in the UK and this is the most useful place to begin in terms of seeking guidance on which course to apply for. The BABCP has a voluntary accreditation process for training courses. This process sets out criteria for courses in terms of syllabus content and assessment methods for students undertaking CBT training. These criteria recommend students undertaking CBT training be assessed on their clinical skills though the submission of audio and/or videotapes of their CBT clinical practice (which are rated on an appropriate scale) and academically through the submission of case studies and essays demonstrating an understanding of the links between CBT theory and clinical practice. A central issue in CBT training is whether the course provides clinical supervision itself or asks the student to find his or her own supervisor. There is much debate regarding the relative merits of each approach. It is the authors' view that a course, which provides inhouse CBT supervision, is going to have more potential to set and monitor quality standards in terms of clinical supervision than a system reliant on the student's finding her own CBT supervisor and then relying on the goodwill of the supervisor to attend any inhouse supervisor development programme. It is important when applying for a formal CBT course that you consider the academic and clinical credibility of the course and seek advice from colleagues as to their knowledge of the different training courses. It is however important to acknowledge that in seeking recommendations the individual giving the guidance may be subject to their own biases and prejudices and so a range of views may be helpful. In this respect it can prove very valuable to speak to ex-students of the course. It is also useful to consider what your training needs are as some courses may better meet these needs than others. This is where, if prior to applying for a formal CBT training you have engaged in a period of supervised clinical practice, your CBT clinical supervisor, through their knowledge of your level of CBT skills and experience, will hopefully have some sense of which CBT course will best meet your needs. One factor to consider here is cost. CBT training is very expensive and it represents a significant investment not just by the student in terms of time, effort and energy but also the organization in terms of cost. It is, therefore, worthwhile considering with your clinical supervisor and manager how to maximize the benefits of the training both while you are undertaking it and once it is completed. This goes beyond giving you funding which, while necessary, is only part of what is needed. It can be helpful to have a mentor while you complete the course to help you with the inevitable stresses as well as provide opportunity to reflect on learning. It is, however, important to maintain a boundary between this type of mentorship or tutoring and clinical supervision which is a different activity with different goals. The authors recommend that different individuals provide these two functions.

Accreditation

Currently in the UK accreditation as a CBT clinician is voluntary. The main organization that offers this facility is the BABCP in conjunction with the United Kingdom Council for Psychotherapy (UKCP), although you need to be accredited by the BABCP in order to be registered with UKCP. In addition the Rational Emotive Behaviour Therapy Association also offers a voluntary accreditation process (linked to UKCP) for individuals who have undertaken CBT training specifically focused on REBT. Details of these accreditation processes can be found on the websites detailed earlier.

While accreditation is currently voluntary some NHS organizations state on job applications for CBT psychotherapy posts that clinicians should be accredited with the relevant accrediting body. This is in line with recommendations for accreditation within other psychotherapy modalities, e.g. family therapy. At present the government is in the process of developing a system for regulating the practice of psychotherapy both within and outside of the NHS. As yet it is unclear which body will regulate the activity of psychotherapy and several models are proposed. There is a possibility that psychotherapy will be recognized as a profession in its own right and in this respect there will be a requirement placed on CBT practioners to work to certain professional standards in terms of the practice of CBT, for example, engaging in a prerequisite minimum amount of CBT focused clinical supervision and maintaining a certain level of CPD. The BABCP already offers guidance in these domains and potentially provides a benchmark in terms of what might be realistically expected as a minimum requirement to achieve accreditation as a CBT clinician.

The BABCP also offers voluntary accreditation as a CBT supervisor and trainer. While these avenues are not as yet likely to be pursued by the readers of this book, it may be something to be considered in the future. However, what may be of benefit to the novice CBT clinician is that you start to keep a detailed record of your CBT-focused CPD in relation to your clinical practice. The BABCP encourages the following activities as counting toward CBT-focused CPD with a minimum of 30 hours per year:

Essential (everyone needs to engage in these activities):

- reading CBT-focused literature combining journal articles and CBT books
- attending CBT skills development workshops
- attending CBT-focused seminars, case presentations, lectures and the like.

Others that can be included:

- CBT-focused teaching of others.
- CBT-focused research.
- CBT publications.

In addition, to be accredited the clinician needs to engage in a minimum of one hour per month CBT focused clinical supervision provided by a supervisor whose main therapeutic modality is CBT.

There is much debate about the value of accreditation and what it means in reality. Undoubtedly, as the professionalization of psychotherapy gathers momentum the debate will continue. The authors would encourage the reader in a spirit of enquiry to consider for themselves the advantages and disadvantages of the accreditation or regulation of CBT practice and its implications for patients as well as clinicians.

Working to a benchmark has in many settings made a significance difference to the quality of service we experience not just in the health service but also in many aspects of our lives and there may be advantages to considering these in relation to CBT practice.

The current health environment supports the use of evidence-based practice and CBT does have a strong evidence base. The clinician who is interested can begin to learn from CBT colleagues from sitting in on sessions and other activities. It is important for the person interested in CBT to acquire a supervisor and showing knowledge and interest will increase the likelihood of that. The person can also use books, the internet and professional bodies to develop his interests and possibly this will lead to a more rewarding career. Training is available at various levels and can lead to accreditation with, in the UK, the BABCP.

Bibliography

Addis, M. E. and Jacobson, N. S. (2000) A closer look at the treatment rationale and homework compliance in cognitive behavioural therapy for depression. *Cognitive Therapy and Research*, 24, 313–326.

American Medical Association (2006) *International Classification of Disease–ICD 9*. Chicago, IL: American Medical Association.

American Psychiatric Association (2005) *DSM-IV*. Washington, DC: American Psychiatric Association.

Barlow, D. H. (1993) *Clinical Handbook of Psychological Disorders*. New York: Guilford Press.

—— (2004) The nature of anxious apprehension, in *Anxiety and Its Disorders: The Nature and Treatment of Anxiety and Panic*, 2nd edn. New York: Guilford Press.

Barlow, D. H., Craske, M. G., Cerny, J. A. and Klosko, J. S. (1989) Behavioural treatment of panic disorder. *Behaviour Therapy*, 20, 261–282.

Barlow, D. H., Hayes, S. C. and Nelson, R. O. (1984) *The Scientist–Practitioner: Research and Accountability in Clinical and Educational Settings*. New York: Pergamon Press.

Beck, A. T. (1967) *Depression: Clinical, Experimental and Theoretical Aspects*. New York: Harper & Row.

—— (1976) *Cognitive Therapy and the Emotional Disorders*. New York: International Universities Press.

Beck, A.T., Emery, G. and Greenberg, R. (1985a) *Anxiety Disorders and Phobias: A Cognitive Perspective*. New York: Basic Books.

Beck, A. T., Freeman. A., Davis, D. D and Associates (2004) *Cognitive Therapy of Personality Disorders*. New York: Guilford Press.

Beck, A. T., Hollon, S. D., Young, J. E., Bedrosian, R. C. and Budenz, D. (1985b) Treatment of depression with cognitive therapy and amitryptyline. *Archives of General Psychiatry*, 42, 142–148.

Beck, A. T., Kovacs, M. and Weissman, A. (1979) Hopelessness and suicidal behavior. *Journal of the American Medical Association*, 234, 1146–1149.

Beck, A. T., Rush, A. J., Shaw, B. F. and Emery, G. (1979) *Cognitive Therapy of Depression*. New York: Guilford Press.

Beck, A. T., Sokol, L., Clark, D. A., Berchick, R. and Wright, F. (1992) A crossover study of focussed cognitive therapy for panic disorder. *American Journal of Psychiatry*, 149, 778–783.

Beck, A. T. and Steer, R. A. (1990) *Manual for the Beck Anxiety Inventory*. New York: The Psychological Corporation.

Beck, A. T., Steer, R. A., Kovacs, M. and Garrison, B. S. (1985c) Hopelessness and eventual suicide: a ten-year prospective study of patients hospitalized with suicidal ideation. *American Journal of Psychiatry*, 142, 559–563.

Beck, A. T., Ward, C. H., Mendelson, M., Mock, J. and Erbaugh, J. (1961) An inventory for measuring depression. *Archives of General Psychiatry*, 4, 561–571.

Beck, A. T., Weissman, A., Lester, D. and Trexler, L. (1974) The measurement of pessimism: the Hopelessness Scale. *Journal of Counseling and Clinical Psychology*, 42, 861–865.

Beck, J. (1995) *Cognitive Therapy: Basics and Beyond*. New York: Guilford Press.

Benca, R. M., Obermeyer, W. H., Shelton, S. E., Droster, J. and Kalin, N. H. (2000) Effects of amygdala lesions on sleep in rhesus monkeys. *Brain Research*, 879, 1–2, 130–138.

Bennett-Levy, J., Butler, G., Fennell, M., Hackmann, A., Mueller, M. and Westbrook, D. (2004) *Oxford Guide to Behavioural Experiments in Cognitive Therapy*. Oxford: Oxford University Press.

Blackburn, I. M., Bishop, S., Glen, I. M., Whalley, L. J. and Christie, J. E. (1981) The efficacy of cognitive therapy in depression: a treatment trial using cognitive therapy and pharmacotherapy each alone and in combination. *British Journal of Psychiatry*, 139, 181–189.

Blackburn, I. M., Eunson, K. M. and Bishop, S. (1986) A two-year naturalistic follow-up of depressed patients treated with cognitive therapy, pharmacotherapy and a combination of both. *Journal of Affective Disorders*, 10, 67–75.

Blackburn, I. M. and Twaddle, V. (1996) *Cognitive Therapy in Action*. London: Souvenir Press.

Bordin, E. S. (1979) The generalisability of the psychoanalytic concept of the working alliance. *Psychotherapy: Theory, Research and Practice*, 16, 252–260.

Borkovec, T. D. and Costello, E. (1993) Efficacy of applied relaxation and cognitive-behavioural therapy in the treatment of generalised anxiety disorder. *Journal of Consulting and Clinical Psychology*, 51, 611–619.

Borkovec, T. D. and Inz, J. (1990) The nature of worry in generalised anxiety disorder: a predominance of thought activity. *Behaviour Research and Therapy*, 28, 2, 153–158.

Bowlby, J. (1980) *Attachment and Loss. Vol. 3: Loss, Sadness and Depression*. New York: Basic Books.

Boyd, J. H.and Weissman, M. M. (1981) Epidemiology of affective disorders: a reexamination and future directions. *Archives of General Psychiatry*, 38, 9, 1039–1046.

Bryant, M. J., Simons, A. D. and Thase, M. E. (1999) Therapist skill and patient variables in homework compliance: controlling and uncontrolled variable in cognitive therapy outcome research. *Cognitive Therapy and Research*, 23, 381–399.

Burns, D. D. (1990) *The Feeling Good Handbook*. New York: Penguin.

Burns, D. D. and Nolen-Hoeksema, S. (1992) Therapeutic empathy and recovery from depression in cognitive behavioural therapy: a structural equation model. *Journal of Consulting and Clinical Psychology*, 60, 441–449.

Butler, G. (1998) Clinical formulation, in A. S. Bellack and M. Hersen (eds) *Comprehensive Clinical Psychology*. Oxford: Pergamon Press.

Butler, G., Fennell, M. J. V., Robson, P. and Gelder, M. (1991) A comparison of behaviour therapy and cognitive-behaviour therapy in the treatment of generalised anxiety disorder. *Journal of Consulting and Clinical Psychology*, 59, 167–175.

Butler, G. and Hope, T. (1995) *Manage Your Mind: The Mental Fitness Guide*. Oxford: Oxford University Press.

Chadwick, P. D., Birchwood, M. J. and Trower, P. (1996) *Cognitive Therapy for Delusions, Voices and Paranoia*. Chichester: John Wiley & Sons.

Chambless, D. L. and Ollendick, T. H. (2001) Empirically supported psychological interventions: controversies and evidence. *Annual Review of Psychology*, 52, 685–716.

Clark, D. M (1986) A cognitive approach to panic. *Behaviour Research and Therapy*, 24, 461–470.

Clark, D. M., Salkovskis, P. M., Hackmann, A., Middleton, H., Anastasiades, P. and Gelder, M. (1994) A comparison of cognitive therapy, applied relaxation and imipramine in the treatment of panic disorder. *British Journal of Psychiatry*, 164, 759–769.

Clark, D. M., Salkovskis, P. M., Hackmann, A., Wells, A., Ludgate, J. and Gelder, M. (1999) Brief cognitive therapy of panic disorder: a randomised controlled trial. *Journal of Consulting and Clinical Psychology*, 67, 583–589.

Clark, D. M. and Wells, A. (1995) A cognitive model of social phobia, in R. Heimberg, M. Liebowitz, D. A. Hope and F. R. Schneier (eds) *Social Phobia: Diagnosis, Assessment and Treatment*. New York: Guilford Press.

Davey, G. C. L. (1992) Classical conditioning and the acquisition of human fears and phobias: a review and synthesis of the literature. *Advances in Behaviour Research and Therapy*, 14, 29–66.

—— (ed.) (1999) *Phobias: A Handbook of Theory, Research and Treatment*. Chichester: John Wiley & Sons.

Department of Health (2001) *Treatment Choice in Psychological Therapies*. London: Department of Health.

DeRubeis, R. J. and Feeley, M. (1991) Determinants of change in cognitive therapy for depression. *Cognitive Therapy and Research*, 14, 5, 469–482.

Dobson, K. S. and Khatri, N. (2000) Cognitive therapy: looking backward, looking forward. *Journal of Clinical Psychology, Special Issue: Advances in Clinical Psychology*, 56, 7, 907–923.

Dryden, W. (1992) *The Incredible Sulk*. London: Sheldon.

—— (1995) *Brief Rational Emotive Behaviour Therapy*. Chichester: John Wiley & Sons.

—— (1999) *Rational Emotive Behaviour Therapy: A Personal Approach*. Bicester: Winslow.

Dyer, J. A. T. and Kreitman, N. (1984) Hopelessness, depression and suicidal intent in parasuicide. *British Journal of Psychiatry*, 144, 127–133.

D'Zurilla, T. J. and Nezu, A. M. (2000) *Problem Solving Therapy*. New York: Springer-Verlag.

Ellis, A. (1962) *Reason and Emotion in Psychotherapy*. Secaucus, NJ: Lyle Stuart.

—— (1985) *Overcoming Resistance: Rational Emotive Therapy with Difficult Clients*. New York: Springer-Verlag.

Espie, C. A. (2002) Insomnia: conceptual issues in the development, persistence, and treatment of sleep disorder in adults. *Annual Review of Psychology*, 53, 1, 215–243.

Fairburn, C. G., Cooper, Z. and Shafran, R. (2003) Cognitive behaviour therapy for eating disorders: a 'transdiagnsotic' theory and treatment. *Behaviour Research and Therapy*, 41, 509–528.

Fennell, M. J. V. (1989) Depression, in K. Hawton, P. M. Salkovskis, J. Kirk and D. M. Clark (eds) *Cognitive Behavioural Therapy for Psychiatric Problems: A Practical Guide*. Oxford: Oxford University Press.

—— (1997) Low self-esteem: a cognitive perspective. *Behavioural and Cognitive Psychotherapy*, 25, 1–26.

—— (1999) *Overcoming Low Self-esteem*. London: Robinson.

Ford, D. E. and Kamerow, D. B. (1989) Epidemiologic study of sleep disturbances and psychiatric disorders. *Journal of the American Medical Association*, 262, 1479–1484.

Freeston, M. H., Rheaume, J. and Ladouceur, R. (1996) Correcting faulty appraisals of obsessional thoughts. *Behaviour Research and Therapy*, 34, 433–446.

Freud, S. (1936) *The Basic Writings of Sigmund Freud*. New York: Random House.

Garland, A. (1996) A case of bulimia nervosa, in I. M. Blackburn and V. Twaddle (eds) *Cognitive Therapy in Action*. London: Souvenir Press.

Garland, A. and Scott, J. (2005) Depression, in N. Kazantzis, F. P. Deane, K. R. Ronan and L. L'Abate (eds) *Using Homework Assignments in Cognitive Behavior Therapy*. New York: Routledge.

Gelder, M. G. and Marks, I. M. (1968) Desensitization and phobias: a crossover study. *British Journal of Psychiatry*, 114, 323–328.

Gilbert, P. (1992) *Depression: The Evolution of Powerlessness*. New York: Guilford Press.

—— (1996) Personal communication.

—— (2000a) *Counselling for Depression*. London: Sage.

—— (2000b) *Overcoming Depression*. London: Robinson.

Grant, A., Mills, J., Mulhern, R. and Short, N. (2004) *Cognitive-behavioural Therapy in Mental Health Care*. Oxford: Sage.

Greenberger, D. and Padesky, C. A. (1995) *Mind over Mood: A Cognitive Therapy Treatment Manual for Clients*. New York: Guilford Press.

Haaga, D. (2000) Introduction to the special edition on stepped care models in psychotherapy. *Journal of Consulting and Clinical Psychology*, 68, 4, 547–548.

Hammen, C., Ellicott, A., Gitlin, M. and Jamison, K. R. (1989) Sociotropy/autonomy and vulnerability to specific life events in uni-polar and bipolar patients. *Journal of Abnormal Psychology*, 98, 154–160.

Hammen, C., Marks, T., de Mayo, R. and Mayol, A. (1985) Self-schemas and risks for depression: a prospective study. *Journal of Personality and Social Psychology*, 49, 1147–1159.

Harvey, A. G., Watkins, E., Mansell, W. and Shafran, R. (2004) *Cognitive-behavioural Processes across Psychological Disorders: A Transdiagnostic Approach to Research and Treatment*. Oxford: Oxford University Press.

Hauck, P. (1981) *How to Stand Up for Yourself*. London: Sheldon.

Hawton, K., Salkovskis, P. M., Kirk, J. and Clark, D. M. (1989) *Cognitive Behavioural Therapy for Psychiatric Problems: A Practical Guide*. Oxford: Oxford University Press.

Hayes, S. C. Follette, V. M. and Linehan, M. M. (eds) (2004a) *Mindfulness and Acceptance: Expanding the Cognitive-behavioral Tradition*. New York: Guilford Press.

Hayes, S. C., Strosahl, K. D. and Wilson, K. G. (2004b) *Acceptance and Commitment Therapy; An Experiential Approach to Behavioural Change*. New York: Guilford Press.

Hodgson, R. J. and Rachman, S. (1977) Obsessional-compulsive complaints. *Behaviour Research and Therapy*, 15, 389–395.

Howe, D. (1993) *On Being a Client: Understanding the Process of Counselling and Psychotherapy*. London: Sage.

Ingram, R. E., Miranda, A. and Segal Z. V. (1998) *Cognitive Vulnerability to Depression*. New York: Guilford Press.

Jacobson, C. R, Addis, M. E., Jacobson N. S. and Martell, C. R. (2001) *Depression in Context: Strategies for Guided Action*. New York: Norton.

James, I. J. (1999) Using a cognitive rationale to conceptualise anxiety in people with dementia. *Behavioural and Cognitive Psychotherapy*, 27, 4, 345–351.

Kazantzis, N., Deane, F. P., Ronan, K. R. and L'Abate, L. (2005) *Using Homework Assignments in Cognitive Behaviour Therapy*. New York: Routledge.

Kennerley, H. (1997) *Overcoming Anxiety*. London: Robinson.

Klosko, J. S. and Sanderson, W. C (1999) *Cognitive-behavioural Treatment of Depression*. New York: Aronson.

Krishnamurti, J. (1996) *Commentaries on Living. Vol. 1*. New York: Quest.

Lazarus, R. S. (1999) *Stress and Emotion*. London: Free Association Books.

Leahy, R. L. (2001) *Overcoming Resistance in Cognitive Therapy*. New York: Guilford Press.

—— (2003) *Cognitive Therapy Techniques: A Practitioner's Guide*. New York: Guilford Press.

Leahy, R. and Hollon, S. J. (2000) *Treatment Plans and Interventions for Depression and Anxiety Disorders*. New York: Guilford Press.

Linehan, M. M. (1993) *Cognitive Behavioural Treatment of Borderline Personality Disorder*. New York: Guilford Press.

Linehan, M. M., Armstrong, H. E., Saurez, A., Allman, D. and Heard, H. L. (1991) Cognitive-behavioural treatment of chronically parasuicidal borderline patients. *Archives of General Psychiatry*, 48, 1060–1064.

Lovell, K. and Richards, D. (2000) Multiple access points and levels of entry (MAPLE): ensuring choice, accessibly and equity for CBT services. *Behavioural and Cognitive Psychotherapy*, 28, 379–391.

Mace, C., Moorey, S. and Roberts, B. (2000) *Evidence in the Psychological Therapies: A Critical Guide for Practitioners*. London: Routledge.

MacLeod, A. K., Williams, J. M. G. and Linehan, M. M. (1992) New developments in the understanding and treatment of suicidal behaviour. *Behavioural Psychotherapy*, 20, 193–218.

Marks, I. M. (1987) *Fears, Phobias and Rituals: Panic, Anxiety and their Disorders*. New York: Oxford University Press.

Marks, I. M., Grey, S., Cohen, S. D., Hill, R., Mawson, D., Ramm, E. M. and Stern, R. S. (1983) Imipramine and brief therapist aided exposure in agoraphobics having self-exposure homework: a controlled trial. *Archives of General Psychiatry*, 40, 153–162.

Mathews, A. M. (1976) Imaginal flooding and exposure to real phobic situations: treatment outcome with agoraphobic patients. *British Journal of Psychiatry*, 129, 362–371.

Mathews, A. M. and MacLeod, C. (1985) Selective processing of threat cues in anxiety states. *Behaviour Research and Therapy*, 23, 563–569.

Mooney, K. A., and Padesky, C. A. (2000) Applying client creativity to recurrent problems: constructing possibilities and tolerating doubt. *Journal of Cognitive Psychotherapy, Special Issue: Creativity in the Context of Cognitive Therapy*, 14, 2, 149–161.

Moore, R. G. and Garland, A. (2003) *Cognitive Therapy for Chronic and Persistent Depression*. Chichester: John Wiley & Sons.

National Institute for Clinical Excellence (NICE) (2002) *Issues Guidance on Computerised Cognitive-behavioural Therapy for Anxiety and Depression: Technology Appraisal Guidance No. 51*. London: NICE.

—— (2004a) *Management of Anxiety in Adults in Primary, Secondary and Community Care*. London: NICE.

—— (2004b) *Management of Depression in Primary and Secondary Care*. London: NICE.

Neenan, M. and Dryden, W. (2002) *Life Coaching: A Cognitive Behavioural Approach*. London: Routledge.

Newman, M. G. and Borkovec T. D. (2002) Cognitive therapy for worry and generalised anxiety disorder, in G. Simos (ed.) *Cognitive-behavioural Therapy: A Guide for the Practising Clinician*. London: Routledge.

Nolen-Hoeksema, S., Morrow, J. and Fredrickson, B. L. (1993) Response styles and the duration of episodes of depressed mood. *Journal of Abnormal Psychology*, 102, 20–28.

Nolen-Hoeksema, S., Parker, L. E. and Larson, J. (1994) Ruminative coping with depressed mood following loss. *Journal of Personality and Social Psychology*, 67, 92–104.

Ogden, J. (2003) *The Psychology of Eating: From Healthy to Disordered Behaviour*. Oxford: Blackwell.

Ost, L.-G. (1989) A maintenance programme for behavioural treatment of anxiety disorders. *Behavioural Research and Therapy*, 27, 123–130.

—— (2002) *CBT for Anxiety Disorders: What Progress have we made after 35 Years of Randomised Clinical Trials?* Keynote address, British Association of Behavioural and Cognitive Psychotherapies, Warwick.

Padesky, C. A. (1993) *Socratic Questioning: Changing Minds or Guided Discovery?* Keynote address, European Congress of Behavioural and Cognitive Psychotherapies, London, September.

—— (1996) Developing cognitive therapist competency: teaching and supervision models, in P. M. Salkovskis (ed.) *Frontiers of Cognitive Therapy*. New York: Guilford Press.

Padesky, C. A. and Greenberger, D. (1995) *Clinician's Guide to Mind over Mood*. New York: Guilford Press.

Pavlov, I. P. (1927) *Conditioned Reflexes*. Oxford: Oxford University Press.

Paykel, E. S., Scott, J., Teasdale, J. D., Johnson, A. L., Garland, A., Moore, R., Jenaway, A., Cornwall, P. L., Hayhurst, H., Abbott, R. and Pope, M. (1999) Prevention of relapse in residual depression by cognitive therapy: a controlled trial. *Archives of General Psychiatry*, 56, 829–835.

Persons, J. (1989) *Cognitive Therapy in Practice: A Case Formulation Approach*. New York: Norton.

Persons, J. B. and Burns, D. D. (1985) Mechanism of action of cognitive therapy: relative contribution of technical and interpersonal intervention. *Cognitive Therapy and Research*, 9, 5, 539–551.

Petrie, K., Chamberlain, K. and Clarke, D. (1988) Psychological predictors of future suicidal behaviour in hospitalized suicide attempters. *British Journal of Clinical Psychology*, 27, 247–257.

Power, M. J. and Dalgliesh T. (1997) *Cognition and Emotion: From Order to Disorder*. Chichester: John Wiley & Sons.

Purdon, C. (1999) Thought suppression and psychopathology. *Behaviour Research and Therapy*, 37, 11, 1029–1054.

Rachman, S. J. (1980) Emotional processing. *Behaviour Research and Therapy*, 18, 51–60.

Rachman, S. and de Silva, P. (1978) Abnormal and normal obsessions. *Behaviour Research and Therapy*, 16, 233–248.

Richards, D. A. and McDonald, B. (1990) *Behavioural Psychotherapy: A Handbook for Nurses*. Oxford: Heinemann Medical Books.

Robb, H. B. (1992) Why you don't have a 'perfect right' to anything. *Journal of Rational Emotive and Cognitive Behavioural Therapy*, 10, 4, 259–270.

Rogers, C. R. (1957) The necessary and sufficient conditions of therapeutic personality change. *Journal of Counselling Psychology*, 21, 95–103.

Roth, P. and Fonagy, A. (1996) *What Works for Whom?* New York: Guilford Press.

Safran, J. D. and Segal, Z. V. (1996) *Interpersonal Processes in Cognitive Therapy*. New York: Basic Books.

Safran, J. D., Segal, Z. V., Vallis, T. M., Shaw, B. F. and Samstag, L. W. (1993) Assessing patient suitability for short-term cognitive therapy with an interpersonal focus. *Cognitive Therapy and Research*, 17, 1, 23–38.

Salkovskis, P. M. (1985) Obsessional-compulsive problems: a cognitive behavioural analysis. *Behaviour Research and Therapy*, 25, 571–583.

—— (1989) Somatic problems, in K. Hawton, P. M. Salkovskis, J. Kirk and D. M. Clark (eds) *Cognitive Behavioural Therapy for Psychiatric Problems: A Practical Guide*. Oxford: Oxford University Press.

—— (1991) The importance of behaviour in the maintenance of anxiety and panic: a cognitive account. *Behavioural Psychotherapy*, 19, 1, 6–19.

—— (2002) Empirically grounded clinical interventions: cognitive-behavioural therapy progresses through a multidimensional approach to clinical science. *Behavioural and Cognitive Psychotherapy*, 30, 3–9.

Salkovskis, P. M., Atha, C. J. and Storer, D. (1990) Cognitive-behavioural problem-solving in the treatment of patients who repeatedly attempt suicide: a controlled trial. *British Journal of Psychiatry*, 157, 871–876.

Salkovskis, P. M. and Harrison, J. (1984) Abnormal and normal obsessions: a replication. *Behaviour Research and Therapy*, 22, 549–552.

Salkovskis, P. M. and Kirk, J. (1997) Obsessive compulsive disorder, in D. M. Clark and C. G. Fairburn (eds) *Science and Practice of Cognitive Behavioural Therapy*. Oxford: Oxford University Press.

Salkovskis, P. M. and Warwick, H. M. C. (1986) Morbid preoccupations, health anxiety and reassurance: a cognitive behavioural approach to hypochondriasis. *Behaviour Research and Therapy*, 24, 597–602.

Scott, C. S., Scott, J., Tacchi, M. J. and Jones, R. H. (1994) Abbreviated cognitive therapy for depression: a pilot study in primary care. *Behavioural and Cognitive Psychotherapy*, 22, 1, 57–64.

Scott, J. (1988) Cognitive therapy with depressed in-patients, in W. Dryden and P. Trower (eds) *Developments in Cognitive Psychotherapy*. London: Sage.

—— (1992) Chronic depression: can cognitive therapy succeed where other treatments fail? *Behavioural and Cognitive Psychotherapy*, 20, 25–36.

—— (2001) *Overcoming Mood Swings*. London: Robinson.

Scott, J., Garland, A. and Moorhead, S. (2001) A pilot study of cognitive therapy in bipolar disorder. *Psychological Medicine*, 31, 3, 459–467.

Segal, Z. V., Teasdale, J. D. and Williams, J. M. G. (2004) Mindfulness-based cognitive therapy: theoretical rationale and empirical status, in S. C. Hayes, V. M. Follette and M. M. Linehan (eds) *Mindfulness and Acceptance: Expanding the Cognitive-behavioral Tradition*. New York: Guilford Press.

Segal, Z. V., Williams, J. M. G. and Teasdale, J. D. (2002) *Mindfulness-based Cognitive Therapy for Depression: A New Approach to Preventing Relapse*. New York: Guilford Press.

Seligman, M. E. P. (1975) *Helplessness: On Depression, Development and Death*. San Francisco: Freeman.

Shakespeare, W. (2006) *Hamlet*. London: Penguin.

Sharoff, K. (2002) *Cognitive Coping Therapy*. London: Routledge.

Silove, D. and Manicavasagar, V. (2001) *Overcoming Panic*. London: Robinson.

Simos, G. (2002) Cognitive behavioural therapy of panic disorder, in *Cognitive Behavioural Therapy: A Guide for the Practising Clinician*. London: Routledge.

Teasdale, J. D. (1993) Emotion and two kinds of meaning: cognitive therapy and applied cognitive science. *Behaviour Research and Therapy*, 31, 339–354.

Teasdale, J. D., Moore, R. G., Hayhurst, H., Pope, M., Williams, S. and Segal, Z. V. (2002) Metacognitive awareness and prevention of relapse in depression: empirical evidence. *Journal of Consulting and Clinical Psychology*, 70, 2, 275–287.

Veale, D. and Wilson, R. (2005) *Overcoming Obsessive-compulsive Disorder*. London: Robinson.

Vita, P. and Owen, N. (1995) A perspective on the behavioural epidemiology, the determinants and the stages of exercise involvement. *Australian Psychologist*, 30, 2, 135–140.

Wells, A. (1997) *Cognitive Therapy of Anxiety Disorders: A Practical Manual*. Chichester: John Wiley & Sons.

—— (2000) *Emotional Disorders and Metacognition: Innovative Cognitive Therapy*. Chichester: John Wiley & Sons.

Wells, A. and Clark, D. M. (1997) Social phobia: a cognitive approach, in G. C. L. Davey (ed.) *Phobias: A Handbook of Description, Treatment and Theory*. Chichester: John Wiley & Sons.

Wetzel, R. D. (1976) Hopelessness, depression and suicidal intent. *Archives of General Psychiatry*, 33, 1069–1073.

Whittal, M. L. and O'Neill, M. L. (2002) Cognitive-behavioral therapy for obsessive-compulsive disorder and body dysmorphic disorder, in L. VandeCreek and T. L. Jackson (eds) *Innovations in Clinical Practice: A Source Book, Vol. 20*. Sarasota, FL: Professional Resource Press.

Williams, C. J. (2003) *Overcoming Anxiety: A Five Areas Approach*. London: Hodder Arnold.

—— (2006) *Overcoming Depression and Low mood: A Five Areas Approach*. Second edn. London: Hodder Arnold.

Williams, J. M. G. (1992) *The Psychological Treatment of Depression*. London: Routledge.

—— (1997) Depression, in D. M. Clark and C. G. Fairburn (eds) *Science and Practice of Cognitive Behaviour Therapy*. Oxford: Oxford Medical Publications.

Williams, J. M. G., Watts, F. N., MacLeod, C. and Mathews, A. (1997) *Cognitive Psychology and Emotional Disorders*, 2nd edn. Chichester: John Wiley & Sons.

Wills, F. and Sanders, D. (1997) *Cognitive Therapy: Transforming the Image*. Chichester: John Wiley & Sons.

Wright, J. H. (1996) Inpatient cognitive therapy, in P. M. Salkovskis (ed.) *Frontiers of Cognitive Therapy*. New York: Guilford Press.

Wright, J. H., Thase, M. E., Beck, A. T. and Ludgate, J. W. (1993) *Cognitive Therapy with In-patients: Developing a Cognitive Milieu*. New York: Guilford Press.

Young, J. E. (1994) *Cognitive Therapy for Personality Disorders: A Schema-focused Approach*. Sarasota, FL: Professional Resource Press.

Young, J., Klosko, J. and Weishaar, M. E. (2003) *Schema Therapy: A Practitioner's Guide*. New York: Guilford Press.